Practical Eclipse Rich Client Platform Projects

Vladimir Silva

Apress®

Practical Eclipse Rich Client Platform Projects

Copyright © 2009 by Vladimir Silva

ISBN-13 (pbk): 978-1-4302-1827-2

ISBN-13 (electronic): 978-1-4302-1828-9

9 8 7 6 5 4 3 2 1

Lead Editor: Tom Welsh
Technical Reviewer: Sumit Pal
Editorial Board: Clay Andres, Steve Anglin, Mark Beckner, Ewan Buckingham, Tony Campbell,
    Gary Cornell, Jonathan Gennick, Michelle Lowman, Matthew Moodie, Jeffrey Pepper, Frank Pohlmann,
    Ben Renow-Clarke, Dominic Shakeshaft, Matt Wade, Tom Welsh
Project Managers: Douglas Sulenta, Susannah Davidson Pfalzer
Senior Copy Editor: Marilyn Smith
Associate Production Director: Kari Brooks-Copony
Production Editor: Ellie Fountain
Compositor: Molly Sharp
Proofreader: Linda Seifert
Indexer: Broccoli Information Management
Artist: Kinetic Publishing Services, LLC
Cover Designer: Kurt Krames
Manufacturing Director: Tom Debolski

Distributed to the book trade worldwide by Springer-Verlag New York, Inc., 233 Spring Street, 6th Floor, New York, NY 10013. Phone 1-800-SPRINGER, fax 201-348-4505, e-mail orders-ny@springer-sbm.com, or visit http://www.springeronline.com.

For information on translations, please contact Apress directly at 2855 Telegraph Avenue, Suite 600, Berkeley, CA 94705. Phone 510-549-5930, fax 510-549-5939, e-mail info@apress.com, or visit http://www.apress.com.

Apress and friends of ED books may be purchased in bulk for academic, corporate, or promotional use. eBook versions and licenses are also available for most titles. For more information, reference our Special Bulk Sales–eBook Licensing web page at http://www.apress.com/info/bulksales.

The source code for this book is available to readers at http://www.apress.com.

Contents at a Glance

About the Author...xi

About the Technical Reviewer xiii

Introduction xv

CHAPTER 1   Foundations of Eclipse RCP.......................................1

CHAPTER 2   Plug-ins: A First Glimpse 21

CHAPTER 3   RCP Basics 53

CHAPTER 4   User Interface Concepts 77

CHAPTER 5   Forms API and Presentation Framework.............................107

CHAPTER 6   Help Support...141

CHAPTER 7   2D Graphics with GEF and Zest 173

CHAPTER 8   3D Graphics for RCP with OpenGL..................................209

CHAPTER 9   Professional Reports with the Business Intelligence and
                Report Toolkit...261

CHAPTER 10 Automated Updates 291

INDEX 325

Contents

About the Author..xi

About the Technical Reviewer xii

Introduction xv

■CHAPTER 1   Foundations of Eclipse RCP 1

Benefits of Eclipse..1
How Is RCP Different from the Eclipse Workbench? 2
Eclipse RCP Architecture 2
    Equinox OSGi 3
    Core Platform 3
    Standard Widget Toolkit 4
    JFace 5
    The Eclipse Workbench...6
Hands-on Exercise: Getting Your Feet Wet with the OSGi Console........6
    Starting a New Plug-in Project..6
    Creating the Plug-in..9
    Testing the Plug-in..12
    Using OSGi Console Commands 15
    Using Logging Services...16
Summary...19

■CHAPTER 2   Plug-ins: A First Glimpse 21

Introducing the Eclipse Plug-in Model 21
    The Plug-in Class and BundleContext 22
    Manifests..23
    Plug-in Fragments and Features...24
Adding Extension Points...24
    Perspectives 25
    Views 28
    View Actions 29
    Editors 31
    Pop-up Menus 33
    Commands 35

Hands-on Exercise: Fun with a Web Browser Plug-in 38

    Adding a Perspective Extension Point 39

    Adding a Perspective Factory 40

    Adding Views and Content 41

    Testing the Plug-in 48

    Enhancing the Web Browser 49

Summary 50

▪CHAPTER 3   **RCP Basics** 53

Components of an RCP Application 53

    Extension Points for an RCP Application 55

    OSGi Manifest 59

    Plug-in Manifest 60

    Advisor Classes 61

    Plug-in Class 63

Defining and Branding Products 65

Using Features 67

Product Testing and Packaging 67

Hands-on Exercise: An RCP Application for the Web Browser Plug-in . . . 68

    Adding an Application Extension Point 68

    Changing the Default Perspective 70

    Modifying Advisor Classes 70

    Adding Menu and Toolbar Extension Points 72

    Adding Commands, Key Bindings, and Handlers 73

    Creating the Product Configuration File 75

Summary 76

▪CHAPTER 4   **User Interface Concepts** 77

Hierarchical Navigation with the Common Navigator Framework 77

    CNF Basics 78

    Using CNF Within RCP 79

Concurrency Infrastructure 83

    Jobs API Basics 84

    Using the Concurrency Infrastructure 86

Hands-on Exercise: A CNF File System Navigator 93

    Creating an RCP Project Template 93

    Adding CNF Extension Points 94

    Implementation Classes 96

Summary 106

CHAPTER 5   Forms API and Presentation Framework 107

Forms API Basics 107
    Common Controls 109
    Form Look and Feel 111
    Custom Layouts 115
    Complex Controls 115
Complex Forms 124
    Managed Forms 124
    Master/Details Form 125
    Multipage Editors 125
Hands-on Exercise: A Web Look for the Mail Template 127
    Customizing the Workbench Window 128
    Customizing the Window Contents 129
    Modifying the Navigation View 132
    Modifying the Mail View 134
Summary 138

CHAPTER 6   Help Support 141

Configuring a Product to Use the Help System 141
    Adding the Dependency Plug-ins 142
    Updating the Menu Bar 142
Adding Help Content 144
    Help System Extension Points 146
    TOC File 147
    Index File 148
    Internationalization 150
Adding Context Help Support 150
    Product Plug-in Modifications 151
    Help Plug-in Modifications 152
Customizing the Help System 154
Hands-on Exercise: Create an Infocenter from Custom Documentation . . . 156
    Splitting the Documentation into Topic HTML/XHTML Files 156
    Creating the Help Contents Plug-in 157
    Creating the Infocenter Plug-in 158
    Adding a Product Configuration File to the Infocenter Plug-in 159
    Adding a TOC to the Help Contents Plug-in 160
    Adding a Help Menu to the Infocenter Plug-in 162
    Adding Help System Dependencies to the Product Configuration . . . 163
    Testing the Infocenter Plug-in 164

Deploying the Infocenter Plug-in. 166

Starting the Infocenter from the Command Line 166

Customizing the Infocenter. 168

Summary. 170

■CHAPTER 7 **2D Graphics with GEF and Zest** 173

Draw2d—The Big Picture 173

Using GEF 175

Displaying Figures 176

Exploring the GEF Shapes Example 176

Adding EditPolicies 185

Adding a Palette. 187

Using Zest. 190

Zest Components. 191

Zest Layouts 193

Hands-on Exercise: Build Your Own Advanced 2D Graphics Editor 195

Creating the RCP Product. 196

Building a Zest Plug-in 200

Testing the Final Product 206

Summary. 207

■CHAPTER 8 **3D Graphics for RCP with OpenGL** 209

OpenGL and SWT 209

The Device-Independent Package 210

OpenGL Bindings for SWT 211

Creating OpenGL Scenes with JOGL and SWT. 211

Setting Up for the OpenGL Scenes 212

Creating the Wire Cubes Scene. 220

Creating the 3D Chart Scene 228

Rotating and Moving the Scene. 236

Refreshing the Scene 241

Putting the Scene into an RCP View. 241

Hands-on Exercise: Build a Powerful 3D Earth Navigator. 242

WWJ Basics 242

Setting Up the Earth Navigator Project. 245

Creating the Earth Navigator View 248

Flying to a Location Within a Globe. 250

Finding Latitude and Longitude with the Yahoo Geocoding API. . . 251

Creating the Layer Navigator View with Geocoding. 256

Summary. 258

CHAPTER 9   Professional Reports with the Business Intelligence and Report Toolkit 261

Using the Report Designer Within the Eclipse IDE 261
    Installing BIRT Using the Software Updates Manager 262
    Report Anatomy 263
    Getting Your Feet Wet with the Report Designer 263
Using BIRT Within a Servlet Container 269
    Deploying the BIRT Runtime 269
    Using the Report Viewer Servlet 270
    Using the JSP Tag Library 272
Using the Report Engine API 275
    Configuring and Creating a Report Engine. 276
    What Kinds of Operations Can Be Done with the Report Engine? . . . 277
Hands-on Exercise: Report Generation from the OSGi Console. 283
    Extending the OSGi Console. 283
    Generating the Report 285
    Running the Report Generator Plug-in 289
Summary. 290

CHAPTER 10   Automated Updates 291

Updating and Installing Software the Eclipse Way. 291
    Defining and Configuring a Product 292
    Grouping Plug-ins in Features 295
    Grouping Plug-ins Within Fragments 296
    Building an Update Site Project 296
Software Update UI Tools 296
    Using the Software Updates and Add-ons Dialog. 297
    Installing Software from the Command Line. 298
Product Build Automation with the Headless Build System 300
    Build Configuration 302
    Build Phases 304
Hands-on Exercise: Automated Updates and Builds for RCP 305
    Creating a Feature 305
    Creating an Update Site 306
    Testing and Publishing 308
    Building the Product Headless. 314
    Building the Product Headless from a CVS Repository 318
Summary. 323

INDEX 325

About the Author

VLADIMIR SILVA was born in Quito, Ecuador. He received a System's Analyst degree from the Polytechnic Institute of the Army in 1994. In the same year, he came to the United States as an exchange student pursuing a Master's degree in Computer Science at Middle Tennessee State University. After graduation, he joined IBM's Web-Ahead technology think tank. His interests include grid computing, neural nets, and artificial intelligence. Vladimir also holds numerous IT certifications, including Oracle Certified Professional (OCP), Microsoft Certified Solution Developer (MCSD), and Microsoft Certified Professional (MCP).

About the Technical Reviewer

SUMIT PAL has about 15 years of experience with software design and development and architecture on a variety of platforms, including Java and J2EE. Sumit worked in the Microsoft SQL Server Replication group for 2 years, and with Oracle's OLAP Server group for 7 years.

Currently, he works as an OLAP architect for LeapFrogRx, which provides advanced analytics to pharmaceutical companies.

Along with certifications like IEEE Certified Software Development Professional (CDSP) and J2EE Architect, Sumit has a Master's degree in Computer Science.

Sumit has a keen interest in search engine internals, data mining, database internals, and algorithms. He has invented some basic generalized algorithms to find divisibility between numbers and also to find divisibility rules for prime numbers less than 100.

In his spare time, Sumit loves to play badminton and swim, and also help organizations like Akshaya Patra Foundation (http://foodforeducation.org/) raise funds.

Introduction

Eclipse Rich Client Platform (RCP) has become the leading open development platform, capturing close to 70% of the open integrated development environment (IDE) market. I wrote this book to give you a clear and technical guide to Eclipse development, and to help you achieve your goals quickly. If you use Eclipse, you must become familiar with RCP. It gives you all the tools you need to build commercial-quality applications and deploy them quickly, thus saving time and increasing the return on investment.

In *Practical Eclipse Rich Client Platform Projects*, I explain the necessary technical concepts approachably, with plenty of source code and images, in a detailed and engaging (I hope) way. This book will show you how to apply modern graphical user interface (GUI) concepts to your applications using real-world examples. Each chapter explains the concepts carefully, and then puts them to the test with a hands-on exercise.

We start with the architecture and foundations of Eclipse RCP, taking a tour of Equinox, the core platform, Standard Widget Toolkit (SWT), and the Eclipse IDE workbench. Next, you learn about the details of the plug-in architecture, always with a focus on RCP components: perspectives, advisor classes, basic branding, and product configuration. In Chapter 4, we look at common concurrency concepts used in modern GUI development with the Jobs API: job classes, scheduling rules, resource management, and more.

In Chapter 5, you learn how to spice up your GUI with the powerful Forms API. Among the areas covered are look and feel, form controls, and advanced topics—in short, everything you need to improve the look of your RCP application.

A good help system is an important component of any application. Chapter 6 tackles this subject with detailed descriptions of how to build your help files, required help plug-ins, dependencies, and configuration.

If you ever work on graphics-enabled applications, you will find Chapters 7 and 8 of special interest. They cover 2D and 3D graphics in depth. In the 2D arena, you learn how to use Draw2D, Graphical Editing Framework (GEF), and the Zest visualization toolkit. If 3D is your thing, you'll want to take a look at how OpenGL can be used to build a powerful Earth navigator (Google style) in a snap.

Chapter 9 shows you how to create powerful reports using the Business Intelligence and Report Toolkit (BIRT), which you will find particularly useful if your application is targeted to a business environment.

Finally, Chapter 10 explains how to pack your work and deploy it automatically to an update site using the automated build system.

Practical Eclipse Rich Client Projects covers all the major needs of a modern application. It will help you get things done. If you are interested in the source code, you can download it from this book's details page at the Apress web site (`http://www.apress.com`).

■ ■ ■

## CHAPTER 1

Foundations of Eclipse RCP

The Eclipse philosophy is simple and has been critical to its success. The Eclipse Platform was designed from the ground up as an integration framework for development tools. Eclipse also enables developers to easily extend products built on it with the latest object-oriented technologies.

Although Eclipse was designed to serve as an open development platform, it is architected so that its components can be used to build just about any client application. The minimal set of modules needed to build a rich client is collectively known as the *Rich Client Platform* (RCP).

This chapter focuses on the foundations of RCP. It begins with a summary of the benefits of Eclipse, and then discusses the architecture of RCP. Finally, you'll work through a practical exercise that demonstrates the power of this dynamic modular technology.

Benefits of Eclipse

Eclipse is an integrated development environment (IDE) written primarily in Java. However, it goes well beyond a Java development platform in the following ways:

- It is open and extensible. Extensible software can function as a component of a larger system. Eclipse's openness permits greater interoperability, opportunity, and choice.

- It provides multilanguage support. Eclipse supports an army of programming languages, including Java, Java Platform, Enterprise Edition (Java EE), AspectJ, C/C++, Ruby, Perl, COBOL, and many others.

- It provides a consistent feature set across all platforms. This allows developers to concentrate on the problem rather than the specific platform. More important, it functions the same way on each of these platforms.

- It provides a native look and feel, which is required by today's professional applications.

- A very active community is willing to help with any problem. Moreover, since Eclipse is the foundation for a number of commercial software products, many vendors offer additional support.

- Eclipse is at the forefront of the software tools industry. This means that you can depend on it as a viable, industrial-strength tool for the foreseeable future.

The bottom line is that Eclipse is extensible, configurable, free, and fully supported. It is so well designed for these purposes that many developers find it a pleasure to work with. Newcomers from other languages, especially C/C++ on Unix, will discover this after learning the basics.

How Is RCP Different from the Eclipse Workbench?

Many people struggle to understand the difference between the Eclipse IDE workbench and RCP. The answer is simple: there is no difference—well almost no difference. Both are based on a dynamic plug-in model, and the user interface (UI) for the workbench and RCP is built using the same toolkits and extension points. However, RCP has the following distinguishing features:

- In RCP, the layout and function of the Eclipse IDE workbench is under fine-grained control of the plug-in developer. In fact, the Eclipse IDE workbench itself is an RCP application for software development. Here is where the line between these two becomes thin.

- In RCP, the developer is responsible for defining the application and customizing the look and feel of the Eclipse IDE workbench to fit the needs of the application.

- In RCP, the platform application needs only the plug-ins `org.eclipse.ui` and `org.eclipse.core runtime` to run. However, RCP applications are free to use any platform plug-ins they need to provide their feature set.

Eclipse RCP Architecture

RCP employs a lightweight software component framework based on plug-ins. This architecture provides extensibility and seamless integration. Everything in RCP (and Eclipse, for that matter), with the exception of the runtime kernel, is a plug-in. It could be said that all features are created equal, as each plug-in integrates with Eclipse in exactly the same way. A plug-in can be anything: a dialog, a view, a web browser, a database explorer, a project explorer, and so forth.

RCP is architected so that its components can be put together to build just about any client application using a dynamic plug-in model, toolkits, and extension points. The layout and function of the workbench is under the fine-grained control of the plug-in developer. Under the covers, the following components constitute RCP:

- Equinox

- Core platform

- Standard Widget Toolkit

- JFace

- Eclipse IDE workbench

Let's take a closer look at each of these components.

Equinox OSGi

According to its developers, OSGi[1] is a dynamic module system for Java. OSGi was designed as a technology to tackle software complexity created by monolithic software products. Its focus is the development of new software, as well as the integration of existing software into new systems. By providing standards for the integration of software, the OSGi framework improves reusability and reliability, and reduces development costs.

At its core, OSGi provides a software framework that allows applications to be constructed from small, reusable, and collaborative components. These components, in turn, can be included in a bigger application and deployed.

Equinox is Eclipse's implementation of the OSGi framework. It defines an application life-cycle management model, a service registry, an execution environment, and modules. On top of this framework, a large number of OSGi layers, application program interfaces (APIs), and services have been defined.

An important concept in the OSGi framework is the *bundle*. A bundle is a dynamic component that can be remotely installed, started, stopped, updated, and uninstalled without requiring a reboot.

Life-cycle management is done via APIs, which allow for remote downloading of management policies. Such a dynamic component model is missing from today's stand-alone Java Virtual Machine (JVM) environments.

OSGi provides a powerful dynamic component model, which is why the Eclipse Foundation selected it as the underlying runtime for Eclipse RCP and the IDE.

Core Platform

The core platform includes a runtime engine that starts the platform base and dynamically discovers and runs plug-ins.

Core Platform Responsibilities

The core platform is responsible for the following:

- Defining a structure for plug-ins and the implementation details: bundles and class-loaders

- Finding and executing the main application, and maintaining a registry of plug-ins, their extensions, and extension points

- Providing miscellaneous utilities, such as logging, debug trace options, adapters, a preference store, and a concurrency infrastructure

The runtime is defined by the plug-ins `org.eclipse.osgi` and `org.eclipse.core.runtime` on which all other plug-ins depend. It effectively holds all the pieces together.

---

1. OSGi originally stood for Open Services Gateway initiative, but that name is now obsolete. Visit `http://www.osgi.org` for more information about OSGi.

■**Note** Because plug-ins are implemented using the OSGi framework, a plug-in is essentially the same thing as an OSGi bundle. I will use these terms interchangeably, unless discussing particular framework classes.

Runtime Plug-in Model

The plug-in model is structured around the following concepts:

Plug-in: A plug-in is a structured bundle of code and/or data that contributes functionality to the system. Some plug-ins can contribute to the UI using an extension point model. Others supply class libraries that can be used to implement system extensions.

Extension points: An extension point is a well-defined place where other plug-ins can add functionality. Plug-ins can add extensions to the platform by implementing an extension point. Defining an extension point can be thought of as defining an API, with the difference that the extension point is declared in Extensible Markup Language (XML) instead of code.

OSGi manifest and plug-in manifest: These manifests allow the plug-in to describe itself to the system. The extensions and extension points are declared in the plug-in manifest file, which is called plugin.xml. The platform maintains a registry of installed plug-ins and the functions they provide in the MANIFEST.MF file.

Dynamic loading: In the OSGi services model, software bundles do not pay a memory or performance penalty for components that are installed but not used. A plug-in can be installed and added to the registry, but it will not be activated unless a function that it provides is requested at runtime.

Resource management: Resources within the user's workspace are managed by the plug-in org.eclipse.core.resources. This plug-in provides services for accessing the projects, folders, and files stored in the user's workspace or alternate file systems, such as network file systems or a database. This plug-in is most useful for Eclipse IDE applications.

The overall philosophy of the core platform revolves around the idea of building plug-ins to extend the system. For example, the Eclipse Software Development Kit (SDK) includes the basic platform plus two major tools: the full-featured Java development tools (JDT) and a Plug-in Developer Environment (PDE) to facilitate the development of plug-ins and extensions. These tools provide an example of how new tools can be composed by building plug-ins that extend the system.

Standard Widget Toolkit

The Standard Widget Toolkit (SWT) is the graphical widget toolkit used by Eclipse. Originally developed by IBM, it was created to overcome the limitations of the Swing graphical user interface (GUI) toolkit introduced by Sun. Swing is 100% Java and employs a lowest common denominator to draw its components by using Java 2D to call low-level operating system primitives. SWT, on the other hand, implements a common widget layer with fast native access to multiple platforms.

SWT's goal is to provide a common API, but avoid the lowest common denominator problem typical of other portable GUI toolkits. SWT was designed for the following:

Performance: SWT claims higher performance and responsiveness, and lower system resource usage than Swing.[2]

Native look and feel: Because SWT is a wrapper around native window systems such as GTK+ and Motif, SWT widgets have the exact same look and feel as native ones. This is in contrast to the Swing toolkit, where widgets are close copies of native ones. This is clearly evident just by looking at Swing applications.

Extensibility: Critics of SWT may claim that the use of native code does not allow for easy inheritance and hurts extensibility. However, both Swing and SWT support writing new widgets using Java code only.

Perhaps a shortcoming is that, unlike Swing, SWT requires manual object deallocation, as opposed to the standard automatic garbage collection of Swing. SWT objects must be explicitly disposed of; otherwise, memory leaks or other unintended behavior may result. This is due to the native nature of SWT, as widgets are not tracked by the JVM, which is unable to garbage-collect them. Some claim that this increases development time and costs for the average Java developer. But the truth of the matter is that the only SWT objects a developer must explicitly dispose of are the subclasses of Image, Color, and Font objects.

JFace

JFace is a window-system-independent GUI toolkit for handling many common programming tasks. JFace is designed to work with SWT without hiding it, and implements a model-view-controller (MVC) architecture.

The following are some of the UI components in JFace:

- Image and font registries
- Text, dialog, preference, and wizard frameworks
- Viewers
- Actions

Viewers are used to simplify the interaction between an underlying data model and the widgets used to present that model. Table and tree viewers are the most typical examples.

Actions are essential for the developer. They may fire when a toolbar button or a menu item is clicked or when a defined key sequence is invoked. They are most useful when contributed to the workbench declaratively in plugin.xml.

---

2. See "Why I choose SWT against Swing" (November 19, 2004), on Ozgur Akan's blog. (http://weblogs. java.net/blog/aiqa/archive/2004/11/why_i_choose_sw.html).

The Eclipse Workbench

The Eclipse IDE workbench is the basic development environment in Eclipse. It is built around the following concepts:

Perspectives: A perspective defines the initial set and layout of the views in your workbench window. Perspectives are focused on a specific development task, such as Java, Java EE, plug-in, and so on.

Views: Views are the small windows and sidebars around the edges of the workbench. Views are used to navigate the workbench and present information in different ways.

Editors: Editors are used to do the actual coding. For example, you might use editors to code in Java, JavaScript, Hypertext Markup Language (HTML), or Cascading Style Sheets (CSS).

Workspaces: A workspace is the disk folder where the actual work will be stored.

Projects: A project is a container used by the workbench to group associated folders and files.

Note All the exercises in this book were written using Eclipse 3.4 (Ganymede). This is important, as the UI is somewhat different from that of version 3.3.

Hands-on Exercise: Getting Your Feet Wet with the OSGi Console

Programming with Eclipse can be thought of as a game. The more you practice, the better you get at it. The goal of this exercise is to get you started by building a plug-in project that uses the OSGi console. We'll go beyond of the typical Hello World example.

In this exercise, you will write a plug-in to embed a tiny Jetty web server that uses Equinox to define a simple servlet class that returns the headers of the HTTP request. This plug-in will use the extension point org.eclipse.equinox.http.registry.servlets to define the servlet alias /servlet1, which will be accessed through the browser as http://localhost:8080/servlet1.

Starting a New Plug-in Project

Starting a new plug-in project is easy with the Plug-in Project wizard.

1. From the Eclipse IDE main menu, select File ➤ New Project (or click the New Project icon on the toolbar) and choose Plug-in Project, as shown in Figure 1-1. Then click Next.

2. Enter a project name and use the default target platform, as shown in Figure 1-2. Click Next to continue.

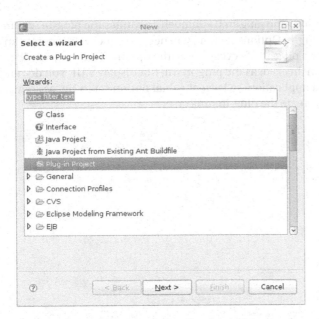

Figure 1-1. *Selecting to create a plug-in project*

Figure 1-2. *Naming and targeting the plug-in project*

3. Enter the plug-in information. The plug-in ID uniquely identifies the plug-in within the core runtime. In the Plug-in Options section, you need to choose to generate an activator class to control the plug-in life cycle. Leave the option "This plug-in will make contributions to the UI" unchecked, as the plug-in will not display a UI. You do not want to create a rich client application, so leave the final option set to No, as shown in Figure 1-3. Click Finish to create the plug-in project.

Figure 1-3. *Specifying plug-in content*

The wizard builds the project, and then presents the plug-in manifest editor, as shown in Figure 1-4. The two most important files are Activator.java and MANIFEST.MF.

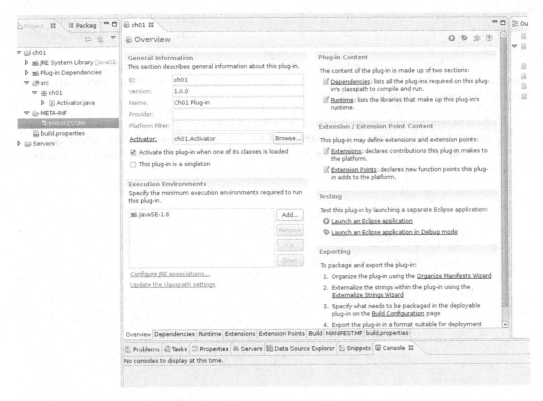

Figure 1-4. *Plug-in manifest editor for this exercise*

Creating the Plug-in

The activator class controls the life-cycle aspects and overall semantics of a plug-in. A plug-in can implement specialized functions for the start and stop aspects of its life cycle. Each life-cycle method includes a reference to a BundleContext, as follows:

```
public void start(BundleContext context) throws Exception {
    super.start(context);
    plugin = this;

    log.info("Activator Start");
}

public void stop(BundleContext context) throws Exception {
    plugin = null;
    super.stop(context);

    log.info("Activator Stop");
}
```

BundleContext is a reference that contains information related to the plug-in and other bundles/plug-ins in the system. Chapter 2 provides more information about the BundleContext methods.

The Dependencies tab of the plug-in manifest editor is used to add references to other bundles. You also need to add an extension point and implement the servlet, which you can do through the Extensions tab of the editor.

1. To add references to other bundles, click the Dependencies tab, and then click the Add button in the Required Plug-ins section. This displays the Plug-in Selection dialog, as shown in Figure 1-5. For this exercise, add the following references, which are required by the servlet extension point:

   - javax.servlet
   - org.eclipse.equinox.http.jetty
   - org.eclipse.equinox.http.registry
   - org.eclipse.equinox.http.servlet

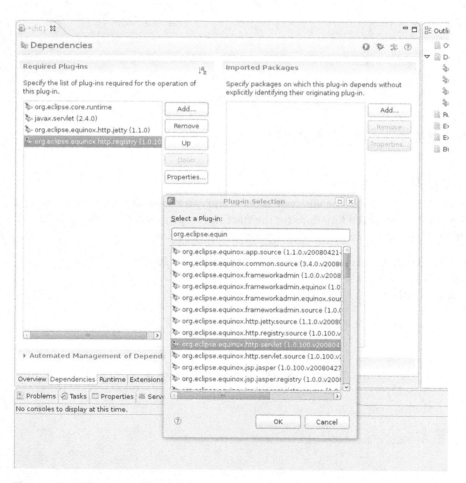

Figure 1-5. *Adding dependencies*

2. Click the Extensions tab. Click the Add button and select the extension point `org.eclipse.equinox.http.registry.servlets`. A servlet class name and alias will be inserted automatically. The servlet alias (`/servlet1`) will be used to reference the servlet from a web browser. Internally, the XML for this extension point looks like this:

```
<?xml version="1.0" encoding="UTF-8"?>
<?eclipse version="3.2"?>
<plugin>
   <extension
         point="org.eclipse.equinox.http.registry.servlets">
      <servlet
           alias="/servlet1"
           class="ch01.Servlet1">
      </servlet>
   </extension>
</plugin>
```

3. To implement the servlet class, click the class label link in the Extensions tab, as shown in Figure 1-6. This launches the New Java Class wizard.

■**Note** You can also implement a new class manually by adding the class name (`ch01.Servlet1` in this example) to the plug-in manifest editor, and then right-clicking the plug-in project folder and selecting New ➤ Java Class.

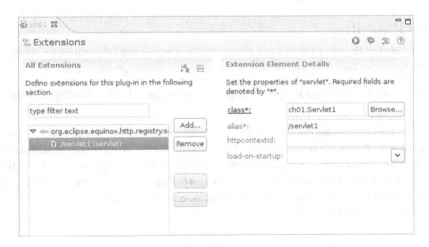

Figure 1-6. *Servlet extension point details*

4. Enter the class information, select `javax.servlet.http.HttpServlet` as the superclass, and click Finish. The Java class will be created automatically.

5. Use the plug-in manifest editor to override the `doGet` method to return the headers of the HTTP request to the browser, as follows:

```
@Override
protected void doGet(HttpServletRequest req, HttpServletResponse resp)
        throws ServletException, IOException
{
        resp.setContentType("text/html");
        dumpHttpHeaders(req, resp.getWriter());
}

@SuppressWarnings("unchecked")
private void dumpHttpHeaders(HttpServletRequest req, PrintWriter out)
{
        out.println("URI:" + req.getRequestURI() + "<br/>");

        Enumeration<String> names = req.getHeaderNames();

        while (names.hasMoreElements()) {
            final String name = names.nextElement();
            out.println(name + "=" + req.getHeader(name) + "<br/>");
        }
}
```

Testing the Plug-in

Now that you've created the plug-in, you can test it. You'll see that the OSGi console is very useful for examining the OSGi framework and debugging missing dependencies.

1. From the main menu, select Run ➤ Configurations to open the Run Configurations dialog.

2. To create a new configuration under the OSGi framework, right-click and select New. Make sure your plug-in is selected in the Bundles list, under Workspace, as shown in Figure 1-7. You must also select all required bundles under Target Platform. To make sure all required bundles are selected, unselect all bundles under Target Platform, and then click Add Required Bundles. This will ensure only the required dependencies are used at runtime. Then click Run.

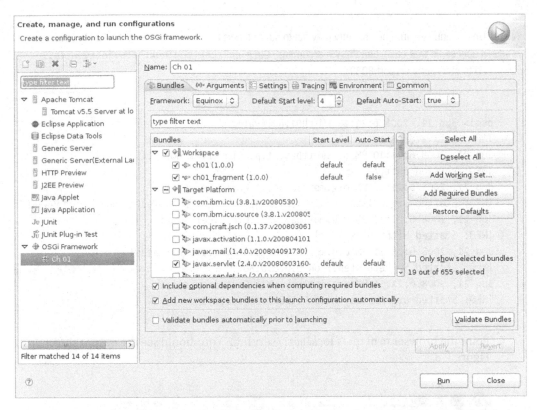

Figure 1-7. *Run configuration dialog showing both the exercise plug-in (ch01) and the logging fragment (ch01_fragment) discussed later in this chapter*

3. Click the Arguments tab. Note the runtime arguments:

- os ${target.os}: The target operating system

- ws ${target.ws}: The target window system

- arch ${target.arch}: The target architecture

- nl ${target.nl}: The locale

- Console: Start the OSGi console; handy for investigating the state of the system

Also note the VM argument:

- osgi.noShutdown: If true, the VM will not exit after the Eclipse application has ended; useful for examining the OSGi framework after the application has ended

When the plug-in runs, the console starts and is ready to receive user commands. This is a handy tool to inspect the state of the system. From the following output, you can see that Jetty started on port 80, which is the default in Windows.

Note Under Linux environments, Jetty may fail to start on port 80, as ports lower than 1024 require sysadmin access. In that case, add the VM argument `-Dorg.eclipse.equinox.http.jetty.http.port=8080` to start Jetty on port 8080.

```
osgi> Jun 21, 2008 6:21:10 PM ch01.Activator start
INFO: Activator Start
Jun 21, 2008 6:21:10 PM org.mortbay.http.HttpServer doStart
INFO: Version Jetty/5.1.x
Jun 21, 2008 6:21:11 PM org.mortbay.util.Container start
INFO: Started org.eclipse.equinox.http.jetty.internal.Servlet25Handler@1a99561
Jun 21, 2008 6:21:11 PM org.mortbay.util.Container start
INFO: Started HttpContext[/,/]
Jun 21, 2008 6:21:11 PM org.mortbay.http.SocketListener start
INFO: Started SocketListener on 0.0.0.0:80
Jun 21, 2008 6:21:11 PM org.mortbay.util.Container start
INFO: Started org.mortbay.http.HttpServer@1ea0252
osgi>
```

4. Point the browser to `http://localhost/servlet1`. You should see the output shown in Figure 1-8.

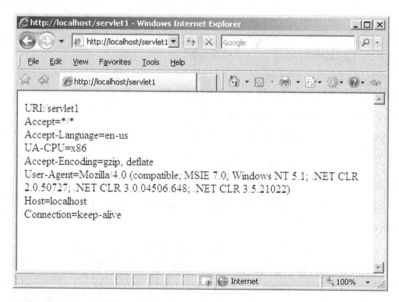

Figure 1-8. *Output of the exercise*

Using OSGi Console Commands

The console is a handy tool to inspect your plug-in and identify problems. The following are some of the most useful commands:

- start [<id>|<name>]: Starts a bundle given an ID or symbolic name
- stop [<id>|<name>]: Stops a bundle given an ID or symbolic name
- install {URL}: Adds a bundle given a URL for the current instance
- uninstall [<id>|<name>]: Removes a bundle given a URL for the current instance
- ss: Lists a short status of all the bundles registered in the current instance
- help: Shows information about all available commands

For example, to look at all the registered bundles, use the ss command, as follows:

```
osgi> ss

Framework is launched.

Id  State       Bundle
0   ACTIVE      org.eclipse.osgi_3.4.0.v20080605-1900
1   ACTIVE      org.eclipse.osgi.services_3.1.200.v20071203
2   ACTIVE      org.eclipse.core.jobs_3.4.0.v20080512
3   RESOLVED    ch01_fragment_1.0.0
                Master=12
4   ACTIVE      org.mortbay.jetty_5.1.14.v200806031611
5   ACTIVE      org.eclipse.core.runtime.compatibility.auth_3.2.100.v20070502
6   ACTIVE      org.eclipse.equinox.http.servlet_1.0.100.v20080427-0830
7   ACTIVE      org.eclipse.equinox.registry_3.4.0.v20080516-0950
                Fragments=16
8   ACTIVE      org.apache.commons.logging_1.0.4.v20080605-1930
9   ACTIVE      org.eclipse.core.runtime_3.4.0.v20080512
10  ACTIVE      org.eclipse.equinox.http.registry_1.0.100.v20080427-0830
11  ACTIVE      org.eclipse.core.contenttype_3.3.0.v20080604-1400
12  ACTIVE      org.apache.log4j_1.2.13.v200806030600
                Fragments=3
13  ACTIVE      javax.servlet_2.4.0.v200806031604
14  ACTIVE      org.eclipse.equinox.common_3.4.0.v20080421-2006
15  ACTIVE      ch01_1.0.0
16  RESOLVED    org.eclipse.core.runtime.compatibility.registry_3.2.200.v20070717
                Master=7
17  ACTIVE      org.eclipse.equinox.preferences_3.2.200.v20080421-2006
18  ACTIVE      org.eclipse.equinox.app_1.1.0.v20080421-2006
19  ACTIVE      org.eclipse.equinox.http.jetty_1.1.0.v20080425

osgi>
```

To start and stop your plug-in, simply use the bundle ID. (The bundle name can also be used, but who wants to type such long names?)

```
osgi> stop 15
271770 [OSGi Console] INFO  ch01.Activator  - Activator Stop
Jun 21, 2008 6:25:42 PM ch01.Activator stop
INFO: Activator Stop

osgi> start 15
Jun 21, 2008 6:25:47 PM ch01.Activator start
INFO: Activator Start
277188 [OSGi Console] INFO  ch01.Activator  - Activator Start
```

Using Logging Services

Enabling a logging service within a plug-in is somewhat different from logging in a traditional Java application. It is a bit trickier because of the dynamic component nature of the runtime.

To enable log4j in a traditional Java application, for example, the developer would create a log4j.properties file in the project classpath, and then use statements such as the following:

```
// Log4J Logger
private static final Logger logger = Logger.getLogger(Activator.class);

public void start(BundleContext context) throws Exception {
    super.start(context);
    plugin = this;

    logger.info("Activator Start");
}
```

However, putting log4j.properties in the plug-in class will not work, because the OSGi framework manages a per-bundle classpath. It returns this message:

```
log4j:WARN No appenders could be found for logger (ch01.Activator).
log4j:WARN Please initialize the log4j system properly.
```

The solution is to have the plug-in find log4j.properties in the classpath at runtime and use it. However, this is a little tricky. One way to handle this is to create a plug-in fragment and set the host plug-in ID to org.apache.log4j, as shown in Figure 1-9. This fragment will have a log4j.properties file at the main level. Then, at runtime, the fragment will attach itself to the log4j bundle classpath, thus finding the required log4j.properties file. The fragment must also be included in the run configuration for the plug-in.

■**Note** *Fragments* are separately packaged files whose contents are treated as if they were in the original plug-in archive file. They are useful for adding plug-in functionality, such as additional language translations, to an existing plug-in after it has been installed. Fragments are discussed further in Chapter 2.

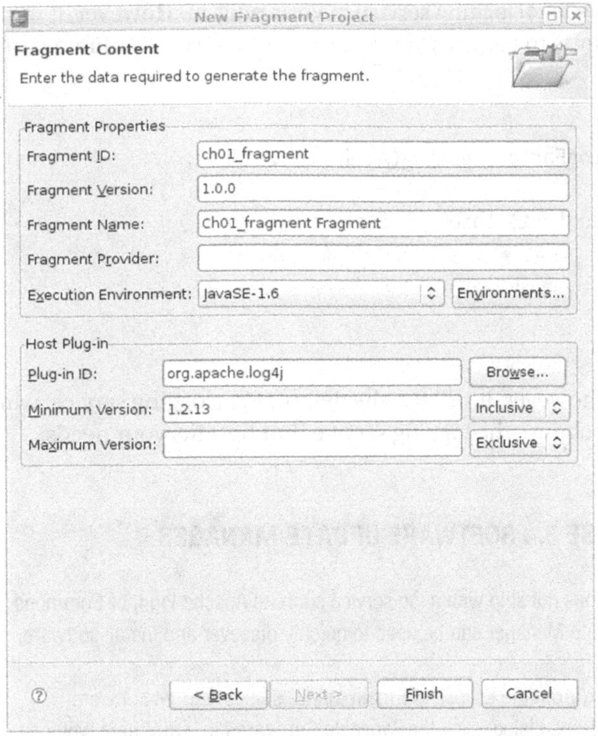

Figure 1-9. *Attaching a log4j.properties to the log4j bundle at runtime using a fragment*

Here is the procedure to create the fragment for this example:

1. From the Eclipse IDE main menu, select File ➤ New ➤ Other ➤ Plug-in Development ➤ Plug-in Fragment.

2. In the New Fragment Project dialog, enter the plug-in information as shown in Figure 1-9. Make sure the host plug-in points to org.apache.log4j. You can click the Browse button to find and select that plug-in ID. Then click Finish.

3. In the fragment folder, add a log4j.properties file with the log configuration shown in the following fragment. To add a text file, right-click the fragment folder and select New ➤ File. Make sure the file name is log4j.properties.

```
# Set root logger level to debug and its only appender to default.
log4j.rootLogger=debug, default

# default is set to be a ConsoleAppender.
log4j.appender.default=org.apache.log4j.ConsoleAppender

# default uses PatternLayout.
log4j.appender.default.layout=org.apache.log4j.PatternLayout
log4j.appender.default.layout.ConversionPattern=%-4r [%t] %-5p %c %x - %m%n
```

This technique should enable the log4j logging service in your plug-in. However, if this seems too complicated, a simpler way is to use the Commons Logging service within the main plug-in, using this code:

```
// Commons Log
private static final  Log log = LogFactory.getLog(Activator.class);

public void start(BundleContext context) throws Exception {
    super.start(context);
    plugin = this;
    log.info("Activator Start");
}
```

This fragment is much simpler; however, it will use the default Java logging service, which I personally dislike. It is up to you to choose the logging service that best fits your needs.

USING THE ECLIPSE 3.4 SOFTWARE UPDATE MANAGER

The Eclipse 3.4 (Ganymede) distribution does not ship with a log service such as Apache log4j or Commons Logging. However, the new Software Update Manager can be used to quickly discover and install software, including logging plug-ins.

To use the Software Update Manager, from the Eclipse IDE main menu, select Help ➤ Software Updates. In the Software Updates and Add-ons dialog, click the Available Software tab. From here, you can search for and install the Jakarta log4j and Commons Logging plug-ins.

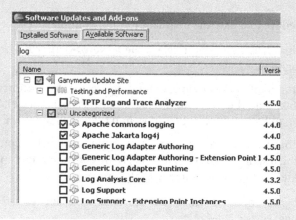

This concludes the exercise in this chapter. The goal of this exercise has been to provide an introduction to the power of the OSGi console and the basic plug-in life cycle, using a simple Jetty servlet extension point to listen for HTTP requests.

Summary

This chapter introduced Eclipse RCP. The following are the important points to take away from this chapter:

- In today's heterogeneous software world, there is a quest for openness and extensibility. A platform that addresses interoperability challenges and supports collaboration is of critical importance.

- Eclipse provides a consistent feature set on multiple platforms. It allows developers to concentrate on the problem at hand, rather than the details of the specific platform.

- The plug-in architecture makes it possible for Eclipse to support many programming languages and development paradigms.

- Eclipse is open source, free, and fully supported.

- Eclipse is designed to be extensible and configurable.

- Eclipse is at the forefront of the software tools industry. This means that you can depend on it as a viable, industrial-strength tool for the foreseeable future.

- The foundation of RCP includes Equinox, the core platform, SWT, JFace, and the Eclipse workbench.

  - Equinox is an implementation of the OSGi framework, a dynamic component model for remote component management. This is something that is missing in stand-alone JVM environments.

  - The core runtime implements the basic plug-in model based on extension points declared in XML in a manifest file (plugin.xml). The extension model provides a structured way for plug-ins to describe the ways they can be extended, and for client plug-ins to describe the extensions they supply.

  - SWT is a GUI toolkit with fast native access to multiple platform widget sets, providing a common API. It is designed for performance, native look and feel, and extensibility.

  - JFace is a window-system-independent GUI toolkit for handling many common programming tasks. It implements text, dialog, preference, and wizard frameworks, as well as actions and data viewers.

  - The workbench is the basic development environment in the Eclipse universe. It is divided into perspectives, viewers, editors, workspaces, and projects.

CHAPTER 2

■■■

Plug-ins: A First Glimpse

As you learned in Chapter 1, the RCP framework is based on plug-ins; nearly everything in Eclipse is a plug-in. Obviously, RCP developers need to understand the Eclipse plug-in model, as well as the extensions and extension points that are used to work with plug-ins. This chapter will explain these concepts and then demonstrate them with a hands-on web browser plug-in project.

Introducing the Eclipse Plug-in Model

The Eclipse Platform runtime plug-in model is a structured component that contributes code or data to the system. Plug-ins are the perfect mechanism for lightweight software component development because they provide seamless integration, extensibility, and a broad range of tools.

Plug-ins let your application use other developers' functionality or extend existing functionality. As noted in Chapter 1, an *extension point* is a well-defined place where other plug-ins can add functionality. The Eclipse workbench UI is an example of a plug-in that defines a number of extension points where other plug-ins can contribute menu and toolbar actions, drag-and-drop operations, dialogs, wizards, views, and editors.

As you learned in Chapter 1, all information about a plug-in is described in its manifest (plugin.xml). The declarative nature of this model provides a small memory footprint and fast performance, as the runtime can determine which extension points and extensions are supplied, without running the plug-in. Thus, many plug-ins may be installed, but none will be activated until a function is requested by the user. This is a critical feature for scalability and robustness.

With the Eclipse plug-in model, you get a number of tools, including the following:

- A workbench with every imaginable component required by today's applications: menus, toolbars, editors, wizards, and more

- A resource management framework for the manipulation of projects, folders, and files, and for organizing and storing development artifacts on disk

- Team support for programming, repository access, and versioning

- Debug support for other plug-ins to implement language-specific program launchers and debuggers

- A help system with an optimized web server and document-integration facility to contribute documentation as viewable books

- Multilanguage development tools for languages such as Java and C/C++

But perhaps the most compelling reason to use the Eclipse plug-in model is the market share Eclipse has captured. One study by BZ Research[1] found that Eclipse gained significant market share in 2005 with steady growth. Eclipse usage grew 9% in 2005, and at the time of writing, it had captured 65.1% of the open source IDE market. In another study by QA Systems,[2] among more than 1,400 developers—software architects and software managers worldwide—Eclipse was found to be the Java IDE with the largest market share (see Figure 2-1).

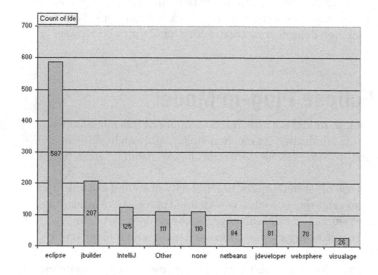

Figure 2-1. *Eclipse market share (from Java IDE Market Share Survey by QA Systems)*

The Plug-in Class and BundleContext

The plug-in class usually extends the class AbstractUIPlugin, which supplies the structure for managing UI resources. AbstractUIPlugin is an abstract class that provides default implementations to manage images, dialog settings, and a preference store during the plug-in's lifetime.

1. "Java Use and Awareness" by BZ Research (publishers of *SD Times* and *Eclipse Review*), available online at http://ianskerrett.wordpress.com/2006/03/11/eclipse-gains-market-share-in-2005/.
2. Java IDE Market Share Survey by QA Systems, available online at http://www.qa-systems.com/products/qstudioforjava/ide_marketshare.html.

The plug-in class centralizes the life-cycle aspects and overall semantics of a plug-in. Two methods, start and stop, define this life cycle, each receiving a reference to a BundleContext with additional information about the runtime.

BundleContext provides the bundle with execution context used to grant access to the framework. BundleContext is a reference that contains information related to the plug-in and other bundles/plug-ins in the system. BundleContext methods allow a bundle to do the following:

- Subscribe to events published by the framework.

- Register service objects with the service registry.

- Retrieve service references from the framework service registry.

- Install new bundles in the framework.

- Get the list of bundles installed.

- Get the Bundle object for a bundle.

- Create files in a persistent storage area provided for the bundle.

The plug-in class's start method is best used to initialize and register objects, but it must be used with care. Registration activities such as adding listeners or starting background threads are appropriate if they can be done quickly; otherwise, it is better to trigger these actions when the data is accessed. Data initialization should be done lazily (when first accessed), rather than at bundle startup. This ensures that large data structures are created when needed.

Caution Beware of premature initialization! It is important to look closely at your plug-in's initialization tasks and consider alternatives, as premature initialization can cause your plug-in's code and data to be loaded long before it is necessary.

Manifests

As explained in Chapter 1, a plug-in is described by the files MANIFEST.MF and plugin.xml. The sample MANIFEST.MF definition shown in Listing 2-1 includes information such as the bundle name, symbolic name (or plug-in ID), version, vendor, bundle dependencies, and classpath.

Listing 2-1. *Sample MANIFEST.MF File*

```
Manifest-Version: 1.0
Bundle-ManifestVersion: 2
Bundle-Name: My Plug-in
Bundle-SymbolicName: org.eclipse.ui.examples.mytool; singleton:=true
Bundle-Version: 3.3.0.qualifier
```

```
Bundle-ClassPath: readmetool.jar
Bundle-Activator: org.eclipse.ui.examples.mytool.MyPlugin
Bundle-Vendor: ACME
Bundle-Localization: plugin
Require-Bundle: org.eclipse.ui,
 org.eclipse.core.resources,
 org.eclipse.core.runtime,
 org.eclipse.ui.views,
 org.eclipse.ui.ide,
Eclipse-AutoStart: true
Eclipse-AutoStart-comment:
```

The format of MANIFEST.MF consists of key/value pairs separated by semicolons, as in Bundle-Name: My Plug-in. Multiple values are separated by commas (as in bundle dependencies).

Most of the file information is self-describing; however, some values are obscure. For example, Eclipse-AutoStart: true tells the runtime to start the plug-in at boot time, and Eclipse-AutoStart-comment displays descriptive text for the plug-in when started within the OSGi console.

Plug-in Fragments and Features

A *plug-in fragment* is a component that provides extra functionality to an existing, installed plug-in. For example, a fragment might provide localization for different languages; add features incrementally, so a full release of the plug-in isn't necessary; or supply platform-specific functionality, such as native code.

At runtime, the fragment attaches itself to the host plug-in. The main difference between a fragment and a plug-in is that a fragment does not have a plug-in class, and its life cycle is managed by its target plug-in. Otherwise, they are essentially the same.

A *feature*, on the other hand, is the packaging of a group of related plug-ins into a product, and it is described by a file called feature.xml. It includes information such as references to the plug-ins, copyright, and licensing. Chapters 3 and 9 include more details on using features.

Adding Extension Points

The workbench defines extension points that allow plug-ins to contribute behaviors to existing views and editors or to provide implementations for new views and editors.

The easiest way to add extension points to your plug-in is to use the plug-in manifest editor. Click the Extensions tab, and then click the Add button to start the New Extension wizard, as shown in Figure 2-2. You can select to add an existing extension point using the Extension Points tab or create a new extension using the Extension Wizards tab. All extension points are described with XML in the plug-in manifest (plugin.xml).

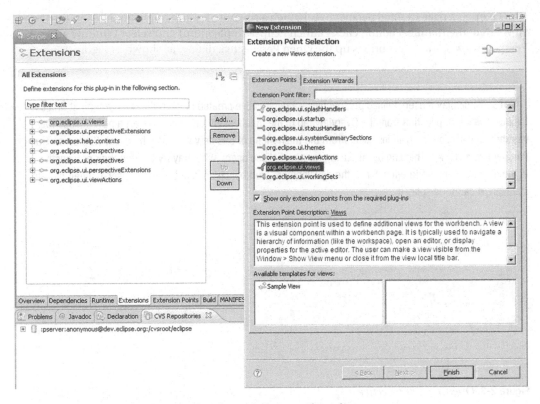

Figure 2-2. *Adding an extension point through the manifest editor*

Let's take a look at some of the most commonly used extension points:

- org.eclipse.ui.perspectives
- org.eclipse.ui.views
- org.eclipse.ui.viewActions
- org.eclipse.ui.editors
- org.eclipse.ui.popupMenus
- org.eclipse.ui.commands

Perspectives

A *perspective* is a visual container for a set of views and editors. A view is typically used to navigate a hierarchy of information, open an editor, or display properties for the active editor.

The Eclipse designers compare a perspective to a page within a book. Like a page, only one perspective is visible at any time.

To open a user-defined perspective, launch a separate Eclipse application (from the Overview tab of the manifest editor, click Launch Eclipse Application) and select Window ➤ Open Perspective ➤ Other. This brings up the Open Perspective dialog, as shown in Figure 2-3.

Note To display a user-defined perspective—a perspective created in your plug-in—you must first click Launch Eclipse Application from the Overview tab of the manifest editor. This will start a new Eclipse IDE workbench with your plug-in installed. From the main menu of this new workbench, select Window ➤ Open Perspective ➤ Other. This can be confusing for new Eclipse users, who may try to open their perspective in the development workbench. Since the development workbench does not have the user-defined plug-in installed, it cannot display it.

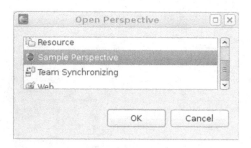

Figure 2-3. *Opening a perspective*

A perspective can be easily created using the Extension wizard, but behind the scenes, it is described by the plug-in xml. For example, the Sample Perspective shown in Figure 2-3 (sample.Perspective1) is defined as shown in Listing 2-2.

Listing 2-2. *Sample Perspective Extension (in plugin.xml)*

```
<extension
      point="org.eclipse.ui.perspectives">
   <perspective
        class="sample.Perspective1"
        icon="icons/sample.gif"
        id="sample.Perspective1"
        name="Sample Perspective">
   </perspective>
</extension>
```

In this definition, the class attribute is the perspective implementation class, which can be used to programmatically add views, action sets, wizard shortcuts, and so on. The id attribute uniquely identifies the perspective within the workbench. The name and icon attributes define the visual layout.

The org.eclipse.ui.perspectives extension point allows plug-ins to add perspectives to the workbench. As an example, you could create a new perspective extension to the perspective sample.Perspective1 with two views: the Sample view and the JDT Package Explorer view, as shown in Figure 2-4. The XML for this example is shown in Listing 2-3.

Listing 2-3. *Perspective Extension Point to Add Package Explorer and Sample Views (in plugin.xml)*

```
<extension
      point="org.eclipse.ui.perspectiveExtensions">
   <perspectiveExtension
         targetID="sample.Perspective1">
      <view
            id="org.eclipse.jdt.ui.PackageExplorer"
            minimized="false"
            ratio="0.5"
            relationship="left"
            relative="sample.views.SampleView">
      </view>
      <view
            id="sample.views.SampleView"
            minimized="false"
            ratio="0.5"
            relationship="right"
            relative="org.eclipse.jdt.ui.PackageExplorer">
      </view>
   </perspectiveExtension>
</extension>
```

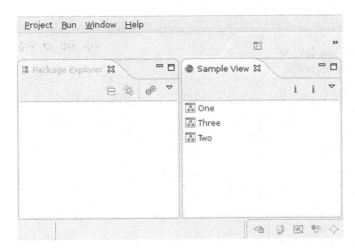

Figure 2-4. *The Sample Perspective extended with the Package Explorer and Sample views*

The most important attribute of this perspective extension is targetID, which is the unique identifier of the perspective. This ID can be used to reference the perspective programmatically.

The perspective in Listing 2-3 contains the view org.eclipse.jdt.ui.PackageExplorer (which is the built-in Java Package Explorer) and the user-defined view sample.views. SampleView. Each view is identified by a unique id attribute, followed by these attributes:

- minimized: Indicates whether or not the view is minimized.

- ratio: Sets the percentage of the relative view area for this view extension.

- relationship: Indicates the placement of the view (left or right).

- relative: Indicates positioning (stacking) relative to an existing view.

Views

The org.eclipse.ui.views extension point allows plug-ins to add views to the workbench. A *view* is a workbench part that performs a visual task such as navigating a hierarchy of information or displaying properties for an object. Listing 2-4 shows the XML for the Sample view shown in Figure 2-5.

Listing 2-4. *Sample View Extension (in plugin.xml)*

```
<extension
      point="org.eclipse.ui.views">
   <category
        name="Sample Category"
        id="Sample">
   </category>
   <view
        name="Sample View"
        icon="icons/sample.gif"
        category="Sample"
        class="sample.views.SampleView"
        id="sample.views.SampleView">
   </view>
</extension>
```

Figure 2-5. *Sample view*

The category element's name attribute is used to group the view within the workbench view registry (accessible through the main menu Window ➤ Show View ➤ Other). The implementation class method createPartControl(Composite parent) is used to add visual components, as follows:

```
public class SampleView extends ViewPart {
    ...

    public void createPartControl(Composite parent) {
        /**
         * Layout the user interface
         */
    }
    ...
}
```

View Actions

View actions contribute behavior to views that already exist in the workbench. The org. eclipse.ui.view extension point allows plug-ins to contribute menu items, submenus, and toolbar icons to an existing view's local pull-down menu and local toolbar. Listing 2-5 shows the XML for a sample view action.

Listing 2-5. *Sample View Action Extension (in plugin.xml)*

```
<extension
        point="org.eclipse.ui.viewActions">
    <viewContribution
            id="sample.view.Contribution1"
            targetID="org.eclipse.jdt.ui.PackageExplorer">
        <action
                class="sample.actions.ViewActionDelegate1"
                icon="icons/releng_gears.gif"
                id="sample.Action1"
                label="Sample Action 1"
                menubarPath="additions"
                style="push"
                toolbarPath="additions"
                tooltip="Sample Action1">
        </action>
    </viewContribution>
</extension>
```

The view to which you are adding the action is specified in the targetID. In this case, a new action is contributed to the JDT Package Explorer. The action will display as an addition to the view's menu and toolbar.

To provide the action behavior, the implementation class `sample.actions.ViewActionDelegate1` must implement the `IViewActionDelegate` interface, as shown in Listing 2-6.

Listing 2-6. *Sample Action Class to Display an Information Message Dialog*

```
public class ViewActionDelegate1 implements IViewActionDelegate {

    @Override
    public void init(IViewPart view) {
    }

    @Override
    public void run(IAction action) {
        MessageDialog.openInformation(
            PlatformUI.getWorkbench(). getActiveWorkbenchWindow().getShell()
                , "Sample View"
                , "Sample Message");
    }

    @Override
    public void selectionChanged(IAction action, ISelection selection) {
    }
}
```

Figure 2-6 shows the view contribution added to the toolbar of the Package Explorer with the associated action delegate. The view's menu can be accessed by clicking the down arrow on the right side of the view's toolbar.

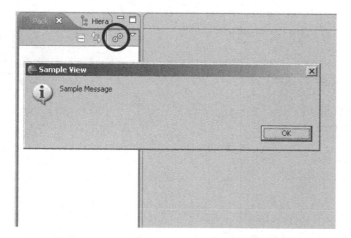

Figure 2-6. *View action added to the Java Package Explorer*

Editors

The org.eclipse.ui.editors extension point allows plug-ins to add editors to the workbench. An *editor* is a workbench part that allows a user to edit an object (often a file). Editors operate in a manner similar to file system editing tools, except that they are tightly integrated into the platform UI. Only one editor can be open for any particular object type in a workbench page. (You can open another editor on the same file from another window or perspective.)

Listing 2-7 shows an example of a the XML for the multipage editor extension shown in Figure 2-7.

Listing 2-7. *Sample Multipage Editor Extension (in plugin.xml)*

```
<extension
        point="org.eclipse.ui.editors">
  <editor
     name="Sample Multi-page Editor"
     extensions="mpe"
     icon="icons/sample.gif"

     contributorClass="editorsample.editors.MultiPageEditorContributor"
     class="editorsample.editors.MultiPageEditor"
     id="editorsample.editors.MultiPageEditor">
  </editor>
</extension>
```

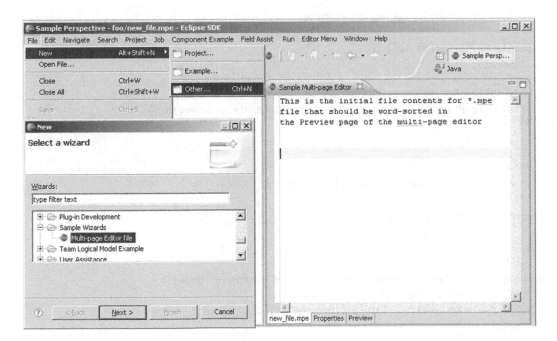

Figure 2-7. *Multipage editor with a wizard*

The contributorClass attribute is responsible for providing editor-related actions and global action handlers. For example, the following code adds global action handlers to add cut/copy functionality to the editor within the contributor class:

```
IActionBars actionBars = getActionBars();
actionBars.setGlobalActionHandler(
    ActionFactory.DELETE.getId(),
    getAction(editor, ITextEditorActionConstants.CUT));
actionBars.setGlobalActionHandler(
    ActionFactory.UNDO.getId(),
    getAction(editor, ITextEditorActionConstants.COPY));
```

Listing 2-8 shows the skeleton and UI of a multipage editor.

Listing 2-8. *Multipage Editor Sample Class*

```
public class MultiPageEditor extends MultiPageEditorPart
  implements IResourceChangeListener
{

 /** The text editor used in page 0. */
 private TextEditor editor;

 ...

 /**
  * Creates a multi-page editor example.
  */
 public MultiPageEditor() {
   super();

   // Listen for resource change events
   ResourcesPlugin.getWorkspace().addResourceChangeListener(this);
 }


 /**
  * Creates the pages of the multi-page editor.
  */
 protected void createPages() {
   // Create pages here
 }

 public void resourceChanged(final IResourceChangeEvent event){
   // Fires on resource change
   // Could be used to close all project files on project close.
   ...
 }
 ...
}
```

Pop-up Menus

The org.eclipse.ui.popupMenus extension point allows a plug-in to contribute to the pop-up menus of other views and editors. Pop-up menus belong to two different categories:

- objectContribution: The menu item will appear in pop-up menus for views or editors where objects of the specified type are selected (for example, an object of type IFile, which is a regular file).

- viewerContribution: The menu item will appear in the pop-up menu of a view or editor specified by ID.

Listing 2-9 shows the XML for a pop-up with the label New Submenu for all viewers where an object of type IFile is selected.

Listing 2-9. *Sample Pop-up Menu Extension (in plugin.xml)*

```
<extension
      point="org.eclipse.ui.popupMenus">
   <objectContribution
         objectClass="org.eclipse.core.resources.IFile"
           nameFilter="*.txt"
         id="SamplePopupMenu.contribution1">
      <menu
            label="New Submenu"
            path="additions"
            id="SamplePopupMenu.menu1">
         <separator
               name="group1">
         </separator>
      </menu>
      <action
            label="New Action"
            class="popupmenu.popup.actions.NewAction"
            menubarPath="SamplePopupMenu.menu1/group1"
            id="SamplePopupMenu.newAction">
      </action>
   </objectContribution>
</extension>
```

The action "New Action" is contributed for the object class IFile. This means that any view containing IFile objects will show the contribution if IFile objects are selected. The selection criteria can be further restricted with a name filter (nameFilter="*.txt") and for single selections (enablesFor="1").

The registration of this menu does not run any code from your plug-in until the menu item is actually selected. When the menu item is selected, the workbench will run the specified action class. Listing 2-10 shows the NewAction class for the extension point in Listing 2-9.

Listing 2-10. *Action Class for the Action Extension Point*

```
public class NewAction implements IObjectActionDelegate
{
  public NewAction() {
      super();
  }

  public void run(IAction action) {
      Shell shell = new Shell();
      MessageDialog.openInformation(shell,
          "SamplePopUp Plug-in",
          "New Action was executed.");
  }
}
```

Figure 2-8 shows the pop-up menu New Submenu showing when an object file is selected within any view. When it is selected, the specified action class will fire.

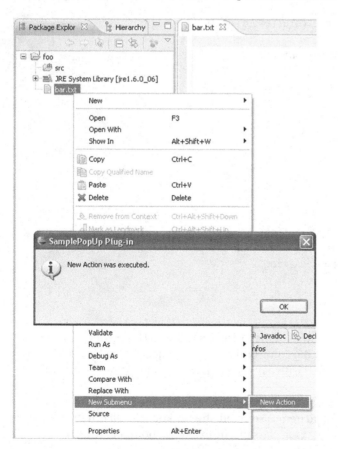

Figure 2-8. *Pop-up menu contribution object and related action class*

Commands

Command contributions can be used to add custom menus to the menu bar and buttons to the toolbar. Both items can then invoke a custom action. The following extension points are used to implement commands:

- `org.eclipse.ui.commands`: Describes the command and associated category.
- `org.eclipse.ui.handlers`: Describes the handler that will fire when the command is invoked.
- `org.eclipse.ui.bindings`: Used to bind a character sequence to the command.
- `org.eclipse.ui.menus`: Used to add menus to the main menu bar, toolbar, or pop-up menus.

Let's take a look at each of these extension points.

Commands

The `org.eclipse.ui.commands`: extension point allows a plug-in to contribute the command name and category. Listing 2-11 shows an example of the XML for a category and command.

Listing 2-11. *Sample Command and Category Extension (in plugin.xml)*

```
<extension
      point="org.eclipse.ui.commands">
   <category
         name="Sample Category"
         id="SampleCommand.commands.category">
   </category>
   <command
         name="Sample Command"
         categoryId="SampleCommand.commands.category"
         id="SampleCommand.commands.sampleCommand">
   </command>
</extension>
```

The `name` attribute defines the category or command name for display in the UI. (Command names typically use an imperative verb.) The `id` attribute is a unique identifier for the category or command. Related commands are usually grouped by categories.

Handlers

Handlers describe the custom action that fires when the command is selected. Listing 2-12 shows an example of an `org.eclipse.ui.handlers` extension point.

Listing 2-12. *Sample Handler Extension (in plugin.xml)*

```
<extension
     point="org.eclipse.ui.handlers">
   <handler
        commandId="SampleCommand.commands.sampleCommand"
        class="command.handlers.SampleHandler">
   </handler>
</extension>
```

The most important attributes are commandID and class. The commandID attribute is the id of the command to associate with the handler implementation. The class attribute defines a class that implements org.eclipse.core.commands or extends org.eclipse.core.command. AbstractHandler.

The basic handler implementation is shown in Listing 2-13.

Listing 2-13. *SampleHandler Class*

```
public class SampleHandler extends AbstractHandler
{
public Object execute(ExecutionEvent event)
throws ExecutionException
{
    IWorkbenchWindow window = HandlerUtil.getActiveWorkbenchWindowChecked(event);
    MessageDialog.openInformation(window.getShell(),
        "SampleCommand Plug-in",
        "Hello, World");
     return null;
  }
}
```

Bindings

Key bindings bind a character sequence with a command. Listing 2-14 shows an example of an org.eclipse.ui.bindings extension point.

Listing 2-14. *Sample Binding Extension (in plugin.xml)*

```
<extension
     point="org.eclipse.ui.bindings">
   <key
        commandId="SampleCommand.commands.sampleCommand"
        contextId="org.eclipse.ui.contexts.window"
        sequence="CTRL+6"
        schemeId="org.eclipse.ui.defaultAcceleratorConfiguration">
   </key>
</extension>
```

The following are the most important attributes:

- commandId: The ID of the command to be executed when this binding is triggered.

- sequence: The character sequence for the binding. Keys are separated by +. Examples of sequences are CTRL+6, ALT+F1, SHIFT+1, and M1.

- contextId: Identifier for the context where the binding is active.

- schemeId: Identifier for the scheme where the binding is active.

Menus

Menu contributions add menus to the menu bar or toolbar, or create pop-up menus. Listing 2-15 shows an example of an org.eclipse.ui.menus extension point, which adds the menu and toolbar item shown in Figure 2-9.

Listing 2-15. *Sample Menu Extension (in plugin.xml)*

```
<extension
        point="org.eclipse.ui.menus">
  <menuContribution
        locationURI="menu:org.eclipse.ui.main.menu?after=additions">
        <menu
             label="Sample Menu"
             mnemonic="M"
             id="SampleCommand.menus.sampleMenu">
          <command
               commandId="SampleCommand.commands.sampleCommand"
               mnemonic="S"
               id="SampleCommand.menus.sampleCommand">
          </command>
        </menu>
  </menuContribution>
  <menuContribution
     locationURI="toolbar:org.eclipse.ui.main.toolbar?after=additions">
        <toolbar
             id="SampleCommand.toolbars.sampleToolbar">
          <command
               commandId="SampleCommand.commands.sampleCommand"
               icon="icons/sample.gif"
               tooltip="Say hello world"
               id="SampleCommand.toolbars.sampleCommand">
          </command>
        </toolbar>
    </menuContribution>
</extension>
```

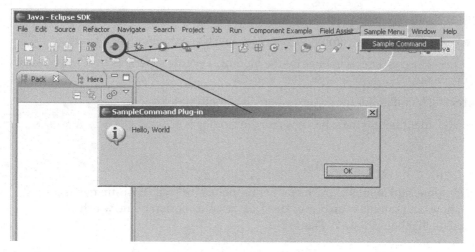

Figure 2-9. *Command implementation with menu and toolbar contributions*

The locationURI attribute defines the URI of the insertion point for the menu addition. The format is as follows:

<scheme>:*<id>*?*<placement>*=*<id>*

where:

- *scheme* is the type of manager used to handle the contribution: menu, popup, or toolbar.
- *id* is the identifier of an existing menu, view, or editor.
- placement is either before or after.

We have covered the most common extension points used to contribute to the workbench UI. There are plenty more, which you can explore at your leisure.

Hands-on Exercise: Fun with a Web Browser Plug-in

Now it is time to put your newly acquired skills to use. The goal of this exercise is to build a perspective that includes two views: a Web Browser view and a Bookmarks view, as shown in Figure 2-10.

The Web Browser view has a toolbar and menu to enter a URL, as well as the typical Home, Back, Forward, and Add Bookmark buttons. When the Add Bookmark button is clicked, an action will be triggered to add the target URL to the Bookmarks view. The Bookmarks view will listen for double-clicks and browse to the specific URL. It will also include an action to delete a bookmark.

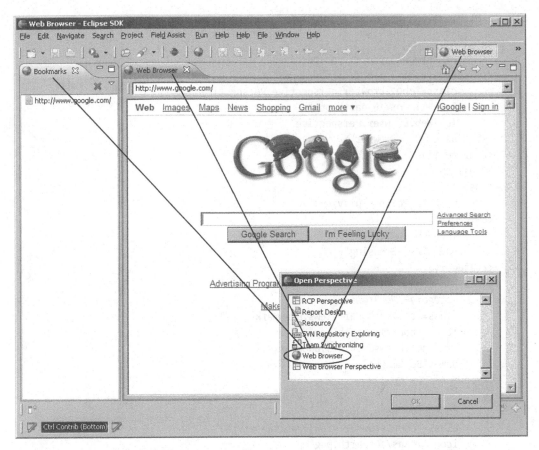

Figure 2-10. *Web browser plug-in showing the browser, bookmarks, and perspective selection components*

You'll use two extensions for this exercise: `org.eclipse.ui.perspectives` and `org.eclipse.ui.views`.

To begin, from the OSGi console, create a new plug-in project (File ➤ New ➤ Project ➤ Plug-in Development ➤ Plug-in Project) with the default settings, as described in Chapter 1. Give it a name such as `Web Browser`. Make sure the "This plug-in will make contributions to the UI" option is checked and the "Would you like to create a rich client application?" option is set to No. (Chapter 3 discusses the Plug-in Project wizard options in more detail.)

Adding a Perspective Extension Point

As explained earlier in the chapter, a perspective is a critical container for visual elements such as views and toolbars. In this case, the perspective defines two views: Web Browser and Bookmarks. Create this extension point with the manifest editor as shown in Listing 2-16.

Listing 2-16. *Perspective Extension Point for the Web Browser Plug-in*

```
<extension
    point="org.eclipse.ui.perspectives">
  <perspective
      class="ch02.browser.perspective.PerspectiveFactory"
      icon="icons/16-earth.png"
      id="Web.Browser.Perspective"
      name="Web Browser">
  </perspective>
</extension>
<extension
    point="org.eclipse.ui.views">
  <category
      id="WebBrowser"
      name="Web Browsing">
  </category>
  <view
      category="WebBrowser"
      class="ch02.browser.views.BookMarksView"
      icon="icons/16-earth.png"
      id="ch02.browser.views.BookMarksView"
      name="Bookmarks">
  </view>
  <view
      category="WebBrowser"
      class="ch02.browser.views.WebBrowserView"
      icon="icons/16-earth.png"
      id="ch02.browser.views.WebBrowserView"
      name="Web Browser"
      restorable="true">
  </view>
</extension>
```

Listing 2-16 creates the perspective Web Browser with the views Web Browser and Bookmarks. Theses views will be accessible from the Window ➤ Open Perspective ➤ Other menu of the workbench when the plug-in is started. Notice that the extension point requires three implementation classes for the perspective factory and the two views: ch02.browser. perspective.PerspectiveFactory, ch02.browser.views.BookMarksView, and ch02.browser. views.WebBrowserView. The next sections explain these in more detail.

Adding a Perspective Factory

The job of the perspective factory class is to lay out the views in the workbench window. The fragment shown in Listing 2-17 lays out the Bookmarks view on the left, taking 20% of the real estate, and the Web Browser view on the right, taking the other 80%. Insert the code in Listing 2-17 into the perspective factory class of your project (ch02.browser.perspective. PerspectiveFactory.java).

Listing 2-17. *Perspective Factory for the Exercise in (ch02.browser.perspective.*
PerspectiveFactory.java)

```
public class PerspectiveFactory implements IPerspectiveFactory
{
  public void createInitialLayout(IPageLayout layout) {
      String editorArea = layout.getEditorArea();
      layout.setEditorAreaVisible(false);

      layout.addView(BookMarksView.ID, IPageLayout.LEFT, 0.2f, editorArea);
      layout.addView(WebBrowserView.ID, IPageLayout.LEFT, 0.8f, editorArea);

  }
}
```

Adding Views and Content

Listing 2-18 shows the layout of the Web Browser view for the plug-in. The view contains the SWT Browser widget, as well as a combo box where URLs can be typed. The view also has a local toolbar with Home, Back, and Forward buttons, and a simple menu to add bookmarks. The code in this listing is a bit long as it implements a custom web browser with toolbars and menus. Insert this code in the ch02.browser.views.WebBrowserView.java file of your project.

Listing 2-18. *Web Browser View (in ch02.browser.views.WebBrowserView.java)*

```
public class WebBrowserView extends ViewPart {
    static public String ID = WebBrowserView.class.getName();

    // View widgets
    private Combo urlCombo;
    private Browser browser;

    // Local view actions
    private Action actionBack;
    private Action actionForward;
    private Action actionHome;
    private Action actionAddBookmark;

    // Start URL
    private final String startUrl = "http://www.google.com/";

    // View icon
    public static ImageDescriptor ICON_HOME = BrowserActivator
            .getImageDescriptor("icons/16x16-home.gif");

    private IStatusLineManager statusLine;
```

```java
// Create view controls
public void createPartControl(Composite parent) {
    Composite comp = new Composite(parent, SWT.NONE);
    comp.setLayout(new GridLayout(1, true));

    CoolBar coolbar = new CoolBar(comp, SWT.NONE);
    coolbar.setLayoutData(new GridData(GridData.FILL_HORIZONTAL));

    // Create a cool item with a URL combo
    CoolItem item = new CoolItem(coolbar, SWT.NONE);
    item.setControl(createComboView(coolbar, new GridData(
            GridData.FILL_HORIZONTAL))); // gridData));
    calcSize(item);

    /*
     * Web browser widget
     */
    try {
        browser = new Browser(comp, SWT.BORDER); // MOZILLA);
    } catch (SWTError e) {
        BrowserActivator.showErrorMessage(getViewSite().getShell(),
                "Error creating browser:" + e);
        return;
    }

    browser.setLayoutData(new GridData(GridData.FILL_BOTH));
    browser.setUrl(startUrl);

    browser.addLocationListener(new LocationListener() {
        public void changed(LocationEvent event) {
            locChanged(event);
        }

        public void changing(LocationEvent event) {
            locChanging(event);
        }
    });

    // Progress listener
    browser.addProgressListener(new ProgressListener() {
        public void changed(ProgressEvent event) {
            onProgress(event);
        }

        public void completed(ProgressEvent event) {
        }
    });
```

```java
        makeActions();
        contributeToActionBars();

        // Status line
        statusLine = getViewSite().getActionBars().getStatusLineManager();
    }

    @Override
    public void setFocus() {
        browser.setFocus();
    }

    /**
     * Creates the urlCombo box view
     */
    private Control createComboView(Composite parent, Object layoutData) {
        urlCombo = new Combo(parent, SWT.NONE);
        urlCombo.setLayoutData(layoutData);
        urlCombo.addSelectionListener(new SelectionListener() {

            public void widgetDefaultSelected(SelectionEvent e) {

                final String url = ((Combo) e.getSource()).getText();
                browser.setUrl(url);
                urlCombo.add(url);
            }

            public void widgetSelected(SelectionEvent e) {
                browser.setUrl(((Combo) e.getSource()).getText());
            }

        });

        return urlCombo;
    }

    /**
     * Helper method to calculate the size of the cool item
     */
    private void calcSize(CoolItem item) {
        Control control = item.getControl();
        org.eclipse.swt.graphics.Point pt = control.computeSize(
                SWT.DEFAULT, SWT.DEFAULT);
        pt = item.computeSize(pt.x, pt.y);
        item.setSize(pt);
    }
```

```java
// Create local actions
private void makeActions() {
    actionBack = new Action() {
        public void run() {
            browser.back();
        }
    };
    actionBack.setText("Back");
    actionBack.setToolTipText("Back");
    actionBack.setImageDescriptor(PlatformUI.getWorkbench()
            .getSharedImages().getImageDescriptor(
                    ISharedImages.IMG_TOOL_BACK));

    actionForward = new Action() {
        public void run() {
            browser.forward();
        }
    };
    actionForward.setText("Forward");
    actionForward.setToolTipText("Forward");
    actionForward.setImageDescriptor(PlatformUI.getWorkbench()
            .getSharedImages().getImageDescriptor(
                    ISharedImages.IMG_TOOL_FORWARD));

    actionHome = new Action() {
        public void run() {
            browser.setUrl(startUrl);
        }
    };
    actionHome.setText("Home");
    actionHome.setToolTipText("Home");
    actionHome.setImageDescriptor(ICON_HOME);

    actionAddBookmark = new Action() {
        public void run() {
            addBookmark(urlCombo.getText());
        }
    };
    actionAddBookmark.setText("Add Bookmark");
    actionAddBookmark.setToolTipText("Add Bookmark");
    actionAddBookmark.setImageDescriptor(PlatformUI.getWorkbench()
            .getSharedImages().getImageDescriptor(
                    ISharedImages.IMG_OBJ_FILE));

}
```

```java
private void contributeToActionBars() {
    IActionBars bars = getViewSite().getActionBars();
    fillLocalPullDown(bars.getMenuManager());
    fillLocalToolBar(bars.getToolBarManager());

}

private void fillLocalToolBar(IToolBarManager manager) {
    // Fill local toobar
    manager.add(actionHome);
    manager.add(actionBack);
    manager.add(actionForward);

    // Other plugins can add actions here
    manager.add(new Separator(IWorkbenchActionConstants.MB_ADDITIONS));
}

private void fillLocalPullDown(IMenuManager manager) {
    manager.add(actionAddBookmark);

    // Other plugins can add actions here
    manager.add(new Separator(IWorkbenchActionConstants.MB_ADDITIONS));
}

/**
 * Add bookmark
 *
 * @param url
 */
private void addBookmark(final String url) {
    BookMarksView v = (BookMarksView) BrowserActivator.getView(
            getViewSite().getWorkbenchWindow(), BookMarksView.ID);
    if (v != null)
        v.addBookmark(url);

}

/**
 * Fires after the web browser location has changed
 */
void locChanged(LocationEvent event) {
    urlCombo.setText(event.location);
}
```

```
/**
 * Fires on load progress
 */
private void onProgress(ProgressEvent event) {
    if (event.total == 0)
        return;
    int ratio = event.current * 100 / event.total;

    // Status line
    statusLine.getProgressMonitor().worked(ratio);
}

public void navigateTo(String url) {
    browser.setUrl(url);
}
}
```

Let's look at some of the important parts of the code in Listing 2-18 in more detail.

Adding the Web Browser Widget

The SWT Browser widget allows the user to visualize and navigate through HTML documents. Adding a browser to your application and listening for events is very simple. The following fragment creates a browser and sets the starting URL:

```
try {
    Browser browser = new Browser(parentcomp, SWT.BORDER);
}
catch (SWTError e) {
    System.err.printl(getViewSite().getShell() ,
            "Error creating browser:" + e);
    return;
}

browser.setLayoutData(new GridData(GridData.FILL_BOTH));
browser.setUrl(startUrl);
```

The Browser widget is capable of listening for progress events to display information on the status line:

```
// Web Browser progress event listener
browser.addProgressListener(new ProgressListener() {
  public void changed(ProgressEvent event) {
    onProgress(event);
  }
  public void completed(ProgressEvent event) {
  }
});
```

```
// fires on progress change
private void onProgress (ProgressEvent event) {
        if (event.total == 0) return;
        int ratio = event.current * 100 / event.total;

        statusLine.getProgressMonitor().worked(ratio);

        if ( ratio == 100)
          getViewSite().
          getActionBars().
          getStatusLineManager().
          getProgressMonitor().
          done();
}
```

The ProgressListener interface implements the methods: changed, when progress is made during the loading of the current location, and completed, which is called when the current location has been completely loaded. The method onProgress in the previous fragment simply displays the ratio of the load operation in the status line progress bar, and it hides it when complete.

Filling a View Toolbar

Each view should fill the local toolbar and pull-down menu with local actions:

```
private void fillLocalToolBar(IToolBarManager manager) {
        // Fill local toobar
        manager.add(actionHome);
        manager.add(actionBack);
        manager.add(actionForward);

        // Other plugins can add actions here
        manager.add(new Separator(IWorkbenchActionConstants.MB_ADDITIONS));
}

private void fillLocalPullDown(IMenuManager manager)
{
        manager.add(actionAddBookmark);

        // Other plugins can add actions here
        manager.add(new Separator(IWorkbenchActionConstants.MB_ADDITIONS));
}
```

The action separator, new Separator(IWorkbenchActionConstants.MB_ADDITIONS), allows other plug-ins to contribute actions to the view's toolbar and pull-down menu.

Invoking Methods in Other Views

Finally, to invoke a public method in another view, the view registry from the workbench can be used to get a reference to the target view, and a cast be done. For example, the next two fragments define two utility functions: addBookmark and getView.

```
/**
 * Add a bookmark to the Bookmarks view.
 * This function goes in ch02.browser.views.WebBrowserView.java
 * @param url
 */
private void addBookmark(final String url)
{
    BookMarksView v = (BookMarksView)BrowserActivator.
            getView(getViewSite().getWorkbenchWindow()
                    ,BookMarksView.ID);
    if ( v != null ) v.addBookmark(url);

}


// Get a view from the registry
// This function goes in the plug-in activator class ch02.WebBrowserActivator.java
public static IViewPart getView (IWorkbenchWindow window,  String ViewID)
{
    IViewReference[] refs =  window.getActivePage().getViewReferences();

    for (IViewReference viewReference : refs) {
        f ( viewReference.getId().equals(ViewID) )
            return viewReference.getView(true);
    }
        return null;
}
```

The addBookmark function adds a string URL to the Bookmarks view (the same way you save bookmarks from the web browser). To do this, addBookmark calls getView to load the Bookmarks view (BookMarksView.ID) from the Eclipse view registry. It then calls the BookMarksView.addBookmark() method. Note that getView is a global utility function that should go in the plug-in activator (ch02.WebBrowserActivator.java), but it can be placed anywhere.

Testing the Plug-in

To start the plug-in, click the Launch as Eclipse application link from the manifest editor. A new workbench will be started. Then, from the main menu, select Window ➤ Open Perspective ➤ Other ➤ Web Browser. The resulting perspective should appear as shown earlier in Figure 2-10.

Enhancing the Web Browser

If you have used the Eclipse Web Tools Platform (WTP), which is a subcomponent of Eclipse and bundles a built-in web browser, you may wonder why you need a web browser in the first place. One reason is to get finer control over the browser itself. For example, you could trap content and perform a custom action. In this section, I'll describe how to enhance the browser by trapping the HTTP response when a link is clicked and detecting its content. If the content is a Google Earth XML document, the browser will print information about the HTTP response to the console.

Trapping the HTTP Response Content

Trapping the response content is useful if you wish to perform custom actions when a link is clicked—for example, open an XML editor when an XML document is detected. A technique to trap the response content type is to use the changing event of the LocationListener to get the document content. The code in Listing 2-19 can be used in WebBrowserView.java to perform this task.

Listing 2-19. *Code to Trap the HTTP Response Content from the Web Browser Widget (in WebBrowserView.java)*

```
/**
 * Trap requests content types Fires when the location in the web
 * browser is changing
 * Don't forget to add a location listener to the browser widget
 * as follows:
 *  browser.addLocationListener(new LocationListener() {
 *    public void changing(LocationEvent event) {
 *      locChanging(event);
 *    }
 * });
 */
void locChanging(LocationEvent evt) {
    String location = evt.location;

    if (!location.startsWith("http")) {
        return;
    }

    // handle custom content type
    try {
        // Note: this is a custom HTTP client (available from the book source)
        SimpleHTTPClient client = new SimpleHTTPClient(location);
        String response = client.doGet();

        if (client.isContentTypeKML() || client.isContentTypeKMZ()) {
            evt.doit = false;

            // handle kml/kmz
            // handleKmlKmz( location);
```

```
                    System.out.println(response);
            }
        } catch (IOException e) {
        }
    }
```

■Caution The code in Listing 2-19 is used to trap Google Earth KML/KMZ content for further processing, but has the unfortunate side effect of opening a duplicate HTTP connection (using a custom HTTP client), which makes the browser behave slower. A duplicate connection is opened because the SWT Browser widget does not provide access to the HTTP request object. Perhaps a better technique would be to use JavaXPCOM with the Browser as explained in the Eclipse SWT FAQ page (`http://www.eclipse.org/swt/faq.php#howusejavaxpcom`). Feel free to investigate this approach.

Saving URL Bookmarks on Exit

URL bookmarks can be easily saved by adding a dispose listener to the Web Browser view's `createPartControl` method and writing the contents of the Bookmarks view viewer to the local file system, as shown in Listing 2-20.

Listing 2-20. *Code to Save Bookmarks When the Web Browser View Is Closed (in WebBrowserView.java)*

```
public void createPartControl(Composite parent)
{
  ...
  parent.addDisposeListener(new DisposeListener() {
          public void widgetDisposed(DisposeEvent arg0) {
              // Save bookmarks to the user's home directory?
              saveBookmarks();
          }
  });
  ...
}
```

Summary

This chapter introduced the Eclipse plug-in model and demonstrated how to add extension points. The following are the important points to take away from this chapter:

- A plug-in is a mechanism for the lightweight software component development. It provides seamless integration, extensibility, and a broad range of tools.

- The declarative nature of the plug-in model provides a small memory footprint and fast performance, as plug-ins are activated/deactivated on demand (when requested by the user).

- The plug-in class centralizes the life-cycle aspects and overall semantics of a plug-in. The methods start and stop define this life cycle, each receiving a reference to a BundleContext with additional information.

- The class AbstractUIPlugin provides the structure for managing UI resources and is usually extended by a user's plug-in.

- BundleContext provides the bundle with execution context, including event subscription/registration, bundle retrieval/installation/removal, and persistent storage access.

- A plug-in fragment is a component that provides extra functionality to a host plug-in.

- A feature is the packaging of a group of related plug-ins into a product, and it is described by a file called feature.xml.

- The platform plug-in model can be extended via extension points. Extension points are declared in plugin.xml.

- The most important extension points provided by the workbench are perspectives, views, actions, editors, editor actions, pop-up menus, and commands.

  - A perspective is a container for visual elements like views, editors, and actions for task-oriented interaction with resources.

  - A view is a workbench part to perform a visual task, such as navigating a hierarchy of information or displaying properties for an object.

  - View actions contribute behavior to views that already exist in the workbench.

  - An editor is a workbench part that allows a user to edit an object (usually a file).

  - The pop-up menus extension point allows a plug-in to contribute to the pop-up menus of other views and editors.

  - Command contributions are used to add custom menus to the menu bar and buttons to the toolbar. An action can then be invoked.

CHAPTER 3

■ ■ ■

RCP Basics

Today's Java programmers may be reluctant to admit that their favorite language is not the best for high-quality client-side applications. Even industry visionary Steve Jobs, founder of Apple, said in a *New York Times* interview, "Java's not worth building in. Nobody uses Java anymore."[1] Eclipse RCP aims to change this perception by providing the technologies to create your own commercial-quality programs.

When Eclipse introduced RCP in version 3.0, it created a refactoring of the fundamental parts of Eclipse's UI, allowing RCP to be used for non-IDE applications. Eclipse has succeeded in building a serious platform for high-quality clients—so much so that its competitors have been forced to create their own Java-based rich client platforms. Some important commercial IDEs are built on RCP, including IBM's WebSphere Studio, CodeGear's JBuilder, and collaboration tools such as IBM's Lotus Notes.

RCP applications are built on the plug-in architecture; therefore, the main program must be a plug-in. This chapter covers the basics of creating RCP applications.

Components of an RCP Application

The best way to understand the components of an RCP application is to use the code-generation facilities of the PDE to build a simple template from which to start your application. Let's set up a sample project for writing Java code and generating the default plug-in manifest files.

Start the Plug-in Project wizard by selecting File ➤ New ➤ Project ➤ Plug-in Project. Enter a project name and click Next.

In the Plug-in Content page, enter the following information (see Figure 3-1 for the entries used for this example):

Plug-in ID: A mandatory unique ID for the plug-in. It is recommended that the ID match the plug-in project name.

Plug-in Version: A mandatory version of the form *major.minor.micro.qualifier* (e.g., 1.0.0). The *qualifier* is an optional segment used to indicate changes between builds. Eclipse uses the date as a qualifier, formatted as *YYYYMMDD* (year, month, and day).

Plug-in Name: A descriptive name for the plug-in, which should be translatable to other languages depending on the locale. This field is required.

---

1. "Ultimate iPhone FAQs List, Part 2," *New York Times Technology*, available online at http://pogue. blogs.nytimes.com/2007/01/13/ultimate-iphone-faqs-list-part-2/.

Plug-in Provider: An optional, translatable name for the provider.

Execution Environment: The symbolic representation of a Java Runtime Environment (JRE). By default, the workbench will detect your installed JRE and define an execution environment. However, it can be configured to use the JRE of your choice. This field is optional, but setting it is recommended.

Generate an activator: An activator is a Java class that controls the life cycle of the plug-in. It is necessary only if your application needs to do work upon startup or shutdown.

This plug-in will make contributions to the UI: Affects the code of the activator class, as follows:

- If the plug-in is a UI plug-in, the activator class extends `org.eclipse.ui.plugin.AbstractUIPlugin`.

- If the plug-in is not a UI plug-in (headless), the activator class extends `org.eclipse.core.runtime.Plugin`.

- If the plug-in is targeted for the OSGi framework, the activator class implements the `org.osgi.framework.BundleActivator` interface.

Enable API Analysis: Enables static analysis of API usage from the new project. Static API analysis allows automatic detection of common bugs, confusing code (likely to cause bugs), bad practices, and syntax errors.

Would you like to create a rich client application?: If you select Yes, you will see a set of sample templates in the next page, and you can choose a sample RCP application. Figure 3-2 shows the sample templates available for RCP.

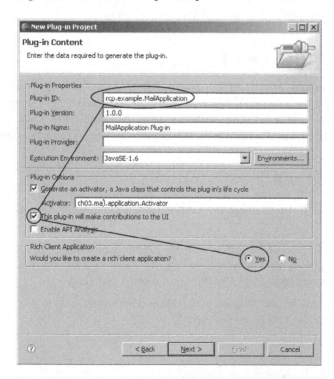

Figure 3-1. *Plug-in content wizard page for the sample Mail Application plug-in*

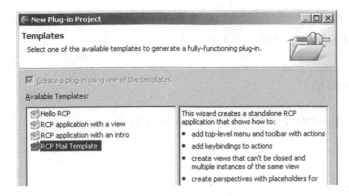

Figure 3-2. *Sample RCP templates*

After setting the Plug-in Content page options, select the RCP Mail Template from the Templates page.

On the final page of the wizard, enter a product name, package name, and application class, and then click Finish. The skeleton of the application and the plug-in manifest editor will be displayed.

Extension Points for an RCP Application

Figure 3-3 shows the Extension tab of the plug-in manifest editor, which lists the extension points required by an RCP application. You can edit extension points visually using the Extensions tab of the editor, or edit them manually using the plugin.xml tab.

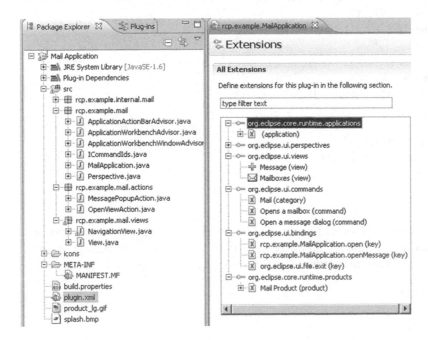

Figure 3-3. *RCP mail template file structure*

Application and Product Extensions

Among the most important extension points for an RCP application are `org.eclipse. core.runtime.products` and `org.eclipse.core.runtime.applications`, which are shown in Listing 3-1. The application extension point describes the name of the main program. A *product* is the Eclipse unit of branding.

Listing 3-1. *Application and Product Extensions for the Mail Application (in plugin.xml)*

```
<extension
      id="Mail Application"
      point="org.eclipse.core.runtime.applications">
   <application>
      <run
            class="rcp.example.mail.MailApplication">
      </run>
   </application>
</extension>

<extension
      id="Mail Product"
      point="org.eclipse.core.runtime.products">
   <product
         application="rcp.example.MailApplication.application"
         name="Mail Product">
      <property
            name="aboutText"
            value="RCP Mail template created by PDE">
      </property>
      <property
            name="windowImages"
            value="icons/sample2.gif">
      </property>
      <property
            name="aboutImage"
            value="product_lg.gif">
      </property>
   </product>
</extension>
```

This XML defines an application (`Mail Application`) that is bound to the class `rcp.example. mail.MailApplication`. It also defines a product (`Mail Product`), with the application ID associated with the product, custom properties to set the text and image to appear in the about dialog, and the window icon. Products are discussed in more detail in the "Defining and Branding Products" section later in the chapter.

Main Program

The org.eclipse.core.runtime.applications extension point defines the main program, as shown in Listing 3-2.

Listing 3-2. *Runtime Applications Extension for the Mail Application (in plugin.xml)*

```
<extension
      id="application"
      point="org.eclipse.core.runtime.applications">
    <application>
       <run
            class="rcp.example.mail.MailApplication">
       </run>
    </application>
</extension>
```

The rcp.example.mail.MailApplication class represents an executable entry point into an application and implements org.eclipse.equinox.app.IApplication, as shown in Listing 3-3.

Listing 3-3. *Basic Skeleton for the Mail Template RCP Application*

```
public class MailApplication implements IApplication
{
 /* (non-Javadoc)
  * @see org.eclipse.equinox.app.IApplication#start()
  */
 public Object start(IApplicationContext context)
 {
   Display display = PlatformUI.createDisplay();
   try {
        int returnCode = PlatformUI.
            createAndRunWorkbench(display, new ApplicationWorkbenchAdvisor());

        if (returnCode == PlatformUI.RETURN_RESTART) {
                return IApplication.EXIT_RESTART;
           }
           return IApplication.EXIT_OK;
   } finally {
        display.dispose();
   }
 }
```

```
/* (non-Javadoc)
 * @see org.eclipse.equinox.app.IApplication#stop()
 */
public void stop() {
        final IWorkbench workbench = PlatformUI.getWorkbench();
        if (workbench == null)
            return;
        final Display display = workbench.getDisplay();
        display.syncExec(new Runnable() {
          public void run() {
            if (!display.isDisposed())
                workbench.close();
          }
        });
    }
}
```

In Listing 3-3, the start method uses org.eclipse.ui.PlatformUI as the central class for access to the Eclipse Platform UI. This class cannot be instantiated and provides static methods to create, access, and close the workbench.

Default Perspective

As discussed in Chapter 2, all RCP applications should define a default perspective with the org.eclipse.ui.perspectives extension point. Listing 3-4 shows the perspective for the Mail Application plug-in.

Listing 3-4. *Perspective Extension for the Mail Application (in plugin.xml)*

```
<extension
      point="org.eclipse.ui.perspectives">
    <perspective
        name="RCP Perspective"
        class="rcp.example.mail.Perspective"
        id="rcp.example.MailApplication.perspective">
    </perspective>
</extension>
```

The Perspective class is used to define the initial layout for a perspective within a page in a workbench window. When a perspective is opened, a new page layout with an editor area is created. This layout is then passed to the default perspective implementation, where additional views and other content can be added. Listing 3-5 shows an example of populating a layout with standard workbench views.

Listing 3-5. *Perpective Implementation for the Extension Point in Listing 3-4*

```
public class Perspective implements IPerspectiveFactory
{
  public void createInitialLayout(IPageLayout layout)
  {
          // Get the editor area.
          String editorArea = layout.getEditorArea();

          // Top left: Resource Navigator view and
          // Bookmarks view placeholder
          IFolderLayout topLeft = layout.
              createFolder("topLeft", IPageLayout.LEFT, 0.25f, editorArea);

          topLeft.addView(IPageLayout.ID_RES_NAV);
          topLeft.addPlaceholder(IPageLayout.ID_BOOKMARKS);

          // Bottom left: Outline view and Property Sheet view
          IFolderLayout bottomLeft = layout.
              createFolder("bottomLeft", IPageLayout.BOTTOM, 0.50f, "topLeft");

          bottomLeft.addView(IPageLayout.ID_OUTLINE);
          bottomLeft.addView(IPageLayout.ID_PROP_SHEET);

          // Bottom right: Task List view
          layout.addView(IPageLayout.ID_TASK_LIST
              , IPageLayout.BOTTOM, 0.66f, editorArea);
  }
}
```

OSGi Manifest

As you've learned, a plug-in is described by the MANIFEST.MF and plugin.xml files. MANIFEST.MF (also known as the *OSGi manifest*) describes bundle information, such as the following:

- Version and name
- Activator class, to control the life cycle
- Bundle dependencies
- Activation policies, to define a mechanism for activating bundles upon the first class load
- An execution environment

This information can be edited visually from the editor's Overview tab, as shown in Figure 3-4, or manually from the MANIFEST.MF tab.

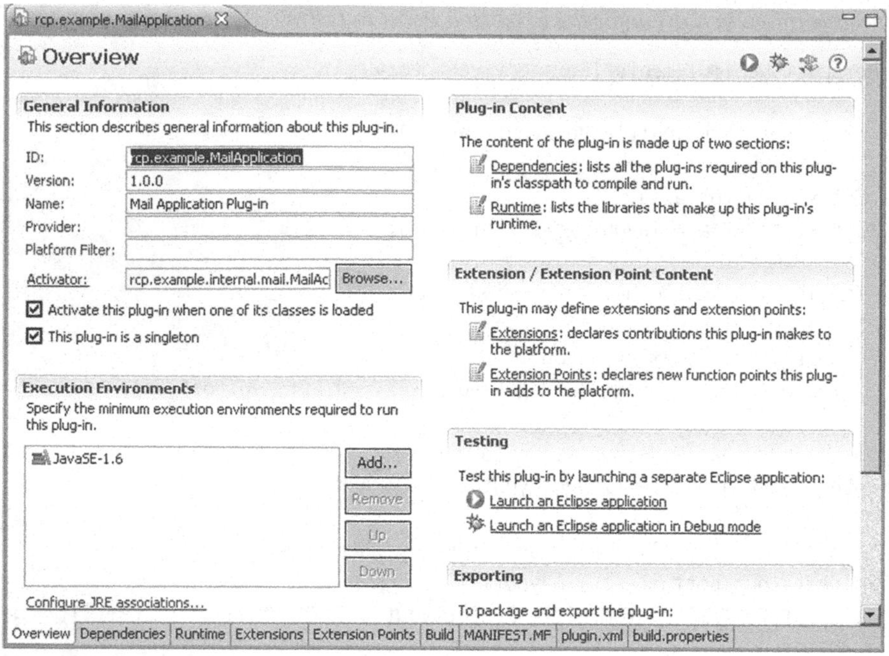

Figure 3-4. *Plug-in manifest editor*

Listing 3-6 shows the OSGi manifest for the Mail Application plug-in.

Listing 3-6. *OSGi Manifest for the Mail Application (MANIFEST.MF)*

```
Manifest-Version: 1.0
Bundle-ManifestVersion: 2
Bundle-Name: Mail Application Plug-in
Bundle-SymbolicName: rcp.example.MailApplication; singleton:=true
Bundle-Version: 1.0.0
Bundle-Activator: rcp.example.internal.mail.MailActivator
Require-Bundle: org.eclipse.ui,
 org.eclipse.core.runtime
Bundle-ActivationPolicy: lazy
Bundle-RequiredExecutionEnvironment: JavaSE-1.6
```

The manifest in Listing 3-6 sets `lazy` as the activation policy. In lazy activation, bundles are not activated until they are needed. Using this model, the application can be started with as few active bundles as possible and activate other bundles on demand, thus reducing its memory footprint.

Plug-in Manifest

The `plugin.xml` file describes information about the RCP application, including the following:

General information: This section describes general information about the plug-in, such as its ID, name, version, activator class, execution environments, and so on.

Dependencies: This section describes plug-in dependencies (packages on which the plug-in depends) and development classpath dependencies.

Runtime: This section describes the packages the plug-in exposes to clients, package visibility, and the plug-in classpath.

Extension points: This section describes the extension points.

Build options: This section describes the folders and files to be included in the source, binary builds, and custom libraries to be built.

As with the OSGi manifest, the plug-in manifest (plugin.xml) can be edited through the Overview tab of the editor (see Figure 3-4) or manually.

Advisor Classes

Advisor classes are used to configure the workbench, the workbench window, and the action bar. The process is started within the main program with a call to PlatformUI. createAndRunWorkbench(Display, ApplicationWorkbenchAdvisor). The advisor classes are WorkbenchAdvisor, WorkbenchWindowAdvisor, and ActionBarAdvisor.

Workbench Advisor

An application should declare a subclass of WorkbenchAdvisor and override methods to configure the workbench for a particular application and define a default perspective, as shown in Listing 3-7.

Listing 3-7. *Basic Skeleton for an RCP Application Workbench Window*

```
public class ApplicationWorkbenchAdvisor extends WorkbenchAdvisor
{

    private static final String PERSPECTIVE_ID =
        "rcp.example.MailApplication.perspective";

    // Define an application workbench window
    public WorkbenchWindowAdvisor createWorkbenchWindowAdvisor(
        IWorkbenchWindowConfigurer configurer)
    {
        return new ApplicationWorkbenchWindowAdvisor(configurer);
    }

    // Define a default perspective
    public String getInitialWindowPerspectiveId() {
        return PERSPECTIVE_ID;
    }
}
```

Workbench Window Advisor

The workbench window advisor is created once for a workbench window, and it is used to configure the window. An application should declare a subclass of WorkbenchWindowAdvisor and override methods to configure the workbench for the particular application. The following methods provide default implementations; however, they can be overridden to configure the workbench window:

- preWindowOpen: Called as the window is being opened. Use it to configure aspects of the window other than action bars.

- postWindowRestore: Called after the window has been re-created from a previously saved state. Use it to adjust the restored window.

- postWindowCreate: Called after the window has been created, either from an initial state or from a restored state. Use it to adjust the window.

- openIntro: Called immediately before the window is opened in order to create the introduction component, if any.

- postWindowOpen: Called after the window has been opened. Use it to hook up window listeners. For example, you could add a listener to load configuration data when the application starts.

- preWindowShellClose: Called when the window is closed by the user. Use it to prescreen window closings.

Listing 3-8 shows an example of using the preWindowOpen method to set the initial size of the window and have it display a toolbar and status line.

Listing 3-8. *Application Workbench Class Used to Configure the Main Application Window*

```
public class ApplicationWorkbenchWindowAdvisor extends WorkbenchWindowAdvisor
{

  public ApplicationWorkbenchWindowAdvisor(IWorkbenchWindowConfigurer configurer)
  {
      super(configurer);
  }

  public ActionBarAdvisor createActionBarAdvisor(IActionBarConfigurer configurer)
  {
      return new ApplicationActionBarAdvisor(configurer);
  }

  public void preWindowOpen() {
      IWorkbenchWindowConfigurer configurer = getWindowConfigurer();
      configurer.setInitialSize(new Point(600, 400));
      configurer.setShowCoolBar(true);
      configurer.setShowStatusLine(false);
  }
}
```

Action Bar Advisor

The action bar advisor is responsible for creating, adding, and disposing of the actions added to a workbench window. This class is useful for allocating global actions, as well as filling the menu bar, toolbar (known as the cool bar), and status line.

Actions have a label, tool tip, and image, as well as code associated with them. They display as menu options or buttons in a toolbar.

Actions can be classified as local or global. *Local actions* may perform tasks within a local context, such as a view. *Global actions* are commonly used to open and close dialogs, files, and so on. They are usually bound to a key sequence (Ctrl+O to open a file, for example). Any corresponding command key bindings are defined in the `plugin.xml` file.

Figure 3-5 shows the actions added to the Mail Application plug-in, represented as menu options and toolbar buttons.

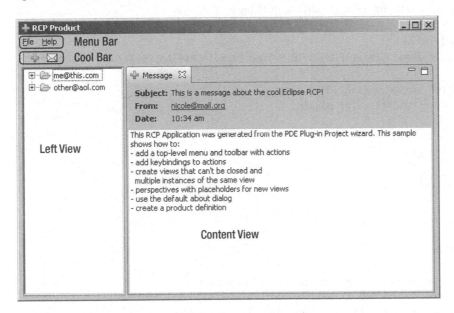

Figure 3-5. *Mail Application RCP template*

Plug-in Class

As explained in Chapter 2, the plug-in class controls the life cycle for plug-ins that integrate with the Eclipse Platform UI. It provides the following:

- Support for plug-in preferences and conversion from the older JFace preference API

- Access to the JFace preference store, which returns a core runtime preferences object

- Ability to set up default values for either preferences using the JFace API (`initializeDefaultPreferences`) or the core runtime API (`initializeDefaultPlugin-Preferences`)

- A dialog store to manipulate dialog settings

- An image registry to store common images

The plug-in class overrides the appropriate life cycle methods in order to react to the life-cycle requests automatically issued by the platform. Instances of the plug-in class are automatically created by the platform in the course of the plug-in activation.

Clients must never instantiate a plug-in class. The singleton pattern can be used to obtain an instance of the plug-in by declaring a static variable in your plug-in class for the singleton. Store the only instance of the plug-in class in the singleton when it is created. Then access the singleton when needed through a static getDefault() method. Listing 3-9 shows the plug-in class for the Mail template with the method getDefault() used to obtain a shared instance of its plug-in. If other plug-ins need to reference the Mail plug-in, a reference can be obtained by calling MailActivator.getDefault().

Listing 3-9. *Plug-in Class for the Mail Template with a Method to Get a Shared Instance*

```java
public class MailActivator extends AbstractUIPlugin {

    // The plug-in ID
    public static final String PLUGIN_ID = "rcp.example.MailApplication";

    // The shared instance (singleton pattern)
    private static MailActivator plugin;

    /**
     * The constructor
     */
    public MailActivator() {
    }

    /*
     * (non-Javadoc)
     *
     * @see org.eclipse.ui.plugin.AbstractUIPlugin#start
     */
    public void start(BundleContext context) throws Exception {
        super.start(context);
        plugin = this;
    }

    /*
     * (non-Javadoc)
     *
     * @see org.eclipse.ui.plugin.AbstractUIPlugin#stop
     */
    public void stop(BundleContext context) throws Exception {
        plugin = null;
        super.stop(context);
    }
```

```
/**
 * Returns the shared instance (singleton pattern)
 *
 * @return the shared instance
 */
public static MailActivator getDefault() {
    return plugin;
}
}
```

Defining and Branding Products

A product definition describes information about the application, and it is required if you wish to distribute your application as a stand-alone product. To create a product, your plug-in must define application and product extension points within the main application, as discussed earlier in this chapter.

To add a Production Definition, from the OSGi console, select File ➤ New ➤ Product Configuration to start the New Product Configuration wizard. Enter a product name, and select the product name defined by your plug-in, as shown in Figure 3-6. Click Finish to bring up the product editor, as shown in Figure 3-7.

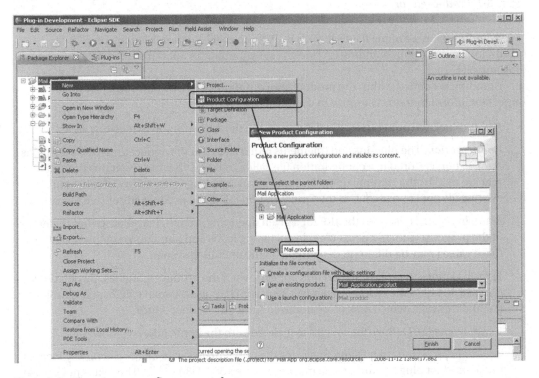

Figure 3-6. *Choosing to configure a product*

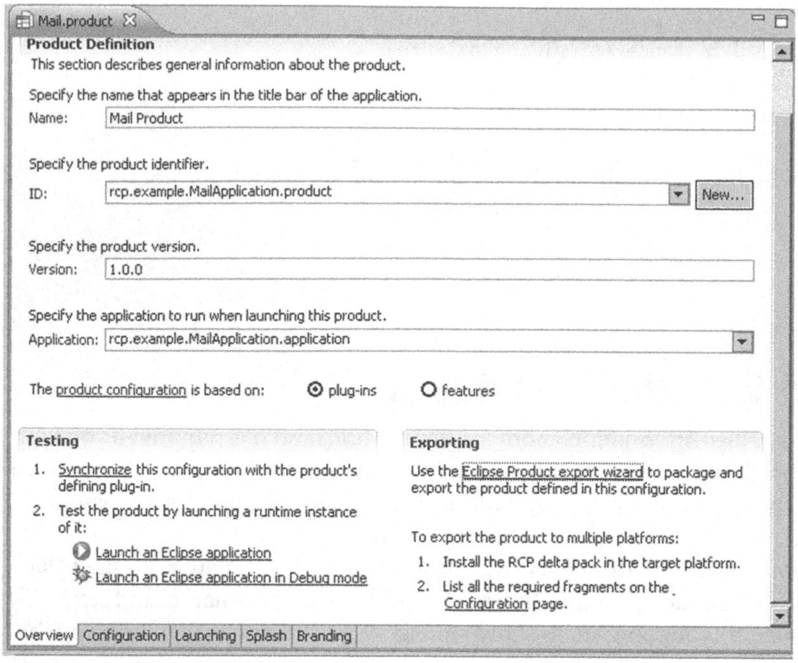

Figure 3-7. *Product editor*

Branding gives a unique flavor to your RCP. If the goal is to distribute the plug-in as a stand-alone application, branding is critical to set your plug-in apart from the default Eclipse look and feel.

Branding is defined within the product configuration file. The following is the most important information to customize in this file:

IDs: Product and application IDs defined within the main plug-in extension points.

Configuration: The plug-ins and fragments required to run the application. By default, this information is stored in a configuration file called config.ini, which contains properties that are read by the runtime upon startup. This file can be generated by default, or an existing file could be used. Use the Configuration tab of the product editor (see Figure 3-7).

Launching: This describes the JRE for a given operating system. It also describes the name of the program launcher or executable, including icons and launching arguments. All these values may be different, depending on the operating system.

Splash: Defines the splash screen that appears when the product launches. By default, the file splash.bmp in the current folder will be used. The splash screen can display a progress bar and message, which may be customized from the product editor.

Window images: Defines the images associated with the application window.

About dialog: Standard text and image for the About dialog. The image is typically located in the product plug-in, and its size must not exceed 500×330 pixels. The text is not shown if the size exceeds 250×330 pixels.

Using Features

As mentioned in Chapter 2, a *feature* is a collection of plug-ins that perform a common function. Consider using features if your application includes many plug-ins for distribution. Features are useful for the following reasons:

- Features help package and manage sets of related plug-ins into logical contributions.

- Features help products that require automatic updates or Java Web Start support.

Features will be discussed in more detail in Chapter 9.

Product Testing and Packaging

Once you've defined the product and branding, you can easily test your application. From the product editor, click the Synchronize link (to publish your changes), and then click the Launch an Eclipse application link (see Figure 3-7).

A very useful tool for deploying the application to a specific location is the Product Export wizard. From the product editor, simply click the Eclipse Product export wizard link (see Figure 3-7). Then enter a destination directory and choose export options, as shown in Figure 3-8.

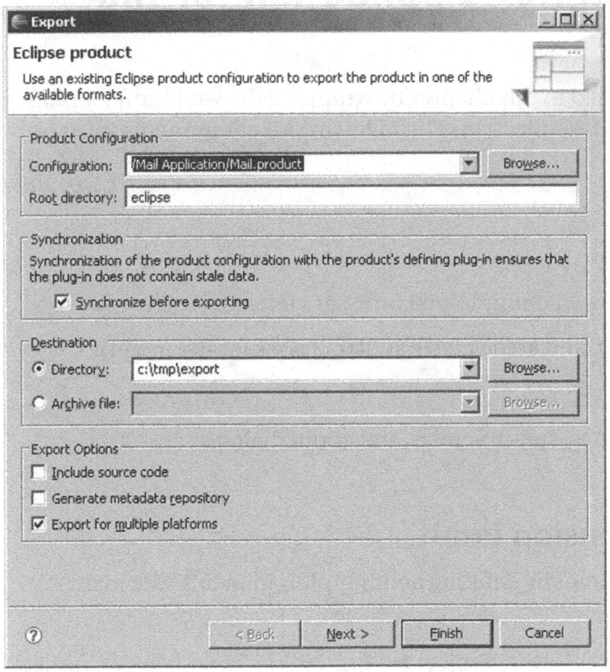

Figure 3-8. *Exporting a product for multiple platforms*

You can even build products for multiple platforms using the Eclipse delta pack. Note that this pack is not distributed with Eclipse by default. You will need to download the delta pack from the Eclipse web site and then install it.

> **MULTIPLATFORM EXPORT WITH THE DELTA PACK**
>
> The Eclipse delta pack is a very useful tool for multiplatform export. However, it is not included by default in the Eclipse download, which means you need to download and install it if you wish to deploy your product on multiple platforms. Here are the steps for installing the delta pack and then using it for a multiplatform export.
>
> 1. Download Eclipse Delta Pack 3.4 (Ganymede) from the product download page. To do so, from the main Eclipse downloads page, select By Project ➤ Eclipse Platform ➤ Latest release (3.4) ➤ Delta Pack.
>
> 2. Unpack the zip file within your Eclipse installation. When prompted, *do not* overwrite existing files; otherwise, your Eclipse installation may fail to start.
>
> 3. Return to the product editor and click the Eclipse Product export wizard link (see Figure 3-7).
>
> 4. Enter a destination folder and check Export for multiple platforms (see Figure 3-8). Then click Next.
>
> 5. In the next wizard page, select the target platforms, and then click Finish. The destination folder now contains all the required plug-ins and binaries.

Hands-on Exercise: An RCP Application for the Web Browser Plug-in

Now you will apply the concepts discussed in this chapter by wrapping the web browser plug-in from Chapter 2 into a stand-alone RCP application. The following UI components must be added:

- An application extension point
- Advisor classes for the application
- A simple menu and toolbar to spawn multiple web browser views
- A set of commands, key bindings, and associated handler classes for the menus
- A product definition
- Branding elements, including icons, splash screen, and about dialog

Adding an Application Extension Point

You can add the application extension point by defining another plug-in to host the main program.

1. From the main menu, select File ➤ New ➤ Project ➤ Plug-in Project and enter a project name (ch03.WebBrowser). Click Next.

2. In the Plug-in Content page, make sure the "This plug-in will make contributions to the UI" option is checked. Set the "Would you like to create a rich client application?" option to Yes. Click Finish. The plug-in manifest editor will open.

3. In the plug-in manifest editor, click the Dependencies tab. Then add a reference to the web browser plug-in you created in Chapter 2. You should now see an application extension point, as well as skeleton advisor classes, as shown in Listing 3-10.

Listing 3-10. *Extension Point for the Web Browser Plug-in (in plugin.xml) and Implementation Class*

```
<extension
      id="application"
      point="org.eclipse.core.runtime.applications">
   <application>
      <run
            class="ch03.browser.BrowserApplication">
      </run>
   </application>
</extension>


/**
 * This class controls all aspects of the application's execution
 */
public class BrowserApplication implements IApplication {

   /*
    * (non-Javadoc)
    */
   public Object start(IApplicationContext context) throws Exception {
      Display display = PlatformUI.createDisplay();
      try {
         int returnCode = PlatformUI.createAndRunWorkbench(display,
               new ApplicationWorkbenchAdvisor());
         if (returnCode == PlatformUI.RETURN_RESTART)
            return IApplication.EXIT_RESTART;
         else
            return IApplication.EXIT_OK;
      } finally {
         display.dispose();
      }

   }

   /*
    * (non-Javadoc)
    */
   public void stop() {
      final IWorkbench workbench = PlatformUI.getWorkbench();
      if (workbench == null)
         return;
      final Display display = workbench.getDisplay();
```

```
display.syncExec(new Runnable() {
    public void run() {
        if (!display.isDisposed())
            workbench.close();
    }
});
    }
}
```

Changing the Default Perspective

The default perspective needs to point to the web browser plug-in perspective from Chapter 2. In the plug-in manifest editor, click the Extensions tab, and then expand the org.eclipse. ui.perspectives Web Browser. Click the Browse button for the perspective class, and then select the WebBrowserPerspective class name from Chapter 2.

Tip If you don't see an org.eclipse.ui.perspectives extension point, that probably means you failed to select it to create a rich client application when creating the plug-in project. Fortunately, you can use the manifest editor to fix it. Just click the Add button in the All Extensions section. In the New Extension Point dialog, select org.eclipse.ui.perspectives, and then click Finish. Finally, add the perspective information, including the ID (ch02.browser.perspective.WebBrowserPerspective), name (Web Browser Perspective), and class (ch02.browser.perspective.WebBrowserPerspective). Remember that the perspective is located in Chapter 2.

Modifying Advisor Classes

The next step is to modify the advisor classes to configure the main window of the application. These classes should have been created by the Plug-in Project wizard. By default, they are named ApplicationWorkbenchAdvisor, ApplicationWorkbenchWindowAdvisor, and ApplicationActionBarAdvisor.

Tip When creating a new RCP plug-in project, remember to choose Yes for the "Would you like to create a rich client application? option. This will ensure that an application extension point and advisor classes are added to the project automatically.

The workbench advisor (ApplicationWorkbenchAdvisor) creates a new workbench window advisor (ApplicationWorkbenchWindowAdvisor), which configures the main window and returns a reference to the default perspective—in this case, the WebBrowserPerspective from the Chapter 2 plug-in. Listing 3-11 shows the required modifications to the ApplicationWorkbenchAdvisor class.

Listing 3-11. *ApplicationWorkbenchAdvisor Class Used to Create a Main Window and Default Perspective*

```
public class ApplicationWorkbenchAdvisor extends WorkbenchAdvisor
{
  public WorkbenchWindowAdvisor
    createWorkbenchWindowAdvisor(IWorkbenchWindowConfigurer configurer)
  {
      // Create a window
      return new ApplicationWorkbenchWindowAdvisor(configurer);
  }

  // Get a default perspective
  public String getInitialWindowPerspectiveId() {
      return  WebBrowserPerspective.ID;
  }
}
```

The ApplicationWorkbenchWindowAdvisor class configures the main window menu, toolbar, and status line. It also creates an instance of the action bar advisor (ApplicationActionBarAdvisor) to set up local menu and toolbar actions. In this case, the main plug-in will not define any local actions, so the action bar advisor will not need to be modified. Listing 3-12 shows the ApplicationWorkbenchWindowAdvisor class which enables a main menu, toolbar, and status line. It also creates an instance of ApplicationActionBarAdvisor.

Listing 3-12. *ApplicationWorkbenchWindowAdvisor Class for the Exercise*

```
public class ApplicationWorkbenchWindowAdvisor extends WorkbenchWindowAdvisor
{

    public ApplicationWorkbenchWindowAdvisor(IWorkbenchWindowConfigurer configurer)
    {
        super(configurer);
    }

    public ActionBarAdvisor createActionBarAdvisor(IActionBarConfigurer configurer)
    {
        return new ApplicationActionBarAdvisor(configurer);
    }

    public void preWindowOpen() {
        IWorkbenchWindowConfigurer configurer = getWindowConfigurer();
        configurer.setShowMenuBar(true);
        configurer.setShowCoolBar(true);
        configurer.setShowStatusLine(true);
    }
}
```

Adding Menu and Toolbar Extension Points

The web browser plug-in should define a toolbar contribution to fire the open web browser command (ch02.WebBrowser.commands.newBrowser), as shown in Listing 3-13.

Listing 3-13. *Menu Contribution to Open a Web Browser (in plugin.xml)*

```
<menuContribution
    locationURI="toolbar:org.eclipse.ui.main.toolbar?after=additions">
        <toolbar
             id="ch02.WebBrowser.toolbars.sampleToolbar">
            <command
                commandId="ch02.WebBrowser.commands.newBrowser"
                icon="icons/16-earth.png"
                id="ch02.WebBrowser.toolbars.newBrowserCommand"
                tooltip="Open Web Browser ">
            </command>
        </toolbar>
 </menuContribution>
```

Notice the locationURI attribute toolbar:org.eclipse.ui.main.toolbar?after=additions. It places a new push button as an addition to the main UI toolbar.

The main application's plug-in is in charge of declaring the main menu using the location URI menu:org.eclipse.ui.main.menu?after=additions. The fragment in Listing 3-14 creates a File menu contribution with two actions—New Browser and Exit—and a Help menu with an About action.

Listing 3-14. *Main Menu Contribution for the Web Browser Plug-in (in plugin.xml)*

```
<extension
 point="org.eclipse.ui.menus">
<menuContribution
    locationURI="menu:org.eclipse.ui.main.menu?after=additions">
 <menu
     id="ch02.WebBrowser.menus.File"
     label="File"
     mnemonic="F">
        <command
                commandId="ch02.WebBrowser.commands.newBrowser"
                mnemonic="S"
                style="push">
        </command>
        <separator
             name="ch02.separator1"
             visible="true">
        </separator>
        <command
             commandId="org.eclipse.ui.file.exit"
             mnemonic="X"
```

```
                     style="push">
            </command>
  </menu>
</menuContribution>
<menuContribution
            locationURI="menu:org.eclipse.ui.main.menu?after=additions">
  <menu
            label="Help"
            mnemonic="H">
        <command
            commandId="org.eclipse.ui.help.aboutAction"
            style="push">
        </command>
  </menu>
</menuContribution>
</extension>
```

Notice the newBrowser command, which is defined in Chapter 2, and the factory commands org.eclipse.ui.file.exit and org.eclipse.ui.help.aboutAction to exit and open the About dialog, respectively.

Adding Commands, Key Bindings, and Handlers

Listing 3-15 shows the command New Browser (defined in Chapter 2) and corresponding key binding (CTRL+6). Note the category extension, which is used to group related commands. The main plug-in (see Chapter 3), on the other hand, defines the factory commands File ➤ Exit and Help ➤ About with associated key bindings (see Listing 3-14), which are not shown here.

Listing 3-15. *Command Extension Point to Open a New Web Browser (in plugin.xml)*

```
<extension
 point="org.eclipse.ui.commands">
<category
        id="ch02.WebBrowser.commands.category"
        name="Web Category">
</category>
<command
        categoryId="ch02.WebBrowser.commands.category"
        id="ch02.WebBrowser.commands.newBrowser"
        name="New Browser">
</command>
</extension>

<extension
 point="org.eclipse.ui.bindings">
<key
        commandId="ch02.WebBrowser.commands.newBrowser"
        contextId="org.eclipse.ui.contexts.window"
```

```
             schemeId="org.eclipse.ui.defaultAcceleratorConfiguration"
             sequence="CTRL+6">
</key>
</extension>
```

You need to add a new handler extension point to the browser plug-in to associate the New Browser command with its handler class, which will be triggered when the command is executed. Listing 3-16 shows the new handler extension point, and Listing 3-17 shows the NewBrowserHandler class.

Listing 3-16. *Extension Point for the Open Web Browser Command Handler (in plugin.xml)*

```
<extension
 point="org.eclipse.ui.handlers">
<handler
      class="ch02.webbrowser.handlers.NewBrowserHandler"
      commandId="ch02.WebBrowser.commands.newBrowser">
</handler>
</extension>
```

Listing 3-17. *Handler Class for the Extension Point in Listing 3-16*

```
public class NewBrowserHandler extends AbstractHandler {
 private int instanceNum = 0;

 /**
  * The command has been executed
  * from the application context.
  */
 public Object execute(ExecutionEvent event)
       throws ExecutionException
 {
       IWorkbenchWindow window = HandlerUtil.
           getActiveWorkbenchWindowChecked(event);
       try {
       window.getActivePage().showView(WebBrowserView.ID
               , Integer.toString(instanceNum++)
               , IWorkbenchPage.VIEW_ACTIVATE);
       }
       catch (PartInitException e) {
           MessageDialog.openError(
               window.getShell(),
               "WebBrowser Plug-in",
               e.getMessage());
       }
       return null;
 }
}
```

Notice the `window.getActivePage().showView()` method in Listing 3-17, which allows multiple instances of a particular view ID to be created. They are disambiguated using an instance counter (or secondary ID) as the second argument. The third argument, `IWorkbenchPage.VIEW_ACTIVATE`, indicates the view should be immediately displayed. Note that if a secondary ID is given, then the view must allow multiple instances by having specified `allowMultiple="true"` in its extension point.

Creating the Product Configuration File

Finally, create a product configuration file, as follows:

1. Right-click the project folder name and select New ➤ Product Configuration.

2. Enter a file name (for example, `WebBrowser.product`) and select the product created by the wizard (`ch3.WebBrowser.product`).

3. In the Overview tab, define general information for the product, including a name (`Web Browser`) and version.

4. In the Configuration tab, check "Include optional dependencies when computing required plug-ins," and then click "Add Required Plug-ins." This will ensure that all required dependencies are included. (Otherwise, the application may fail to start.)

5. From the Overview tab, click Synchronize to publish the changes. Then click the Launch an Eclipse application link to test the product.

Figure 3-9 shows the completed Web Browser RCP application.

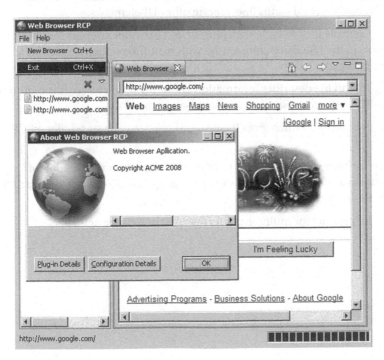

Figure 3-9. *The Web Browser RCP application*

Summary

This chapter covered the fundamentals of RCP. Here are the main points to keep in mind:

- RCP is essentially a refactoring of the fundamental parts of Eclipse's UI, allowing it to be used for non-IDE applications. It provides the technology to create your own commercial-quality programs.

- The main components of an RCP application are application, workbench, and workbench window classes. These classes are typically known as *advisor classes*.

- The application class represents an executable entry point and implements `org.eclipse.equinox.app.IApplication`. It uses the class `org.eclipse.ui.PlatformUI` to access the Eclipse Platform UI.

- Applications should define a default perspective extension point and associated class. The perspective class is used to define the initial layout of the workbench window.

- The application workbench advisor class extends `WorkbenchAdvisor`. It is responsible for defining a default perspective and configuring the workbench (by creating a workbench window advisor).

- The application workbench window advisor class extends `WorkbenchWindowAdvisor`. It is responsible for configuring the main window (set window size, show menu bar, toolbar, status line, and so on), and creating an `ActionBarAdvisor` class.

- The application action bar advisor class extends `ActionBarAdvisor` and is responsible for creating, adding, and disposing of the actions added to a workbench window. It also fills the menu bar, cool bar, and status line, among other UI elements.

- The plug-in class controls the life cycle for a plug-in and provides support for plug-in preferences, access to the JFace preference store with runtime preferences, a dialog store, and an image registry.

- A product configuration file describes information about the application. It is required if you wish to distribute your application as a stand-alone product.

- A product includes branding, which gives the unique flavor to your stand-alone RCP application.

- A product may be described using plug-ins or features. A feature is a collection of plug-ins that perform a common function. Consider using features if your application includes many plug-ins for distribution.

- When exporting the product for multiple platforms, use the Eclipse delta pack.

CHAPTER 4

■■■

User Interface Concepts

As you know, an application's UI provides the interaction between the user and the computer. Because the UI affects the amount of effort the user must expend to perform a given task, it has a big impact of an application's usability.

This chapter explores two useful Eclipse APIs for UIs: the Common Navigator Framework (CNF) and the concurrency infrastructure (Jobs API). The goal of CNF is to provide a general-purpose, configurable navigator that presents an integrated view of resources to the user. The concurrency infrastructure provides the means to perform simultaneous tasks using shared resources. This allows the application to remain responsive while tasks are performed.

Hierarchical Navigation with the Common Navigator Framework

CNF provides a general-purpose navigator view for applications. You can use it to implement all kinds of resource viewers. As just one example, the Eclipse IDE's Project Explorer view is implemented with CNF.

CNF viewers can be shared by many applications working with the same set of resources or other objects, presenting an integrated view to the end user. CNF instances are declared by extension points. CNF content, filters, wizards, and action providers (described shortly) are also declared as extensions, thus maximizing shareability among multiple views.

CNF viewers are highly extensible. You can define one or more CNF viewers and associate each viewer with content extensions, filters, wizards, and sets of actions. You can also use the `org.eclipse.ui.navigator.resources` plug-in to provide reusable components for clients that need to expand on the capabilities of CNF. These resources include actions to open, save, cut, paste, and add filters for resource types (files or custom user objects). Visually, these actions display as menu options in the navigator pop-up menu.

Furthermore, CNF allows for drag-and-drop (DnD) functionality. DnD uses drop assistants associated with a content extension.

Let's look at the basic components of CNF, and then explore the ways of integrating CNF into your RCP applications.

■Tip For a good introduction to CNF, see the RCP Quickstart "Common Navigator Tutorial 1: Hello World," available online at http://rcpquickstart.com/2007/04/25/common-navigator-tutorial-➡ 1-hello-world/.

CNF Basics

Using the CNF classes and configuration elements, you can create navigation systems for your applications. Figure 4-1 shows an example of a CNF viewer in an RCP application.

Figure 4-1. *CNF in action within RCP*

CNF Classes

The backbone of CNF is the class org.eclipse.ui.navigator.CommonNavigator, which uses the following classes:

- CommonViewer to render an extensible tree. Content and labels of the tree are provided by an instance of INavigatorContentService.

- NavigatorActionService to provide actions from extensions for menu and IActionBars contributions.

- INavigatorContentService to manage content extensions for extensible viewers and provide reusable services for filters, sorting, activation of content extensions, and DnD.

Clients are not expected to subclass CommonNavigator for traditional tasks such as workspace navigation. However, some RCP applications, such as file managers, may wish to override this behavior. By default, CNF will let you navigate only workspace resources, which is fine for the IDE, but not enough for an application such as an FTP client. The "Using CNF by Extending the Common Navigator" section later in this chapter discusses ways to overcome this limitation.

CNF Configuration

CNF defines the following for navigator configuration:

Content extensions: CNF uses content extensions to include resources of any type. These extensions provide the following:

- Means of associating objects with appropriate icons, labels, and menu items

- Invocation based on expressions defined within the extension point

- A priority to indicate the category of importance of the extension related to other extensions, which is useful when more than one content extension is enabled for a given object and situation

Filters: Users can specify which resources or objects to exclude.

Wizards: Users can use wizards to create new resources or import/export resources from a CNF viewer.

Action providers: Action providers allow users to programmatically configure the pop-up menu in a CNF viewer. Action providers may be associated with content extensions. This association is useful for enabling cut/copy/paste operations when a file is selected, for example. Action providers are also useful for performing computations to determine which items are added to the pop-up menu.

Using CNF Within RCP

You can use CNF within RCP in two ways:

Contribute to the Common Navigator: You can contribute to the `org.eclipse.ui.navigator.CommonNavigator` view to manipulate workspace resources (see Figure 4-1). This is a bit cumbersome, as the navigator is designed to manipulate workspace resources, not file system resources, by default. However, you can fake file system access by creating a project in the navigator and link the target to a file system location. For example, you could create a project called home and point the location to your home directory, thus giving the viewer access to files in your home directory. This option does not give you a lot of control, but is it very simple and quick to implement.

Extend the Common Navigator: You can extend `org.eclipse.ui.navigator.CommonNavigator` to control the mechanism that discovers a navigator's root node. This requires more work than contributing, but it gives you a higher degree of control over the navigator. You might want to use this approach for applications such as file explorers and FTP clients, for example.

Whichever way you use CNF within your RCP application, the following plug-ins are required to get started:

- `org.eclipse.ui.navigator`

- `org.eclipse.ui.navigator.resources`

- `org.eclipse.ui.ide`

- `org.eclipse.core.resources`

Using CNF by Contributing to the Common Navigator

As I mentioned, contributing to the `org.eclipse.ui.navigator.CommonNavigator` view is the easiest and quickest way to get CNF working within RCP, but gives you a low degree of control, as you must create projects within a workspace to manipulate resources. On the bright side, it bundles a lot of built-in actions to manipulate resources.

The following example demonstrates the steps for contributing to the Common Navigator view. It creates the simple navigator shown earlier in Figure 4-1.

1. Make sure the CNF dependencies are included. As noted, these are `org.eclipse.ui.navigator`, `org.eclipse.ui.navigator.resources`, `org.eclipse.ui.ide`, and `org.eclipse.core.resources`.

2. Add an extension point for the Common Navigator view to your plug-in manifest. Use a custom name and ID, but make sure the class is `org.eclipse.ui.navigator.CommonNavigator`. The following fragment creates a Common Navigator view (within your plug-in) called `Eclipse Navigator`, with the ID `eclipse.navigator.view` (which can be used to reference the view from your main perspective) and a custom icon. Note that the class `org.eclipse.ui.navigator.CommonNavigator` is part of CNF.

```
<extension
    point="org.eclipse.ui.views">
  <view
    class="org.eclipse.ui.navigator.CommonNavigator"
    icon="icons/alt_window_16.gif"
    id="eclipse.navigator.view"
    name="Eclipse Navigator">
  </view>
</extension>
```

3. Add action and content bindings extension points to the plug-in manifest. Action bindings attach built-in actions to a Common Navigator view ID (`eclipse.navigator.view` in this case). This includes all actions under `org.eclipse.ui.navigator.resources`. Content bindings define the navigator content types, filters, and other resources that will be visible. They should include the following:

   - `org.eclipse.ui.navigator.resources`

   - `org.eclipse.ui.navigator.resourceContent`

   - `org.eclipse.ui.navigator.resources.filters`

   - `org.eclipse.ui.navigator.resources.linkHelper`

   - `org.eclipse.ui.navigator.resources.workingSets`

```
<extension point="org.eclipse.ui.navigator.viewer">
<viewerActionBinding
    viewerId="eclipse.navigator.view">
 <includes>
     <actionExtension pattern="org.eclipse.ui.navigator.resources.*" />
 </includes>
</viewerActionBinding>
```

```
<viewerContentBinding viewerId="eclipse.navigator.view">
  <includes>
     <contentExtension
         pattern="org.eclipse.ui.navigator.resourceContent" />
     <contentExtension
         pattern="org.eclipse.ui.navigator.resources.filters.*"/>
      <contentExtension
         pattern="org.eclipse.ui.navigator.resources.linkHelper"/>
       <contentExtension
         pattern="org.eclipse.ui.navigator.resources.workingSets"/>
  </includes>
</viewerContentBinding>
</extension>
```

This fragment binds all navigator actions (org.eclipse.ui.navigator.resources.*) to the Common Navigator view (eclipse.navigator.view). The actions will display as menu options in the navigator context menu.

This fragment also defines viewerContentBinding elements to describe which content extensions and common filters are visible to the viewer. A content extension or common filter is visible if the ID of the content extension or common filter matches an includes statement under a viewerContentBinding. In this case, the content extension org.eclipse.ui.navigator.resourceContent—that is, any resource in the user's workspace—is bound to a viewer matching the ID eclipse.navigator.view. The content extension org.eclipse.ui.navigator.resources.filters.* indicates that the content filter for that viewer will be available in the navigator filters dialog. The content extension org.eclipse.ui.navigator.resources.linkHelper tells the viewer to provide a link with editor support to the navigator.

4. Modify the application WorkbenchAdvisor class to do the following:

    • Get the workspace root as input by overriding the method getDefaultPageInput

    • Load the built-in project opened and closed icons used by CNF by overriding the initialize method (see the next fragment)

```java
@Override
// Override this method to return the workspace root
public IAdaptable getDefaultPageInput() {
    IWorkspace workspace = ResourcesPlugin.getWorkspace();
    return workspace.getRoot();
}


@Override
// Override to initialize the Workbench for CNF:  Load project icons
public void initialize(IWorkbenchConfigurer configurer) {
    // Required to load icons
    WorkbenchAdapterBuilder.registerAdapters();

    final String ICONS_PATH = "icons/full/";
    final String PATH_OBJECT = ICONS_PATH + "obj16/";
```

```
        // Get the workbench plug-in
        Bundle ideBundle = Platform
                .getBundle(IDEWorkbenchPlugin.IDE_WORKBENCH);

        // Load the built-in project opened/closed icons from the plug-in
        declareWorkbenchImage(configurer, ideBundle,
                IDE.SharedImages.IMG_OBJ_PROJECT, PATH_OBJECT
                        + "prj_obj.gif", true);
        declareWorkbenchImage(configurer, ideBundle,
                IDE.SharedImages.IMG_OBJ_PROJECT_CLOSED, PATH_OBJECT
                        + "cprj_obj.gif", true);
    }

    // Declare an image with the workbench
    private void declareWorkbenchImage(IWorkbenchConfigurer configurer_p,
            Bundle ideBundle, String symbolicName, String path,
            boolean shared) {
        URL url = ideBundle.getEntry(path);
        ImageDescriptor desc = ImageDescriptor.createFromURL(url);
        configurer_p.declareImage(symbolicName, desc, shared);
    }
```

5. Finally, add the Common Navigator view to the default perspective factory of your RCP application.

```
public void createInitialLayout(IPageLayout layout) {
    String editorArea = layout.getEditorArea();
    layout.setEditorAreaVisible(false);
    layout.setFixed(true);

    layout.addStandaloneView("eclipse.navigator.view", true,
            IPageLayout.LEFT, 0.5f, editorArea);

    ...
}
```

Now, when the application starts, you should see an empty navigator. To add a file system location, right-click and select New ➤ Project, enter a project name in the wizard, select a target location, and then click Finish. The files in the target location should display in the navigator (see Figure 4-1).

Using CNF by Extending the Common Navigator

Extending the Common Navigator involves more coding, but it gives you a higher degree of control over the behavior of the navigator than can be achieved by contributing to the Common Navigator. An FTP client is a good example of an RCP application that should extend the Common Navigator.

Here are the steps required to extend the Common Navigator:

1. Create an RCP template (using the PDE wizard), if you don't have one.

2. Add the CNF dependencies using the plug-in manifest editor's Dependencies tab.

3. Add a view (`org.eclipse.ui.views`) extension point to the plug-in. Enter an ID, name, and class name for the view. For example, you might use `navigator.view`, `File System Navigator`, and `ch04.navigator.view.FileSystemNavigator`, respectively. This differs from contributing to the Common Navigator, which requires `org.eclipse.ui.navigator.CommonNavigator` as the class.

4. Create the view class. Make sure it extends `org.eclipse.ui.navigator.CommonNavigator`.

5. Add the view to a perspective, either programmatically or through a perspective extension. At this point, you could run the application to see an empty CNF view.

6. Create content classes to serve as the root node in your navigator. The children of the root node will be the first to appear in the navigator tree. These classes are commonly referred as the *model* of the navigator. The root node class should extend `PlatformObject` to provide the required `IAdaptable` interface. These classes are described in detail in the hands-on exercise.

7. Declare an `org.eclipse.ui.navigator.navigatorContent` extension point to define content, filters, and actions. The content element includes classes for content and label providers.

8. Add trigger points that cause the label and content providers to be called.

9. Bind content to the navigator using the `org.eclipse.ui.navigator.viewer` extension. This extension point registers the view as a navigator and binds content and actions using the `viewerContentBinding` and `viewerActionBinding` elements.

10. Run and test the application.

As you can see, there are quite a few steps required and plenty of code to be written. These steps are described in detail in the exercise at the end of this chapter.

Concurrency Infrastructure

The Eclipse Jobs API (`org.eclipse.core.runtime.jobs`) provides a concurrency infrastructure, which allows your application to perform simultaneous tasks, yet remain responsive while these tasks are performed. Obviously, this enhances the usability of your application.

The Jobs API provides the means to do the following:

- Schedule jobs for immediate execution or for execution after a specified delay

- Query, cancel, or suspend scheduled jobs

- Attach rules to jobs to indicate when they can run and whether they can run simultaneously with other jobs

- Acquire and release locks, and also detect and respond to deadlocks

Jobs API Basics

A *job* is an asynchronous task that runs concurrently with other tasks. You create a class that extends the Job class, and then schedule it somewhere within your application. Once a job is scheduled, it is added to a job queue managed by the Eclipse Platform runtime.

The Eclipse Platform runtime manages pending jobs using a background thread. When a job becomes active, the runtime invokes its run() method. When a job completes, it is removed from the queue, and then the runtime decides which job to run next.

Job States

The state of the job changes as the Eclipse Platform runs and completes the job. The following are lifetime states:

- WAITING: Indicates that the job has been scheduled to run, but is not running yet.

- RUNNING: Indicates that the job is running.

- SLEEPING: Indicates that the job is sleeping due to a sleep request or because it was scheduled to run after a certain delay.

- NONE: Indicates that the job is not waiting, running, or sleeping. A job is in this state when it has been created but is not yet scheduled.

Job Operations

You can do many interesting things with jobs by invoking the following methods:

- schedule(): This method starts the job immediately or at a specified interval.

- join(): This method will block the caller until the job has completed, or until the calling thread is interrupted.

- cancel(): This method allows canceling the job. It is up to the job to respond to the cancellation if it has already started. It is a good idea to wait for the job to complete after the job has been canceled: if (!job.cancel()) job.join(). If the cancellation does not take effect immediately, then cancel() will return false, and the caller will use join() to wait for the job to be canceled.

- sleep(): This method will cause the job to be put on hold indefinitely if the job has not yet started running.

- wakeUp(): This method will cause the job to be added to the wait queue, where it eventually will be executed.

Tip To make sure the job completes, use the join() method. It will block the caller until the job has completed or until the calling thread is interrupted. Keep in mind that it is not useful to call join() after scheduling a job, since you get no concurrency by doing so. You might as well do the work from the caller.

Scheduling Rules

A scheduling rule acts as a mutex (semaphore) that prevents a race condition between two jobs running concurrently. Consider the next fragment:

```
class Job1 extends Job {
    public Job1() {
        super("Job 1");
    }
     ...
}
class Job2 extends Job {
    public Job2() {
        super("Job 2");
    }
     ...
}


Job1 job1 = new Job1();
Job2 job2 = new Job1();

job1.schedule();
job2.schedule();
```

Because job1 and job2 run concurrently, we do not know which one will execute first. Even though the order is job1, job2, there is a possibility that job2 will execute first. This race condition can be fixed by adding a scheduling rule to both jobs.

The interface org.eclipse.core.runtime.jobs.ISchedulingRule is used to indicate the need for exclusive access to a resource. This interface defines the methods contains(ISchedulingRule rule) and isConflicting(ISchedulingRule rule), which test if this scheduling rule completely contains or is compatible with another scheduling rule, respectively. If we rewrite the previous fragment as:

```
final Mutext rule = new Mutex();
class Mutex implements ISchedulingRule {
    public boolean isConflicting(ISchedulingRule rule) {
        return rule == this;
    }
    public boolean contains(ISchedulingRule rule) {
        return rule == this;
    }
}
class Job1 extends Job {
    public Job1() {
        super("Job 1");
        setRule(rule);
    }
     ...
}
```

```
class Job2 extends Job {
    public Job2() {
        super("Job 2");
        setRule(rule);
    }
    ...
Job1job1 = newJob1();
Job2job2 = newJob1();

job1.schedule();
job2.schedule();
}
```

When a job has a scheduling rule, the isConflicting() method is used to determine if
the rule conflicts with the rules of any jobs currently running. Thus, your implementation
of isConflicting() can define exactly when it is safe to execute the job. If two jobs have the
identical rule, they will not be run concurrently. In this example, the same rule will ensure the
execution order of the job is always preserved: job1 always runs first.

Locks

A lock defines protocol for granting exclusive access to a shared object. When a job needs
access to the shared object, it acquires a lock for that object. When it is finished manipulating
the object, it releases the lock.

```
IJobManager jobMan = Job.getJobManager();
ILock lock = jobMan.newLock();

try {
  lock.acquire();
  // Update object
} finally {
  lock.release();
}
```

■**Tip** A lock should be created when the shared object is created or first accessed; that is, code that has a
reference to the shared object should also have a reference to its lock.

Using the Concurrency Infrastructure

Let's look at a simple program that demonstrates these concurrency concepts. Our example
is a virtual race in which runners compete. The race will take place in the workbench and will
be shown in the built-in progress view. We will have six runners, split into three teams of two.
Each runner will be a job that uses the run() method to advance through the course. We will
also need a referee (another job) to monitor the race, as well as a racetrack.

The Job Class

The RaceRunner object is shown in Listing 4-1.

Listing 4-1. *Sample Job Class Using the Concurrency Infrastructure*

```java
public class RaceRunner extends Job {
    int maxDistance = 1000;
    private String team;
    private String name;

    // Constructor: takes a runner and team names
    public RaceRunner(final String name, String team) {
        super(name);
        this.team = team;
        this.name = name;
    }

    // Listen to job changes
    public void register(JobChangeAdapter adapter) {
        addJobChangeListener(adapter);
    }

    @Override
    public boolean belongsTo(Object family) {
        return family == team;
    }

    @Override
    protected IStatus run(IProgressMonitor monitor) {
        int count = 0;

        // Perform background work and report progress
        try {
            monitor.beginTask("From team " + team, maxDistance);

            while (count++ < maxDistance) {
                if (monitor.isCanceled())
                    return Status.CANCEL_STATUS;

                int stamina = (int) (Math.random() * 100) + 1;
                final long sleep = (long) (Math.random() * 1000) / stamina;

                monitor.subTask("Elapsed distance " + count + "/"
                        + maxDistance + " stamina " + stamina);
```

```
                    // ... do some work ...
                    monitor.worked(1);
                    Thread.sleep(sleep);
                }

        } catch (InterruptedException e) {
            System.err.println(e);
        } finally {
            monitor.done();
        }
        return Status.OK_STATUS;
    }

    public void race() {
        schedule();
    }

    @Override
    public String toString() {
        return name + " from team " + team;
    }
}
```

The RaceRunner class extends Job and takes a runner and team names as arguments to the constructor. The team name is used to identify the runner within a job family. We'll explore job families in more detail after taking a look at job progress reporting and change listeners.

Progress Reporting

A runner uses the IProgressMonitor.beginTask() to report progress. On each loop interaction, a random sleep value is calculated, and feedback is provided to the monitor. When the number of interactions reaches the maximum distance, the loop completes and Status.OK_STATUS is returned. If the user clicks the Cancel button, monitor.isCanceled() will return false, and the thread will return Status.CANCEL_STATUS (which means the runner has dropped out of the race). Listing 4-2 demonstrates this technique, including a random sleep value to simulate a race. The progress of each runner can be seen in the standard progress view.

Listing 4-2. *Reporting Progress Within the Job Loop*

```
@Override
protected IStatus run(IProgressMonitor monitor) {
        int count = 0;

        try {
            monitor.beginTask("From team " + team, maxDistance);
```

```
            while (count++ < maxDistance) {
                if (monitor.isCanceled())
                    return Status.CANCEL_STATUS;

                final int stamina = (int) (Math.random() * 100) + 1;
                final long sleep = (long) (Math.random() * 1000) / stamina;

                monitor.subTask("Elapsed distance " + count + "/"
                        + maxDistance + " stamina " + stamina);

                // ... do some work ...
                monitor.worked(1);
                Thread.sleep(sleep);
            }

        } catch (InterruptedException e) {
            System.err.println(e);
        } finally {
            monitor.done();
        }
        return Status.OK_STATUS;
}
```

Job Change Listeners

Each runner will register for a race by adding a job change listener (see the register method in Listing 4-1). The listener takes a JobChangeAdapter as an argument, which provides default implementations for the methods described by the IJobChangeListener interface. The goal is to listen for status changes on the runners, such as cancel() or done().

Job Families

Job families make it easy to work with a group of related jobs as a single unit. In this example, a runner declares that it belongs to a team (family) by overriding the belongsTo method:

```
public boolean belongsTo(Object family) {
        return family == team;
}
```

The Race Class

Now we need a racetrack where the runners compete. We also need a referee to monitor the race and a race results container (a java.util.ArrayList should do). Listing 4-3 shows the Race class.

Listing 4-3. *Race Class to Demonstrate Concurrency Concepts*

```java
/**
 * Simple Race class to demonstrate concurrency concepts
 */
public class Race {

    static ArrayList<RaceRunner> results = new ArrayList<RaceRunner>();

    /**
     * The Referee monitors the race
     */
    static class Referee extends Job {
        int numRunners = 6;
        boolean done = false;

        public Referee(String name) {
            super(name);
        }

        @Override
        protected IStatus run(IProgressMonitor monitor) {
            while (!done) {
                if (results.size() >= numRunners)
                    done = true;
                try {
                    Thread.sleep(2000);
                } catch (Exception e) {
                    System.err.println(e);
                }
            }

            System.out.println("Race results");

            // Print race results
            int place = 1;
            for (int i = 0; i < results.size(); i++) {
                RaceRunner runner = results.get(i);

                // If the runner completes successfully
                if (runner.getResult().getCode() == IStatus.OK)
                    System.out.println((place++) + " " + runner);
            }
            return Status.OK_STATUS;
        }

    }
```

```java
    public Race() {
    }

    /**
     * Start the race
     */
    public void start() {
        RaceRunner bob = new RaceRunner("Bob", "US");
        RaceRunner john = new RaceRunner("John", "US");
        RaceRunner hans = new RaceRunner("Hans", "GER");
        RaceRunner lars = new RaceRunner("Lars", "GER");
        RaceRunner harry = new RaceRunner("Harry", "UK");
        RaceRunner ron = new RaceRunner("Ron", "UK");

        // Race referee...monitors results
        Referee ref = new Referee("Referee");
        ref.setSystem(true);
        ref.schedule();

        // This job change simulates a race name
        JobChangeAdapter oneKatNY = new JobChangeAdapter() {
            @Override
            // When the job completes, runners are added to a results array
            public synchronized void done(IJobChangeEvent event) {
                results.add((RaceRunner) event.getJob());
            }
        };

        // Register runners
        bob.register(oneKatNY);
        john.register(oneKatNY);
        hans.register(oneKatNY);
        lars.register(oneKatNY);
        harry.register(oneKatNY);
        ron.register(oneKatNY);

        // Start
        bob.race();
        john.race();
        hans.race();
        lars.race();
        harry.race();
        ron.race();
    }
}
```

Notice the race referee is another job. It simply monitors the results array list and then prints the winners. The referee is set as a system job. Jobs can be classified in two categories:

User jobs: A user job will appear in a modal progress dialog that provides a button for moving the dialog into the background. By defining your job as a user job, the progress feedback will automatically conform to the user preference for progress viewing.

System jobs: A system job is just like any other job, except the corresponding UI support will not set up a progress view or show any other UI elements. System jobs are used for low-level implementation details that you don't want to show to users.

Thus we have six runners: Bob, John, Hans, Lars, Harry, and Ron. They are split into three teams: US, GER, and UK. Each runner registers for a race (oneKatNY in this case) to provide for status updates:

```
JobChangeAdapter oneKatNY = new JobChangeAdapter() {
        @Override
        public synchronized void done(IJobChangeEvent event) {
            results.add((RaceRunner) event.getJob());
        }
};

bob.register(oneKatNY);
john.register(oneKatNY);
```

The runners start racing by calling race(), which simply calls the job's schedule() method. When all runners either complete the race or drop out, the referee will detect a finish and print the results to the console. Finally, to view the race in the workbench, the WorkbenchWindowAdvisor.postWindowOpen event can be overridden to start the race:

```
public class ApplicationWorkbenchWindowAdvisor extends
        WorkbenchWindowAdvisor
{
    // ...

    @Override
    public void postWindowOpen() {
        super.postWindowOpen();
        new Race().start();
    }
}
```

Figure 4-2 shows the virtual workbench race. When the race completes, the referee will print the results:

```
Race results
1 John from team US
2 Bob from team US
3 Hans from team GER
4 Ron from team UK
5 Lars from team GER
6 Harry from team UK
```

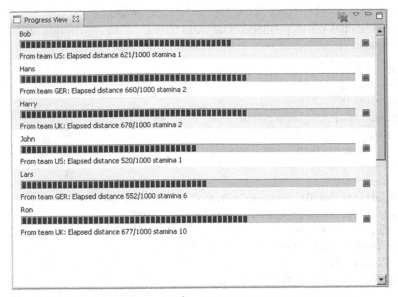

Figure 4-2. *Virtual track race to demonstrate concurrency concepts*

Hands-on Exercise: A CNF File System Navigator

The best way to get started with CNF is to build a real application. In this exercise, you'll build a simple file system navigator. You'll extend the org.eclipse.ui.navigator.CommonNavigator class to obtain a higher degree of control over the resource discovery. The exercise demonstrates using CNF extension points, content and label providers, content binding, resource encapsulation, and perspectives.

Creating an RCP Project Template

The first task is to create an RCP application project, as follows:

1. From the Eclipse IDE main menu, select New ➤ Project ➤ Plug-in Project. Enter a name for the project (such as File Navigator), and then click Next.

2. Make sure the "This plug-in will make contributions to the UI" option is checked and the "Would you like to create a rich client application?" option is set to Yes. Click Next.

3. On the Templates page, select the RCP application with a view template. Click Next.

4. Make sure the Add branding option is selected. This will add a default product extension to the project (otherwise, you must add it to the manifest manually). Click Finish to open the manifest editor.

5. Add a product configuration file by selecting New ➤ Other ➤ Plug-in Development ➤ Product Configuration. Enter a name and select the plug-in product. Click Finish.

6. Test the template by clicking the Launch an Eclipse application link in the product editor.

7. With the template in place, add the CNF dependencies. To add dependencies from the plug-in manifest editor, click the Dependencies tab, and then click the Add button and select the required packages, as highlighted in the following manifest file:

```
Manifest-Version: 1.0
Bundle-ManifestVersion: 2
Bundle-Name: Ch04 Plug-in
Bundle-SymbolicName: ch04; singleton:=true
Bundle-Version: 1.0.0
Bundle-Activator: ch04.Activator
Require-Bundle: org.eclipse.ui,
 org.eclipse.core.runtime,
 org.eclipse.ui.navigator;bundle-version="3.3.100",
 org.eclipse.ui.navigator.resources;bundle-version="3.3.100",
 org.eclipse.ui.ide;bundle-version="3.4.0",
 org.eclipse.core.resources;bundle-version="3.4.0"
Bundle-ActivationPolicy: lazy
Bundle-RequiredExecutionEnvironment: JavaSE-1.6
```

Adding CNF Extension Points

Now, you need some CNF extension points. These include a view, navigator content, and content bindings. The fastest way to add these extension points is to use the plug-in manifest editor's Extensions tab. For example, to add the view extension point, click Add, select org.eclipse.ui.views, and then enter the view attributes. The Extension wizard also provides some extension templates.

View

The view should include the following required attributes:

- id: A unique identifier for the view (navigator.view).

- name: A descriptive name (File System Navigator).

- class: The implementation class name (ch04.navigator.view.FileSystemNavigator). You can create the class by clicking the Class label and using the wizard. Make sure the class extends org.eclipse.ui.navigator.CommonNavigator.

Listing 4-4 shows the view extension point for the file system navigator.

Listing 4-4. *View Extension Point for the File System Navigator*

```
<extension
    point="org.eclipse.ui.views">
  <view
      class="ch04.navigator.view.FileSystemNavigator"
      icon="icons/alt_window_16.gif"
```

```
            id="navigator.view"
            name="FileSystem Navigator">
    </view>
</extension>
```

Navigator Content

The navigator content extension defines the content and label providers, which populate the internal tree widget of the navigator with information. The following are the most important attributes:

- id: A unique ID to identify this extension (ch04.navigatorContent).

- name: The display name for the content extension (ch04.navigatorContent).

- contentProvider: The name of the class that implements a tree content provider. The content provider will be consulted when adding children to the tree. Use an enablement or triggerPoints clause to indicate which kinds of content should trigger a request to this content provider. This example uses the class ch04.navigator. model.NavigatorRoot as the content trigger. This class must be an IAdaptable. This can be achieved by extending org.eclipse.core.runtime.PlatformObject. The content provider is described in further detail a little later in this chapter, when we look at implementing the classes for the example.

- labelProvider: Supplies the name of the class to provide label and image information to the internal tree. Clients may implement the following:

  - ILabelProvider to provide labels and images

  - ICommonLabelProvider for more advanced functionality

  - IStyledLabelProvider to provide styled text labels for version 3.4

Listing 4-5 shows the navigator content extension point for the file system navigator.

Listing 4-5. *Navigator Content Extension Point for the File System Navigator*

```
<extension
        point="org.eclipse.ui.navigator.navigatorContent">
    <navigatorContent
        contentProvider="ch04.navigator.view.TreeContentProvider"
        id="ch04.navigatorContent"
        labelProvider="ch04.navigator.view.LabelProvider"
        name="ch04.navigatorContent">
    <triggerPoints>
        <instanceof
            value="ch04.navigator.model.NavigatorRoot">
        </instanceof></triggerPoints>
    </navigatorContent>
</extension>
```

Content Binding

Finally, you need to bind the navigator view (navigator.view) with the content extension (ch04.navigatorContent) by using the includes clause of the content binding. A content extension may be selected by the exact extension ID. Clients may also use a regular expression pattern to select any content extensions that match the pattern.

Listing 4-6 shows the content binding for the file system navigator.

Listing 4-6. *Content Binding for the File System Navigator*

```
<extension
        point="org.eclipse.ui.navigator.viewer">
    <viewer
          viewerId="navigator.view">
    </viewer>

    <viewerContentBinding
          viewerId="navigator.view">
        <includes>
            <contentExtension
                  pattern="ch04.navigatorContent">
            </contentExtension>

        </includes>
    </viewerContentBinding>
</extension>
```

At this point, you have all the extension points in place. Now, let's proceed to the class implementation steps.

Implementation Classes

The implementation classes can be categorized as follows:

- *Content trigger* (NavigatorRoot): Serves as the root node of the navigator. Its children will be the first to appear in the tree.

- *Resource encapsulator* (FileBean): Encapsulates files to be shown in the navigator.

- *Content provider classes* (TreeContentProvider *and* LabelProvider): Add children to the tree, and add labels and images for the node elements.

- *Navigator class* (FileSystemNavigator): The main CNF class. It extends the Common Navigator to provide initial input to populate the data tree.

- *Perspective factory* (Perspective): Needs to be modified to display the default views when the application starts.

All of these classes are new and must be created, except for Perspective, which is created by the Plug-in Project wizard and only needs modifications.

To create these classes, right-click the plug-in project folder and select New ➤ Class. Then enter the names and package locations. NavigatorRoot, FileBean, and FileSystemNavigator should be created in the package ch04.navigator.model. TreeContentProvider. LabelContentProvider should go in the package ch04.navigator.view.

Tip All of the pieces in this puzzle are bound together by the extension points (in plugin.xml) from Listing 4-4 (describing the view class), Listing 4-5 (describing the navigator content, which references TreeContentProvider, LabelProvider, and NavigatorRoot), and Listing 4-6 (describing the content binding, which binds the navigator content with the view).

The next sections provide more details on the implementation of these classes.

Navigator Root

Listing 4-7 shows the class that serves as the root node of the navigator. It will not appear in the navigator; however, its children will be the first to appear.

Listing 4-7. *Root Node Class for the File System Navigator*

```
package ch04.navigator.model;

import java.io.File;

import org.eclipse.core.runtime.PlatformObject;

public class NavigatorRoot extends PlatformObject {
    private final String OSNAME = System.getProperty("os.name");
    private final boolean isWindows = OSNAME.indexOf("Windows") != -1;

    public FileBean[] getParentBeans() {
        File f = isWindows ? new File("c:/") : new File("/");

        FileBean top = new FileBean(f);
        return top.getChildren();
    }
}
```

This class extends PlatformObject, which in turn implements the IAdaptable interface (nodes of a CNF viewer must implement this interface). The class uses the getParentBeans() method to return the top elements. Notice that the top elements will be file beans from c:\ or /, depending on the operating system: Windows or Linux.

Resource Encapsulator: File Bean

Listing 4-8 shows the FileBean class to encapsulate a file within the file system.

Listing 4-8. *Resource Encapsulator Class for the File System Navigator*

```
package ch04.navigator.model;

import java.io.File;

public class FileBean {
    File file;

    public FileBean(File file) {
        this.file = file;
    }

    @Override
    public String toString() {
        return file.getName();
    }

    public boolean isDirectory() {
        return file.isDirectory();
    }

    public boolean hasChildren() {
        return file.list() != null;
    }

    public FileBean[] getChildren() {
        File[] files = file.listFiles();

        FileBean[] fileBeans = new FileBean[files.length];

        for (int i = 0; i < files.length; i++) {
            fileBeans[i] = new FileBean(files[i]);
        }
        return fileBeans;
    }
}
```

The class constructs an instance from a java.io.File object and has the following methods:

- toString(): Returns the name to be used as the label within the tree.
- isDirectory(): Returns true if the current instance is a directory.

- hasChildren(): Returns true if the current instance has children.

- getChildren(): Returns children file beans for the current instance.

These methods will be useful for the tree and label content provider implementations.

Navigator Class

The navigator class is responsible for getting the initial input to populate the data tree, as well as creating other visual components such as a context menu and action bars. Listing 4-9 shows the navigator class for the file system navigator.

Listing 4-9. *Navigator Class for the File System Navigator*

```
import ch04.navigator.model.NavigatorRoot;

public class FileSystemNavigator extends CommonNavigator {
    private Action action1;

    @Override
    protected IAdaptable getInitialInput() {
        return new NavigatorRoot();
    }

    @Override
    public void createPartControl(Composite parent) {
        super.createPartControl(parent);

        makeActions();
        hookContextMenu();
        contributeToActionBars();
    }

    private void makeActions() {
        action1 = new Action() {
            public void run() {
                showMessage("Action 1 executed");
            }
        };
        action1.setText("Action 1");
        action1.setToolTipText("Action 1 tooltip");
        action1.setImageDescriptor(PlatformUI.getWorkbench()
                .getSharedImages().getImageDescriptor(
                        ISharedImages.IMG_OBJS_INFO_TSK));

    }
```

```java
        private void showMessage(String message) {
            MessageDialog.openInformation(getCommonViewer().getControl()
                    .getShell(), "Sample View", message);
        }

        private void hookContextMenu() {
            MenuManager menuMgr = new MenuManager("#PopupMenu");
            menuMgr.setRemoveAllWhenShown(true);
            menuMgr.addMenuListener(new IMenuListener() {
                public void menuAboutToShow(IMenuManager manager) {
                    FileSystemNavigator.this.fillContextMenu(manager);
                }
            });
            Menu menu = menuMgr.createContextMenu(getCommonViewer()
                    .getControl());
            getCommonViewer().getControl().setMenu(menu);
            getSite().registerContextMenu(menuMgr, getCommonViewer());
        }

        private void contributeToActionBars() {
            IActionBars bars = getViewSite().getActionBars();
            fillLocalPullDown(bars.getMenuManager());
            fillLocalToolBar(bars.getToolBarManager());
        }

        private void fillContextMenu(IMenuManager manager) {
            manager.add(action1);
            manager.add(new Separator());

            // Other plug-ins can contribute their actions here
            manager.add(new Separator(IWorkbenchActionConstants.MB_ADDITIONS));
        }

        private void fillLocalToolBar(IToolBarManager manager) {
            manager.add(action1);
            manager.add(new Separator());
        }

        private void fillLocalPullDown(IMenuManager manager) {
            manager.add(action1);
            manager.add(new Separator());
        }
    }
```

The navigator class overrides the getInitialInput() method and simply returns a new instance of NavigatorRoot. The createPartControl() method can also be overridden to add custom actions. Here, we add a simple action to display a message box. Then we hook the action to the context menu and local toolbar and pull-down menu.

Content Providers

Content providers will be consulted when adding children to the tree and requesting labels and images for the node elements. CNF defines tree and label content providers.

Listing 4-10 shows the tree content provider for the file system navigator.

Listing 4-10. *Tree Content Provider for the File System Navigator*

```
package ch04.navigator.view;

import org.eclipse.jface.viewers.ITreeContentProvider;
import org.eclipse.jface.viewers.Viewer;

import ch04.navigator.model.FileBean;
import ch04.navigator.model.NavigatorRoot;

public class TreeContentProvider implements ITreeContentProvider {

    @Override
    public Object[] getChildren(Object parentElement) {
        FileBean parent = (FileBean) parentElement;
        return parent.getChildren();
    }

    @Override
    public Object getParent(Object element) {
        return null;
    }

    @Override
    public boolean hasChildren(Object element) {
        FileBean file = (FileBean) element;
        return file.hasChildren();
    }

    @Override
    public Object[] getElements(Object inputElement) {
        NavigatorRoot root = ((NavigatorRoot) inputElement);

        return root.getParentBeans();
    }
```

```
@Override
public void dispose() {
}

@Override
public void inputChanged(Viewer viewer, Object oldInput,
        Object newInput) {
}

}
```

The tree content provider overrides the following methods:

- getChildren(): Returns the child elements of the given parent element. This method differs from getElements() in that getElements() is called to obtain the tree viewer's root elements, whereas getChildren() is used to obtain the children of a given parent element in the tree (including a root).

- getElements(): Returns the elements to display in the viewer when its input is set to the given element. These elements can be presented as rows in a table, items in a list, and so on. The result is not modified by the viewer.

- getParent(): Returns the parent for the given element or null, indicating that the parent cannot be computed.

- hasChildren(): Returns whether the given element has children.

- inputChanged(): Notifies this content provider that the given viewer's input has been switched to a different element. A typical use for this method is to register the content provider as a listener for changes on the new input (using model-specific means), and to deregister the viewer from the old input. In response to these change notifications, the content provider should update the viewer.

Notice that the FileBean class methods match the methods of the tree content provider. The method TreeContentProvider.getElements is used to return the files of the top file system using NavigatorRoot.getParentBeans.

The label content provider for the file system navigator is shown in Listing 4-11.

Listing 4-11. *Label Content Provider for the File System Navigator*

```
package ch04.navigator.view;

import java.util.Hashtable;

import org.eclipse.jface.viewers.ILabelProvider;
import org.eclipse.jface.viewers.ILabelProviderListener;
import org.eclipse.swt.graphics.Image;
import org.eclipse.swt.graphics.ImageData;
import org.eclipse.swt.program.Program;
import org.eclipse.ui.ISharedImages;
```

```java
import ch04.Activator;
import ch04.NavigatorApplication;
import ch04.navigator.model.FileBean;

public class LabelProvider implements ILabelProvider {
    // Cached icons
    private Hashtable<Program, Image> iconCache
        = new Hashtable<Program, Image>();

    @Override
    public Image getImage(Object element) {
        FileBean file = (FileBean) element;
        String nameString = file.toString();
        Image image = null;

        int dot = nameString.lastIndexOf('.');

        // Get icon from the file system
        if (dot != -1) {
            // Find the program using the file extension
            String extension = nameString.substring(dot);
            Program program = Program.findProgram(extension);

            // Get icon based on extension
            if (program != null) {
                image = getIconFromProgram(program);
            }
        }

        if (image == null)
            image = Activator.getSharedImage(ISharedImages.IMG_OBJ_FILE);

        return file.isDirectory() ? Activator
                .getSharedImage(ISharedImages.IMG_OBJ_FOLDER) : image;
    }

    @Override
    public String getText(Object element) {
        return element.toString();
    }

    @Override
    public void addListener(ILabelProviderListener listener) {
    }
```

```
@Override
public void dispose() {
}

@Override
public boolean isLabelProperty(Object element, String property) {
    return false;
}

@Override
public void removeListener(ILabelProviderListener listener) {
}

/**
 * Gets an image for a file associated with a given program
 *
 * @param program
 *              the Program
 */
public Image getIconFromProgram(Program program) {
    Image image = (Image) iconCache.get(program);
    if (image == null) {
        ImageData imageData = program.getImageData();
        if (imageData != null) {
            image = new Image(NavigatorApplication.getDefault()
                    .getDisplay(), imageData);
            iconCache.put(program, image);
        }
    }
    return image;
}

}
```

The label content provider returns the text of the object (the file name in this case), but
it also uses a neat trick from the SWT to return the icon associated with a specific program. It
uses the class org.eclipse.swt.program.Program to find the program that is associated with an
extension. Note that a Display object must already exist to guarantee that this method returns
an appropriate result. Program.getImageData is used to return the receiver's image data. This is
the icon that is associated with the receiver in the operating system. The result is a neat display
of files and associated operating system icons in the tree.

Default Perspective

We are almost finished building the file system navigator. The final step is to add the view to
the default perspective factory, as shown in Listing 4-12.

Listing 4-12. *Default Perspective for the File System Navigator*

```java
public class Perspective implements IPerspectiveFactory {
    public static final String ID = Perspective.class.getName();

    public void createInitialLayout(IPageLayout layout) {
        String editorArea = layout.getEditorArea();
        layout.setEditorAreaVisible(false);
        layout.setFixed(true);

        layout.addStandaloneView("navigator.view", true, IPageLayout.LEFT,
                0.33f, editorArea);
    }
}
```

The IPageLayout.addStandaloneView adds a stand-alone view with the given ID to this page layout. A stand-alone view cannot be docked together with other views.

The first argument (navigator.view) is the ID of the view contributed as a workbench's view extension point.

Figure 4-3 shows the final result of this exercise, as well as the example earlier in this chapter. You now have two resource navigators: one built by extending the Common Navigator and the second built by contributing to it. As you saw, extending the Common Navigator is quite a bit of work, but it gives you more control over the content of the navigator.

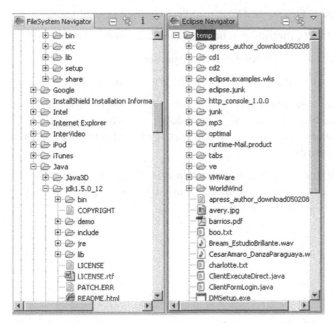

Figure 4-3. *The file system navigator and Common Navigator views side by side*

Summary

This chapter covered the Eclipse CNF and Jobs API. Here are the important points to keep in mind:

- CNF provides a general-purpose navigator view for applications with pluggable content, filters, sorting, and much more.

- CNF has the following benefits: it's shareable, highly extensible, and declarative (using extension points). It also has DnD support and built-in resources support.

- CNF uses content extensions, filters, wizards, and action providers for configuration.

  - Content extensions are used to associate objects with appropriate icons, labels, and menu items.

  - Filters are used to define objects to exclude.

  - Wizards are used to import, export, or create resources.

  - Action providers allow the user to programmatically configure the pop-up menu in a CNF viewer.

- The concurrency infrastructure provides an API for scheduling jobs in the background, an API for attaching rules to indicate when they can run and whether they can run simultaneously, and a generic locking facility for detecting and responding to deadlocks.

- Job states are WAITING, RUNNING, SLEEPING, and NONE (not yet scheduled).

- The IProgressMonitor.beginTask() method can be used to report progress on the job.

- A job change listener can be used to listen for job status updates.

- Job families make it easy to work with a group of related jobs as a single unit.

- Jobs can be categorized as user and system jobs. A user job will appear in a modal progress dialog that provides a button for moving the dialog into the background. A system job is like any other job, except it has no UI support; it will not set up a progress view or show any other UI elements.

- A lock defines a protocol for granting exclusive access to a shared object. When a job needs access to the shared object, it acquires a lock for that object. When it is finished manipulating the object, it releases the lock.

■ ■ ■

## CHAPTER 5

Forms API and Presentation Framework

The Eclipse Forms API is an optional RCP feature that allows you to create portable, web-style UIs. Since its inception, the Forms API's popularity has continued to grow, due to its sophisticated functionality and small footprint. This API gives developers a powerful tool for spicing up their rich client interfaces—without using an embedded browser. Forms allow you to retain full control of the widgets in the UI and to maintain portability across platforms.

This chapter describes how to use the Forms API. In the exercise at the end of the chapter, you'll modify the standard Eclipse Mail template to use forms.

Forms API Basics

The Forms API provides custom widgets, layouts, and support classes to achieve a web look inside your desktop applications, so you don't need to resort to an embedded browser. It is portable across all the platforms where SWT is supported. In fact, as you'll learn in this chapter, it expands the possibilities of the UI well beyond traditional SWT widgets.

The goal of the Eclipse Forms API is to make web-style UIs possible by providing the following:

- A `Forms` object that can be included in content areas such as views and editors.

- A toolkit (`FormToolkit`) that serves as a factory for SWT controls and manages colors as well as other aspects of the form

- New layout managers: `TableWrapLayout`, and `ColumnLayout`

- Complex web-style controls, including text hyperlink, image hyperlink, expandable composite, section, and form text

- Multipage forms or editors, like the plug-in manifest editor itself (see Figure 5-5 later in this chapter)

The Forms API can be easily integrated within an Eclipse view, as shown in Listing 5-1.

Listing 5-1. *Sample View Class Showing Basic Forms API Integration*

```java
public class View extends ViewPart
{
    public static final String ID = View.class.getName();

    /**
     * Eclipse forms support. Requires the plug-in org.eclipse.ui.forms
     */
    private FormToolkit toolkit;
    private ScrolledForm scrolledForm;

    private ImageDescriptor FORM_ICON = Activator
            .getImageDescriptor("icons/alt_window_16.gif");

    /**
     * This is a callback that will allow us to create the viewer and
     * initialize it
     */
    public void createPartControl(Composite parent)
    {
        // Create a Form API toolkit
        toolkit = new FormToolkit(getFormColors(parent.getDisplay()));

        /**
         * Create a scrolled form widget in the provided parent. If you do
         * not require scrolling because there is already a scrolled
         * composite up the parent chain, use 'createForm' instead
         */
        scrolledForm = toolkit.createScrolledForm(parent);

        // Form title and image
        scrolledForm.setFont(new Font(null, "Times", 18, SWT.BOLD
                | SWT.ITALIC));
        scrolledForm.setText("Form Title");
        scrolledForm.setImage(FORM_ICON.createImage());

        /**
         * Takes advantage of the gradients and other capabilities to
         * decorate the form heading using colors computed based on the
         * current skin and operating system.
         */
        toolkit.decorateFormHeading(scrolledForm.getForm());

        /**
         * Add controls
         */
    }
```

```
/**
 * Passing the focus request to the viewer's control.
 */
public void setFocus() {
    scrolledForm.setFocus();
}
}
```

The first step is to create a FormToolkit within the view's createPartControl() callback. The FormToolkit will accept either a Display object or a set of colors (FormColors) to be applied to forms and form widgets. The toolkit can then be used as a factory to create the form and the child widgets.

In Listing 5-1, ScrolledForm is the first control created. It provides scrolling for the instance of the Form class. The ScrolledForm control is created in a parent composite that will allow it to use all the available area.

Common Controls

Child widgets of the form should typically be created using FormToolkit so they match the appearance and behavior of the form and each other. Among the most basic controls are label, text box, and button.

A form label is created as follows:

```
toolkit.createLabel(scrolledForm.getBody(), "Label");
```

A form text box is created as follows:

```
Text text = toolkit.createText(scrolledForm.getBody(), "", SWT.FILL);
```

By default, borders will not be painted for a text box in a form if the global border style is SWT.BORDER. Thus, you should call the method toolkit.paintBordersFor(text.getParent()) to paint flat borders for widgets created by the toolkit, as shown in Listing 5-1.

You can create check boxes and push buttons as follows:

```
Button b1 = toolkit.createButton(scrolledForm.getBody(), "Check Box", SWT.CHECK);
Button b2 = toolkit.createButton(scrolledForm.getBody(), "Push Button", SWT.PUSH);
```

Listing 5-2 shows an example of creating these common controls.

Listing 5-2. *Forms API Common Controls Along with Event Listeners*

```
private void addCommonControls()
{
        // Label
        toolkit.createLabel(scrolledForm.getBody(), "Label");

        // Text box
        Text text = toolkit.createText(scrolledForm.getBody(), "",
                SWT.FILL);
```

```
        // Make the text box grab all available horizontal space
        text.setLayoutData(new TableWrapData(TableWrapData.FILL_GRAB));

        // Paint borders for the text box
        toolkit.paintBordersFor(text.getParent());

        // Check box and push buttons
        Button b1 = toolkit.createButton(scrolledForm.getBody(),
                "Check Box", SWT.CHECK);
        Button b2 = toolkit.createButton(scrolledForm.getBody(),
                "Push Button", SWT.PUSH);

        // Event listeners: The container class must implement the interface
        // org.eclipse.swt.widgets.Listener
        b1.addListener(SWT.Selection, this);
        b2.addListener(SWT.Selection, this);
    }

@Override
public void handleEvent(Event event) {
        System.out.println(event);
    }
```

Tip To have the background of controls match the background of the form, use `toolkit.createLabel(form.getBody(), "Label")` instead of `Label label = new Label(form.getBody(), SWT.NULL)`.

Figure 5-1 shows the form generated by Listing 5-2.

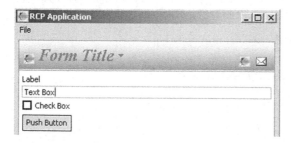

Figure 5-1. *Common form controls*

Form Look and Feel

You can easily customize the look and feel of the form, including the form colors, font, icons, toolbar, and drop-down menu, as shown in Figure 5-2.

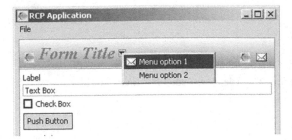

Figure 5-2. *Customized form toolbar, drop-down menu, and gradient colors*

Form Toolbar

Use the getToolBarManager() method from the Form class to access the toolbar manager to manage tool items in the form's title area. The toolbar manager uses the add() method to add an action as a contribution item to this manager. In turn, the action describes the text, tool tip, image, and a default implementation. Listing 5-3 defines a toolbar with two actions, which display simple messages in the form header (see Figure 5-2).

Listing 5-3. *Creating a Forms Toolbar*

```
/**
 * Create a form toolbar
 */
private void createToolBar() {
        // Two toolbar icons
        ImageDescriptor TB_ICON_1 = Activator
                .getImageDescriptor("icons/alt_window_16.gif");
        ImageDescriptor TB_ICON_2 = Activator
                .getImageDescriptor("icons/sample3.gif");

        Form form = scrolledForm.getForm();

        // Toolbar action #1:
        Action toolBtn1 = new Action() {
            public void run() {
                // Show a message in the form header
                setFormMessage("Tool button 1", IMessageProvider.INFORMATION);
            }
        };
```

```
    // Tool button #1
    toolBtn1.setToolTipText("Tool button 1");
    toolBtn1.setText("Tool button 1");
    toolBtn1.setImageDescriptor(TB_ICON_1);

    // Toolbar action #2
    Action toolBtn2 = new Action() {
        public void run() {
            // Show a message in the form header
            setFormMessage("Tool button 2", IMessageProvider.WARNING);
        }
    };
    // Tool button #2
    toolBtn2.setToolTipText("Tool button 2");
    toolBtn2.setText("Tool button 2");
    toolBtn2.setImageDescriptor(TB_ICON_2);

    // Add toolbar actions
    form.getToolBarManager().add(toolBtn1);
    form.getToolBarManager().add(toolBtn2);
    form.getToolBarManager().add(new Separator());

    // Refresh the toolbar after adding buttons
    form.getToolBarManager().update(true);

    // Sets the toolbar vertical alignment relative to the header.
    // Can be useful when there is more free space at the second row
    form.setToolBarVerticalAlignment(SWT.LEFT);
}
```

Tip Don't forget to bring the toolbar manager's underlying widgets up-to-date with any changes by calling the `form.getToolBarManager().update(true)` method. This will refresh the toolbar when the state of a contribution item (such as a button) changes.

Form Drop-Down Menu

Contributing to the drop-down menu is similar to contributing to the toolbar. The main difference is that you must use the method `form.getMenuManager().add(IAction)` instead of `form.getToolBarManager.add(IAction)` to return the menu manager used to access the form's title area and drop-down menu items. Listing 5-4 adds the two menu options shown in Figure 5-2.

Listing 5-4. *Creating a Form Drop-Down Menu*

```
/**
 * Form drop-down menus
 */
private void addFromDropDownMenu() {
        // Drop-down menu icon
        ImageDescriptor DD_ICON_1 = Activator
                .getImageDescriptor("icons/sample3.gif");

        // The inner form from the scrolled form instance variable
        Form form = scrolledForm.getForm();

        // Drop-down menu action #1 with icon and message
        form.getMenuManager().add(new Action("Menu option 1", DD_ICON_1) {
            @Override
            public void run() {
                setFormMessage("Menu option1",
                        IMessageProvider.INFORMATION);
            }
        });

        // Drop-down action 2, no icon or message
        form.getMenuManager().add(new Action("Menu option 2") {
        });
}
```

Form Messages

Form messages are presented with text between the title and the toolbar in the form heading, as shown in Listing 5-5. In addition to the text message, an image icon will be displayed, depending on the message type (defined in org.eclipse.jface.dialogs.IMessageProvider).

Listing 5-5. *Displaying a Form Message*

```
/**
 * Form message handling
 * @param text
 *            Message to display
 * @param type
 *            One of ERROR, NONE, WARNING, or INFORMATION
 */
private void setFormMessage(String text, int type) {
        Form form = scrolledForm.getForm();
```

```
    /**
     * Adds a message hyperlink listener. Messages will be rendered as
     * hyperlinks
     */
    form.addMessageHyperlinkListener(new HyperlinkAdapter());
    form.setMessage(text, type);
}
```

Messages are rendered as static text by default. However, if at least one hyperlink listener is present, messages will be rendered as hyperlinks.

Form Gradient Colors

A form displays a horizontal background gradient whose background and font colors can be manipulated with the class FormColors by using the following constants:

- IFormColors.H_GRADIENT_START: Key for the form header gradient start color.

- IFormColors.H_GRADIENT_END: Key for the form header gradient end color.

- IFormColors.H_BOTTOM_KEYLINE1: Key for the form header bottom keyline 1 color.

- IFormColors.H_BOTTOM_KEYLINE2: Key for the form header bottom keyline 2 color.

- IFormColors.TITLE: Key for the form title foreground color.

Listing 5-6 defines the custom gradient colors used for the form shown in Figure 5-2.

Listing 5-6. *Defining Custom Gradient Colors for a Form*

```
public void createPartControl(Composite parent) {
    // Create a Form API toolkit with custom gradient colors
    toolkit = new FormToolkit(getFormColors(parent.getDisplay()));
    ...
}


// Toolkit color management
public FormColors getFormColors(final Display display) {
    // Gradient colors: start, end
    final Color COLOR_START = new Color(null, 128, 128, 128);
    final Color COLOR_END = new Color(null, 255, 255, 255);

    // Title color
    final Color COLOR_HEADING = new Color(null, 102, 102, 102);

    FormColors formColors;

    formColors = new FormColors(display);
```

```
          // Set gradient colors
          formColors.createColor(IFormColors.H_GRADIENT_START
                  , COLOR_START.getRGB());
          formColors.createColor(IFormColors.H_GRADIENT_END
                  , COLOR_END.getRGB());
          formColors.createColor(IFormColors.H_BOTTOM_KEYLINE1
                  , COLOR_END.getRGB());
          formColors.createColor(IFormColors.H_BOTTOM_KEYLINE2
                  , COLOR_START.getRGB());
          // Set title color
          formColors.createColor(IFormColors.TITLE, COLOR_HEADING.getRGB());
          return formColors;
    }
```

The method getFormColors() from Listing 5-6 changes the header color values, as well as the title foreground color, using custom RGB. getFormColors() is called when creating the form toolkit with toolkit = new FormToolkit(getFormColors(Display)). An SWT Display is required for this customization.

Custom Layouts

Two new custom layouts are provided by the Forms API: TableWrapLayout and ColumnLayout.

The TableWrapLayout layout manager attempts to position controls in the composite using a two-pass HTML table, as recommended by the HTML World Wide Web Consortium (W3C) specification.[1] The main difference from GridLayout is that it makes two passes (meaning it parses the HTML layout twice), and the width and height are not calculated in the same pass. For example, to apply a two-column HTML table layout to a scrollable form, use the following:

```
TableWrapLayout layout = new TableWrapLayout();
 layout.numColumns = 2;

 scrolledForm.getBody().setLayout(layout);
```

The ColumnLayout layout manager arranges children of the parent in vertical columns. All the columns are identically sized, and children are stretched horizontally to fill the column width. The goal is to give the layout a range of column numbers to allow it to handle various parent widths. This is useful in complex forms where the number of columns changes depending on the width of the form. The number of columns drops when the width decreases and grows when allowed by the parent width.

Complex Controls

Complex controls allow your application to use a web-style look without requiring an embedded and bulky web browser. These controls include text hyperlinks, image hyperlinks, expandable composites, sections, and form text, as shown in Figure 5-3.

---

1. The W3C HTML specification is available online at http://www.w3.org/html/wg/.

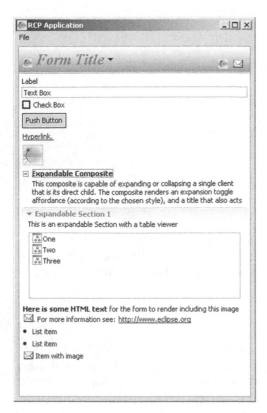

Figure 5-3. *Complex form controls: hyperlink, expandable composite, section, and form text*

Hyperlinks

A form hyperlink mirrors its HTML counterpart. Behind the scenes, it simply draws text in the client area. This text can be wrapped and underlined, just like an HTML hyperlink. Each hyperlink has text, a tool tip, and an activation listener that fires when the link is clicked. Listing 5-7 creates the text hyperlink and image hyperlink shown in Figure 5-3.

Listing 5-7. *Creating a Hyperlink Widget and Related Click Listener*

```
private void createHyperLink() {
      // Hyperlink with listener
      Hyperlink link = toolkit.createHyperlink(scrolledForm.getBody(),
            "Hyperlink.", SWT.WRAP);

      link.addHyperlinkListener(new HyperlinkAdapter() {
         @Override
         public void linkActivated(HyperlinkEvent e) {
            System.out.println(e);
         }
      });
```

```
    // Create a second image hyperlink with icon, text, and click listener
    // Image hyperlink icon
    ImageDescriptor ICON = Activator
            .getImageDescriptor("icons/alt_window_32.gif");
    // Create image hyperlink
    ImageHyperlink ihl = toolkit.createImageHyperlink(scrolledForm
            .getBody(), SWT.WRAP);

    ihl.setImage(ICON.createImage());
    ihl.setToolTipText("Image Hyperlink");
    ihl.addHyperlinkListener(new HyperlinkAdapter() {
        @Override
        public void linkActivated(HyperlinkEvent e) {
            System.out.println(e);
        }
    });
}
```

You can use the addHyperlinkListener(IHyperlinkListener) method to listen for click events from the hyperlink. The class org.eclipse.ui.forms.events.HyperlinkAdapter provides the default implementations for the methods described by the IHyperlinkListener interface.

Tip When the hyperlink has a focus rectangle painted around it, it means the widget has the keyboard focus. Therefore, simply pressing the Enter key will activate it.

Expandable Composite

The expandable composite control is capable of expanding or collapsing a single child label composite. The composite renders a title that also acts as a hyperlink. The left and right arrow keys can be used to control the expansion state. If several expandable composites are created in the same parent, the up and down arrow keys can be used to traverse between them. The expandable text accepts mnemonics, and mnemonic activation will toggle the expansion state. Listing 5-8 creates the expandable composite shown in Figure 5-3.

Listing 5-8. *Creating an Expandable Composite*

```
private void createExpandableComposite() {
    ExpandableComposite ec = toolkit.createExpandableComposite(
        scrolledForm.getBody()                          // Parent widget
        , ExpandableComposite.TREE_NODE        // Use a tree
            // Use a tree with indentation
            | ExpandableComposite.CLIENT_INDENT);

    ec.setText("Expandable Composite");
```

```
        // Text displayed when the control is expanded/collapsed
        String text = "This composite is capable of expanding or collapsing "
                + "a single client that is its direct child. "
                + "The composite renders an expansion toggle "
                + "affordance (according to the chosen style), "
                + "and a title that also acts as a hyperlink.";

        // Create a label for the composite and bind it to the control
        Label client = toolkit.createLabel(ec, text, SWT.WRAP);
        ec.setClient(client);

        // Lay out  the control in a 1 column table style
        TableWrapData td = new TableWrapData();
        td.colspan = 1;
        ec.setLayoutData(td);

        ec.addExpansionListener(new ExpansionAdapter() {
            @Override
            public void expansionStateChanged(ExpansionEvent e) {
                scrolledForm.reflow(true);
            }
        });
    }
```

Listing 5-8 creates an expandable composite with a tree node style and indented text (ExpandableComposite.TREE_NODE and ExpandableComposite.CLIENT_INDENT), in which the plus (+) or minus (–) sign will be used to render the expand/collapse toggle with a single label as child (client).

Notice that overriding the expansion event is required to refresh the UI whenever the user expands or collapses the widget. Use ExpandableComposite.addExpansionListener to override the method expansionStateChanged, and call scrolledForm.reflow(true) (reflow refreshes the body layout and the scrollbars of the form).

Sections

A section is a variation of the expandable composite with an optional description below the title. The section is often used as a basic building block in forms because it provides for logical grouping of information.

The style and colors of the section are supplied by the toolkit, and initialized based on the system colors. For this reason, it is recommended that you create the section with the toolkit, instead of through its own constructor. Listing 5-9 shows a utility method to create a section and set its title, description, style, and the column span of the layout.

Listing 5-9. *Creating an Expandable Section Using an HTMLTableLayout*

```
/**
 * Create an expandable form section. It uses a Layout data in
 * conjunction with HTMLTableLayout.
 */
```

```
private Section createSection(String title, String description
        , int style, int colSpan)
{
        Section section = toolkit.createSection(scrolledForm.getBody(),
                style);

        // Refresh the section
        section.addExpansionListener(new ExpansionAdapter() {
            public void expansionStateChanged(ExpansionEvent e) {
                scrolledForm.reflow(true);
            }
        });

        if (title != null)
            section.setText(title);

        if (description != null)
            section.setDescription(description);

        TableWrapData td = new TableWrapData(TableWrapData.FILL_GRAB);
        td.colspan = colSpan;
        section.setLayoutData(td);

        return section;
}
```

Tip Since Eclipse 3.1, it is possible to use a control for the section's description. A typical way to do this is to use an instance of FormText to provide for hyperlinks and images in the description area. If a control is used for the description, the DESCRIPTION style should not be set.

Listing 5-10 demonstrates a utility method to create a section with a client and inner table. The section client uses a two-column table wrap layout. The inner table then grabs the available horizontal space with a column span of 2.

Listing 5-10. *Creating an Expandable Section with an Inner HTML-Style Table*

```
private TableViewer createExpandableSectionWithTable(String title
        , String description, int style, int colSpan)
{
        /**
         * Create an expandable section with title, description, style
         * (expanded) and column span
         */
```

```
Section section = createSection(title, description, style, colSpan);

// Create the composite as a part of the form.
Composite sectionClient = toolkit.createComposite(section);

/**
 * Give the widgets a flat look
 */
sectionClient.setData(FormToolkit.KEY_DRAW_BORDER,
        FormToolkit.TEXT_BORDER);
toolkit.paintBordersFor(sectionClient);

/**
 * Use the forms HTML like table layout for the contents of the
 * expandable section
 */
TableWrapLayout layout = new TableWrapLayout();
layout.numColumns = 2;

sectionClient.setLayout(layout);

/**
 * Add contents to the section client. A table is wrapped on a
 * table viewer to use label and content providers
 */
Table table = toolkit.createTable(sectionClient, SWT.FILL);

// The table will grab all excess horizontal space with a minimum height
// of 100 pixels. Each table cell will have a span of 2 columns
TableWrapData td = new TableWrapData(TableWrapData.FILL_GRAB);
td.colspan = 2;
td.heightHint = 100;

table.setLayoutData(td);

/**
 * Sets the client of this expandable composite. The client must
 * not be null and must be a direct child of this container
 */
section.setClient(sectionClient);

return new TableViewer(table);
}
```

The subroutine in Listing 5-10 can be called using a custom style and column span. The returned viewer can then set content and label providers, as well as the input, as shown in Listing 5-11. You can see the final expandable section with a table in Figure 5-3.

Listing 5-11. *Adding a Content and Label Provider to an Expandable Section*

```
/**
 * SECTIONS
 */
private void addExpandableSectionWithTable() {
        /**
         * Add an expandable section with a table viewer with an expanded
         * style and column span of 1
         */
        int expanded = Section.DESCRIPTION | Section.TITLE_BAR
                | Section.TWISTIE | Section.EXPANDED;

        int colSpan = 1;

        // Viewer is an instance variable of type TableViewer
        viewer = createExpandableSectionWithTable("Expandable Section 1",
                "This is an expandable section with a table viewer";
                expanded, colSpan);

        // Add content and label providers:
        // ViewContentProvider and ViewLabelProvider
        // These are user-defined classes
        viewer.setContentProvider(new ViewContentProvider());
        viewer.setLabelProvider(new ViewLabelProvider());

        // Set initial input
        viewer.setInput(getViewSite());
}
```

The style Section.DESCRIPTION | Section.TITLE_BAR | Section.TWISTIE| Section. EXPANDED displays a section with a description, title bar, and expanded state. Section.TWISTIE displays a twistie (right- or down-pointing arrow) as the expand/collapse toggle. The section contains a custom TableViewer control, which uses a content provider (ViewContentProvider) to provide objects to the view, and a label provider (ViewLabelProvider) to provide labels and images. These two classes should implement the interface org.eclipse,jface.viewers. IContentProvider and must be defined by the user.

Form Text Control

As shown in Figure 5-4, a form text control is capable of rendering the following:

- Wrapped text
- Text that starts with http:// converted into hyperlinks on the fly
- Formatted XML tags

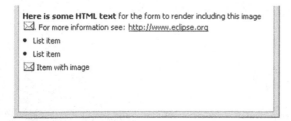

Figure 5-4. *Form text control*

When configured to use formatted XML, the form text control requires the root element `<form>` to be used. The `<p>` and `<li>` tags can be children of the `<form>` element, with the attributes shown in Table 5-1. Table 5-2 lists the tags that can appear as children of the `<p>` and `<li>` tags.

Table 5-1. *Tags That Can Be Children of the <form> Element*

Tag	Description	Attributes
`<p>`	For paragraphs	vspace: If set to `false`, no vertical space will be added (default is `true`).
`<li>`	For list items	vspace: Same as `<p>`.
		style: One of `bullet` (default), `text`, or `image`.
		value: For text, it is the value of the text that is rendered as a bullet. For an image, it is the `href` of the image to be rendered as a bullet. Not used for `bullet` style.
		indent: Number of pixels to indent the text in the list item.
		bindent: Number of pixels to indent the bullet itself.

Table 5-2. *Tags That Can Appear As Children of <p> and <li> Elements*

Tag	Description	Attributes
`<img>`	For images	href: A key to the image set using the `setImage` method. Required.
`<A>`	For hyperlinks	href: A key that will be provided to the hyperlink listeners via the `HyperlinkEvent` object. Required.
		nowrap: When set to `true`, the hyperlink will not be wrapped. Default is `false`. Optional.
`<B>`	For bold font	
` `	For line breaks	
`<span>`	For enclosed text, with color and font specified in the element attributes	Color: A key to the `Color` object set by the `setColor` method to set the color. Optional.
		font: A key to the `Font` object set by the `setFont` method to set the font. Optional.
		nowrap: When set to `true`, blocks wrapping. The default is `false`. Optional.

Tag	Description	Attributes
`<control>`	For a control that is a child of the text control (new in 3.1)	`href`: A key to the `Control` object set using the `setControl` method. Required.
		`fill`: When set to `true`, makes the control fill the entire width of the text. The default is `false`. Optional.
		`width` and `height`: Force the dimensions of the control. Optional.
		`align`: To set the vertical position of the control. Optional.

Tip Since Eclipse 3.1, it is possible to select text. Text selection can be programmatically accessed and also copied to the clipboard. Nontextual objects (images, controls, and so on.) in the selection are ignored.

Listing 5-12 shows a form text control with HTML-style formatting. Note that the HTML must be well formed (in reality, it is XML). The XML contains a `<form>` element with a hyperlink embedded in the first paragraph, and a bulleted item list with text and image elements. The form text also defines a hyperlink listener, where the `href` attribute can be extracted from the event.

Listing 5-12. *Adding a FormText Control to a Form*

```
private void addFormTextControl() {
        ImageDescriptor ICON = Activator
                .getImageDescriptor("icons/sample3.gif");

        FormText formText = toolkit.createFormText(scrolledForm.getBody(),
                true);

        formText.setLayoutData(new TableWrapData(TableWrapData.FILL));

        StringBuffer html = new StringBuffer(
                "<form><p><b>Here is some HTML text</b> for the form to render "
                + "including this image <img href=\"image\"/>. "
                + "For more information see: http://www.eclipse.org</p>");

        html.append("<li>List item</li>");
        html.append("<li>List item</li>");
        html
                .append("<li style=\"image\" value=\"image\">Item with image</li>");
        html.append("</form>");

        // If parseTags is true, formatting tags will be parsed.
        // Otherwise, text will be rendered as is.
        // If expandURLs is true, URLs found in the untagged text will be
        // converted into hyperlinks.
```

```
            boolean parseTags = true;
            boolean expandURLs = true;

            //
            formText.setText(html.toString(), parseTags, expandURLs);
            formText.setImage("image", ICON.createImage());

            formText.addHyperlinkListener(new HyperlinkAdapter() {
                @Override
                public void linkActivated(HyperlinkEvent e) {
                    System.out.println(e.getHref());
                }
            });
    }
```

Note The form text control was designed to render children controls defined with XML tags. However, it is not responsible for creating or disposing of those controls; it only places them relative to the surrounding text. Moreover, none of the elements can be nested. For example, you cannot have a <b> inside a <span> or two nested lists.

Form text is not meant to be an HTML browser. Compared with a web browser, it has the following limitations:

- A form text control supports only a subset of the HTML tags. For example, bold is supported, but not italic. Attributes for vertical alignment of text with respect to images are missing. List support is poor.

- For the sake of simplicity, elements cannot be nested. For example, you cannot have <b> inside a <span>. Note that an exception has been made to this rule to allow nesting of images and text inside the hyperlink.

If you need complex formatting capabilities, use the SWT Browser widget instead. If you need editing capabilities with font and color styles of text, use the SWT StyledText widget. If you need to wrap text, use the SWT Label widget with an SWT.WRAP style.

Complex Forms

The Forms API provides advanced editors customized to manipulate content that is hard to display and edit by hand. These include managed forms, master/details forms, and multipage editors.

Managed Forms

A managed form is a form wrapper that adds life-cycle management and notification to its members. The life-cycle management includes save, commit, focus, selection, dirty state, and others.

■Tip The Form/Managed Form relationship is similar to the one between a Table and TableViewer in JFace.

Master/Details Form

A master/details form follows a common pattern that consists of a tree or table (master) and a list (details) driven by the master's selection. Creating a master/details form involves three steps:

1. Create the master part to drive the details.

2. Contribute actions to the form toolbar. For example, you might add actions to change the master/details orientation between horizontal and vertical.

3. Register details pages for each distinct input from the master. Details pages can contain any number of controls.

Multipage Editors

The goal of a multipage editor is to provide a high-quality GUI to manipulate complex XML documents. Multipage editors are arguably the most powerful feature of the Forms API, and they are used intensively by the plug-in manifest editor itself.

The plug-in manifest editor shown in Figure 5-5 is an example of all the complex form types—managed, master/details, and multipage editor forms—used together.

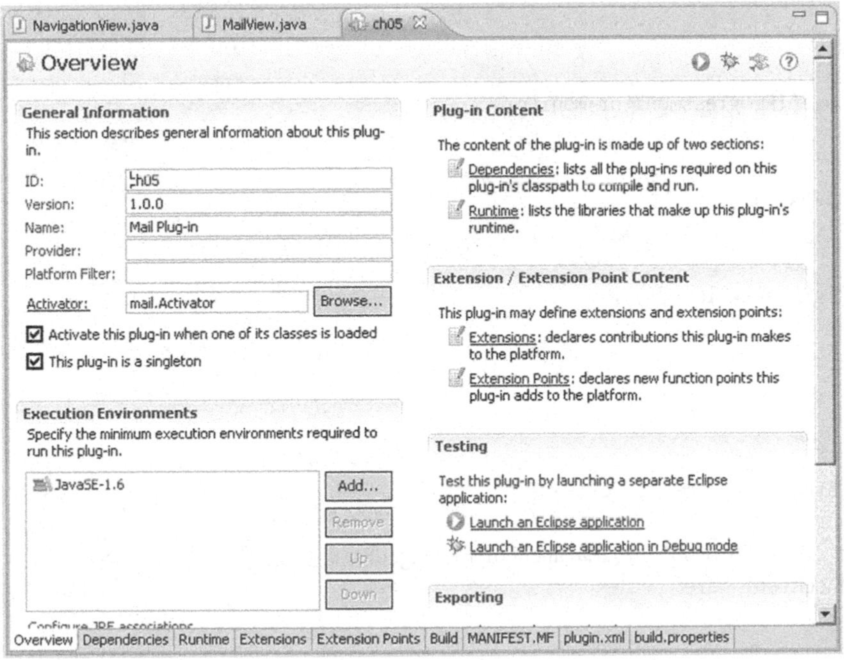

Figure 5-5. *Multipage plug-in manifest editor*

To build a multipage editor, your class should extend FormEditor and add pages by overriding the addPages() method. In turn, each page should implement FormPage and override createFormContent() to add custom content to the page, as shown in Listing 5-13.

Listing 5-13. *Skeleton for a Multipage Form Editor*

```java
// Multi-page form editor
public class MyEditor extends FormEditor {

 public MyEditor() {
 }

 protected FormToolkit createToolkit(Display display) {
  // Create a toolkit that shares colors between editors.
  return new FormToolkit(display);
 }

 protected void addPages() {
  try {
     addPage(new FirstPage(this));
     addPage(new SecondPage(this));
     ...
  }
  catch (PartInitException e) {
   // Handle exception
  }
 }

 public void doSave(IProgressMonitor monitor) {
 }

 public void doSaveAs() {
 }

 public boolean isSaveAsAllowed() {
  return false;
 }
}

// Editor page
public class FirstPage implements FormPage
{
   protected void createFormContent(IManagedForm managedForm) {
     // add page content here
   }
}
```

Hands-on Exercise: A Web Look for the Mail Template

The Mail Template is the built-in application bundled with RCP. It simulates a basic mail client with navigation and details views. The goal of this exercise is to give a web look to the standard Mail template provided by the Plug-in Project wizard, which is shown in Figure 5-6. You'll do this using the Forms API. The changes are simple, yet they have a powerful effect. Here are the modifications you'll make:

- Hide the main menu, cool bar, and status line

- Replace the main menu and cool bar with an image header with a custom toolbar

- Convert each view into a form with a heading and toolbar

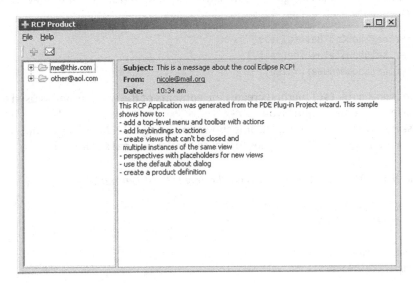

Figure 5-6. *RCP Mail template*

To begin, use the Plug-in Project wizard to create a mail RCP template. Here is how:

1. From the main menu, click File ➤ New ➤ Other ➤ Plug-in Development ➤ Plug-in Project. Click Next.

2. Enter a project name (ch05.Mail). Click Next.

3. In the Plug-in Content page, set Rich Client application to yes. Click Next.

4. In the Templates page, select the RCP Mail Template. Click Next.

5. In the Mail Template details page, set the product name and click Finish.

6. Create a product configuration for the application. Right-click the project folder and select New ➤ Other ➤ Plug-in Development ➤ Product Configuration. Click Next.

7. Enter a file name (Mail.product). Make sure the product ID is selected under Use an existing product. Click Finish.

8. Test the product. From the product editor, click synchronize to publish and launch an Eclipse application to run it.

9. Use this template to customize the application for this exercise.

Customizing the Workbench Window

The first class to be modified is the workbench window advisor (`ApplicationWorkbenchWindowAdvisor`), which configures the main window. This is done by overloading the `preWindowOpen()` and `createWindowContents()` methods.

The `preWindowOpen()` method is called before the window's controls have been created. Typical clients will use the window configurer to tweak the workbench window in an application-specific way. For this exercise, set up the initial size and use the `setShow*` methods on `IWorkbenchWindowConfigurer` to hide the cool bar, status line, and menu bars, as follows:

```
configurer.setShowCoolBar(false);
configurer.setShowStatusLine(false);
configurer.setShowMenuBar(false);
```

The `createWindowContents()` method creates the contents of the window and is used to define custom window contents and layout.

The basic skeleton of the window advisor is shown in Listing 5-14. Note the private composite for the header and two custom images to draw a header and background fill.

Listing 5-14. *Workbench Window Advisor Class for the Forms Mail Template*

```
public class ApplicationWorkbenchWindowAdvisor
 extends WorkbenchWindowAdvisor
{
    // Main window header
    private Composite header;

    // Custom page control
    private Control page;

    // Main window banner image
    private static Image bannerMain = Activator
            .imageDescriptorFromPlugin(Activator.PLUGIN_ID,
                    "icons/banner.png").createImage(); //$NON-NLS-1$

    // Window fill image
    private static Image bannerFill = Activator.imageDescriptorFromPlugin(
            Activator.PLUGIN_ID, "icons/fill.jpg").createImage();

    public ApplicationWorkbenchWindowAdvisor(
            IWorkbenchWindowConfigurer configurer) {
        super(configurer);
    }
```

```java
    public ActionBarAdvisor createActionBarAdvisor(
            IActionBarConfigurer configurer) {
        return new ApplicationActionBarAdvisor(configurer);
    }

    public void preWindowOpen() {
        IWorkbenchWindowConfigurer configurer = getWindowConfigurer();
        configurer.setInitialSize(new Point(700, 500));

        // Hide cool bar, status line, and menu bar
        configurer.setShowCoolBar(false);
        configurer.setShowStatusLine(false);
        configurer.setShowMenuBar(false);
    }

    @Override
    public void createWindowContents(Shell shell) {
        // Add custom window contents
    }

}
```

The most important method is createWindowContents(), which is where the elements and layout are defined.

Customizing the Window Contents

The default implementation of createWindowContents() adds a menu bar, cool bar, status line, perspective bar, and a fast view bar to the main window. Listing 5-15 shows how to customize the window contents for this example.

Listing 5-15. *Adding Window Contents to the Mail Template*

```java
public void createWindowContents(Shell shell) {
    /**
     * Define custom window contents
     */
    final IWorkbenchWindowConfigurer configurer = getWindowConfigurer();

    // Control the position and size of the children of a composite
    // control by using FormAttachments to optionally configure the
    // left, top, right and bottom edges of each child.
    final FormLayout layout = new FormLayout();
    layout.marginWidth = 0;
    layout.marginHeight = 0;
    shell.setLayout(layout);
```

```
// Create a top header in the main window. Set the background to white
this.header = new Composite(shell, SWT.NONE);
this.header.setBackground(Display.getDefault().getSystemColor(
        SWT.COLOR_WHITE));

// Create a 2 column grid layout for the main header
final GridLayout gLayout = new GridLayout(2, false);
gLayout.horizontalSpacing = 0;
gLayout.marginHeight = 0;
gLayout.marginWidth = 0;
gLayout.marginWidth = 0;
gLayout.verticalSpacing = 0;

this.header.setLayout(gLayout);

// The 1st composite in the header is a toolbar
final Composite toolbar = new Composite(this.header, SWT.NONE);

// Fill the background of the toolbar with a fill image (bannerFill)
toolbar.setBackgroundImage(bannerFill);

// Lay out the toolbar in a 1 column grid
toolbar.setLayout(new GridLayout(1, false));

GridData gd = new GridData(SWT.BEGINNING, SWT.CENTER, true, true);
gd.horizontalIndent = 0;

 // Create a toolbar manager for the toolbar
// The main toolbar has 2 actions: Open View, and about
final ToolBarManager tbm = new ToolBarManager(new ToolBar(toolbar,
        SWT.FLAT));
tbm.getControl().setBackgroundImage(bannerFill);
tbm.getControl().setLayoutData(gd);

// Add toolbar actions
// Open View action
tbm.add(new OpenViewAction(configurer.getWindow(),
        "Open Another Message MailView", MailView.ID));

// About action (from the Eclipse factory)
tbm.add(new Action("About", Activator
        .getImageDescriptor("icons/about32.png")) {
    @Override
    public void run() {
        ActionFactory.ABOUT.create(
                PlatformUI.getWorkbench()
                        .getActiveWorkbenchWindow()).run();
    }
});
```

```
        // Refresh toolbar
        tbm.update(true);

        gd = new GridData(SWT.FILL, SWT.FILL, true, true);
        toolbar.setLayoutData(gd);

        // Main header image
        final Label mainImage = new Label(this.header, SWT.NONE);
        mainImage.setImage(bannerMain);

        // Lay out  the header image
        gd = new GridData(SWT.END, SWT.BEGINNING, false, false);
        mainImage.setLayoutData(gd);

        /**
         * Create the page composite, in which the window's pages,
         * and their views and editors, appear
         */
        this.page = configurer.createPageComposite(shell);

        doLayout();
}
```

Listing 5-15 starts by creating a window shell. It uses the form layout and size of the children (via FormAttachments) to configure the left, top, right, and bottom edges.

It then creates a two-column header composite to hold a toolbar and header image. This composite lays out children in a two-column grid, as shown in Figure 5-7.

Figure 5-7. *Header composite with two-column grid layout displaying a toolbar on the left and an image on the right*

On the left of the header, a toolbar and associated manager are created with two actions: open view, to open the mail message view, and the factory About dialog. Note that the toolbar and manager set a background fill image, as shown in Figure 5-8.

Figure 5-8. *Header composite with background fill applied*

On the right, a main image banner is constructed. A very important step before layout is `configurer.createPageComposite(shell)`, which creates the page composite, in which the window's pages and their views and editors appear.

The final step in window customization is to lay out the children by using `FormAttachments` to configure the left, top, right, and bottom edges of the header and page composites, as shown in Listing 5-16.

Listing 5-16. *Configuring the Edges of the Main Window for the Mail Template*

```
private void doLayout() {
        // Lay out header on top of the page
        FormData data = new FormData();
        data.top = new FormAttachment(0, 0);
        data.left = new FormAttachment(0, 0);
        data.right = new FormAttachment(100, 0);
        this.header.setLayoutData(data);

        // Lay out custom page below the header
        data = new FormData();
        data.top = new FormAttachment(this.header, 0, SWT.BOTTOM);
        data.left = new FormAttachment(0, 0);
        data.right = new FormAttachment(100, 0);
        data.bottom = new FormAttachment(100, 0);
        this.page.setLayoutData(data);

        // Refresh
        getWindowConfigurer().getWindow().getShell().layout(true);
        if (this.page != null) {
            ((Composite) this.page).layout(true);
        }
}
```

`FormAttachment` can take two arguments: a numerator, which is the percentage of the form, and an offset of the side from the (0, 0) position. Here, the window header is laid out on top by setting the top-left attachment to (0, 0) and the right attachment to 100% of the width of the window. The content page is laid out below the header by attaching the top side of the page to the bottom side of the header:

```
data.top = new FormAttachment(this.header, 0, SWT.BOTTOM)
```

Here, `FormAttachment` takes three arguments. The bottom-right edge is attached to 100% of the window size.

Modifying the Navigation View

The navigation view contains a sample navigation tree with e-mail addresses. This setup requires the following simple changes to the `createPartControl` method:

- Create a form toolkit and associated form
- Use a column `TableWrap` layout for the form's body to lay out the navigation tree using a one-column table

- Change the navigation tree to use `toolkit.createTree()`
- Have the navigation tree set the layout data used in conjunction with `HTMLTableLayout` with a call to `tree.setLayoutData()`

These changes are outlined in Listing 5-17.

Listing 5-17. *Navigation View for the Mail Template*

```
public class NavigationView extends ViewPart {
    public static final String ID = "Mail.navigationView";
    private TreeViewer viewer;

    private ImageDescriptor FORM_ICON = mail.Activator
            .getImageDescriptor("icons/sample2.gif");

    /**
     * Eclipse forms support.
     */
    private FormToolkit toolkit;
    private Form form;

    // Template code has been removed for simplicity

    /**
     * This is a callback that will allow us to create the viewer and
     * initialize it.
     */
    public void createPartControl(Composite parent) {
        // Create a Form API toolkit
        toolkit = new FormToolkit(parent.getDisplay());
        /**
         * Create a scrolled form widget in the provided parent. If you do
         * not require scrolling because there is already a scrolled
         * composite up the parent chain, use 'createForm' instead
         */
        form = toolkit.createForm(parent);
        form.setText("Navigator");
        form.setImage(FORM_ICON.createImage());

        toolkit.decorateFormHeading(form);

        /**
         * Flat look
         */
        toolkit.paintBordersFor(form.getBody());

        // Add a 1 column layout to the scrolled form contents
        TableWrapLayout layout = new TableWrapLayout();
        layout.numColumns = 1;
```

```
        form.getBody().setLayout(layout);

        Tree tree = toolkit.createTree(form.getBody(), SWT.MULTI
                | SWT.H_SCROLL | SWT.V_SCROLL | SWT.FILL);

        TableWrapData td = new TableWrapData(TableWrapData.FILL_GRAB);
        td.colspan = 1;
        td.heightHint = 300;

        tree.setLayoutData(td);

        viewer = new TreeViewer(tree);
        viewer.setContentProvider(new ViewContentProvider());
        viewer.setLabelProvider(new ViewLabelProvider());
        viewer.setInput(createDummyModel());

        viewer.setData(FormToolkit.KEY_DRAW_BORDER,
                FormToolkit.TEXT_BORDER);

    }

    // Template code has been removed for simplicity...
}
```

Modifying the Mail View

The final step is converting the mail view into a form. This view displays a header with a subject, sender e-mail address, and date labels. It also has a text control with the actual e-mail message. This requires the following additions:

- A form header and icon to display the sender's e-mail address
- A toolbar with a button to close the message

Also, the layout needs to be changed from a GridLayout to a TableWrapLayout, and the widgets must be created using the toolkit. The changes are shown in Listing 5-18.

Listing 5-18. *Contents View for the Mail Template*

```
public class MailView extends ViewPart {

    /**
     * Eclipse forms support
     */
    private FormToolkit toolkit;
    private Form form;

    // Unique ID of this view
    public static final String ID = "Mail.view";
```

```java
    // Form header icon: getImageDescriptor is defined
    // in the Activator plugin class
    private final ImageDescriptor FORM_ICON = Activator
            .getImageDescriptor("icons/sample3.gif");

    /**
     * Create the SWT controls for this workbench part
     */
    public void createPartControl(Composite parent) {
        // Create a Form API toolkit
        toolkit = new FormToolkit(parent.getDisplay());

        /**
         * Create a form widget in the provided parent. Note that this
         * widget does not scroll its content. If you require scrolling,
         * use 'createScrolledForm' instead
         */
        form = toolkit.createForm(parent);
        form.setText("user@aol.com");
        form.setImage(FORM_ICON.createImage());

        // Takes advantage of the gradients and other capabilities
        // to decorate the form heading
        toolkit.decorateFormHeading(form);

        // Flat look
        toolkit.paintBordersFor(form.getBody());

        // Add a 1 column layout to the scrolled form contents
        TableWrapLayout layout = new TableWrapLayout();
        layout.numColumns = 1;

        form.getBody().setLayout(layout);

        // Form toolbar
        createToolBar();

        Composite body = form.getBody();

        // Message subject label
        toolkit.createLabel(body, "Subject:");

        // Subject text
        toolkit.createLabel(body,
                "This is a message about the cool Eclipse RCP!");
        // Sender label
        toolkit.createLabel(body, "From:");
```

```java
        // Sender text as hyperlink with listener
        Hyperlink link = toolkit.createHyperlink(body, "user@aol.com",
                SWT.WRAP);

        link.addHyperlinkListener(new HyperlinkAdapter() {
            @Override
            public void linkActivated(
                    org.eclipse.ui.forms.events.HyperlinkEvent e) {
                MessageDialog.openInformation(getSite().getShell(),
                  "Not Implemented",
                  "Open the address book or a new message being created.");
            }
        });

        // Date
        toolkit.createLabel(body, "Date:");
        toolkit.createLabel(body, new Date().toString());

        // Text widget with sample message
        Text text = new Text(body, SWT.MULTI | SWT.WRAP);
        text.setText("This RCP Application was generated from the PDE "
                + "Plug-in Project wizard. This sample shows how to:\n"
                + "- add a top-level menu and toolbar with actions\n"
                + "- add key bindings to actions\n"
                + "- create views that can't be closed and\n"
                + "  multiple instances of the same view\n"
                + "- perspectives with placeholders for new views\n"
                + "- use the default about dialog\n"
                + "- create a product definition\n");

        text.setLayoutData(new TableWrapData(TableWrapData.FILL_GRAB));
    }

    /**
     * Create a form toolbar
     */
    private void createToolBar() {
        // Toolbar icons
        ImageDescriptor TB_ICON_1 = Activator
                .getImageDescriptor("icons/close16.png");

        // Action #1: Hide view
        Action toolBtn1 = new Action() {
            public void run() {
                MailView.this.getViewSite().getPage().hideView(
                        MailView.this);
```

```java
        }
    };
    toolBtn1.setToolTipText("Hide this View");
    toolBtn1.setText("Hide this View");
    toolBtn1.setImageDescriptor(TB_ICON_1);

    // Add toolbar actions
    form.getToolBarManager().add(toolBtn1);
    form.getToolBarManager().add(new Separator());

    form.getToolBarManager().update(true);

    // Sets the toolbar vertical alignment relative to the header.
    // Can be useful when there is more free space at the second row
    form.setToolBarVerticalAlignment(SWT.LEFT);
}

public void setFocus() {
    form.setFocus();
}

/**
 * Form message handling
 *
 * @param text
 *          Message to display
 * @param type
 *          One of IMessageProvider.ERROR, NONE, WRNING, INFORMATION
 */
@SuppressWarnings("unused")
private void setFormMessage(String text, int type) {
    /**
     * Adds a message hyperlink listener. Messages will be rendered as
     * hyperlinks
     */
    form.addMessageHyperlinkListener(new HyperlinkAdapter());
    form.setMessage(text, type);
}

}
```

The view's createPartControl() method creates a form using a one-column
TableWrapLayout, with a subject, sender, date, and sample message text. It also calls
createToolBar() to fill the form toolbar with an action to hide the view. Note that the
form icons are created with the following method:

```java
ImageDescriptor FORM_ICON = Activator.getImageDescriptor("icons/icon.gif")
```

This is a static method in the plug-in activator class returning an image descriptor for a file within the specified plug-in. `Activator.getImageDescriptor()` simply calls the parent `AbstractUIPlugin.imageDescriptorFromPlugin(PLUGIN_ID, icon_path)`, where `PLUGIN_ID` is the unique ID of the mail plug-in.

The form has a toolbar for the custom actions, and all messages will be displayed as form messages.

Figure 5-9 shows the revised Mail application. Compare it with the standard template, shown earlier in Figure 5-6.

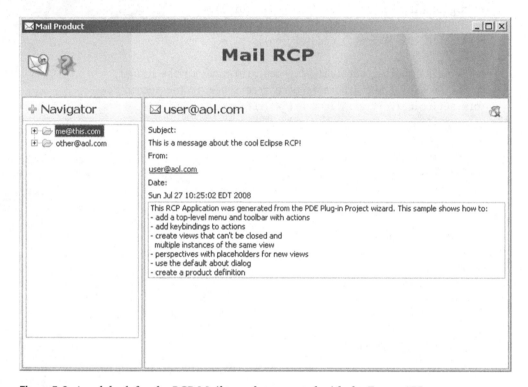

Figure 5-9. *A web look for the RCP Mail template, created with the Forms API*

Summary

This chapter covered the Eclipse Forms API. The following are the important points to keep in mind:

- The Eclipse Forms API lets you spice up your application with a web look without using an embedded browser.

- The Forms API provides custom widgets, layouts, and support classes to achieve the web look.

- Forms are portable and expand the possibilities of the UI well beyond traditional SWT controls.

- A Form object can be included in content areas such as views and editors.

- The Forms API provides two new layout managers: TableWrapLayout and ColumnLayout.

    - TableWrapLayout positions controls in the composite using a two-pass HTML table.

    - ColumnLayout arranges children of the parent in vertical columns. All the columns are identical in size, and children are stretched horizontally to fill the column width. ColumnLayout is useful for complex forms where the number of columns changes depending on the width of the form.

- The Forms API provides custom web-style controls, as well as multipage forms and editors.

- You can convert a view into a form within the createPartControl() method:

```
public void createPartControl(Composite parent) {
        // Create a Form API toolkit
        FormToolkit toolkit = new FormToolkit(parent.getDisplay());
        ScrolledForm scrolledForm = toolkit.createScrolledForm(parent);

        // Form title
        scrolledForm.setText("Form Title");
}
```

- Call toolkit.paintBordersFor(text.getParent()) to paint flat borders for widgets created by the toolkit. Borders will not be painted if the global border style is SWT.BORDER.

- Create form controls using FormToolkit.

    - For labels, use toolkit.createLabel(scrolledForm.getBody(), "Label").

    - For text boxes, use Text text = toolkit.createText(scrolledForm.getBody(), "", SWT.FILL).

    - For buttons, use Button b1 = toolkit.createButton(scrolledForm.getBody(), "Check Box", SWT.CHECK).

- You can control the look and feel of a form by using a custom toolbar, drop-down menu, fonts, and gradient colors.

- Add actions to the form toolbar with form.getToolBarManager().add(Action). Add actions to the form drop-down menu with form.getMenuManager().add(Action).

- Form messages are presented with text between the title and the toolbar of the heading. Set the form message with an indication of the message type with form.setMessage(Text, MessageType). Messages can be rendered as static text or hyperlinks.

- Complex controls include text/image hyperlinks, expandable composites, sections, and form text.

- Create a hyperlink and listen for click events with the following:

```
Hyperlink link = toolkit.createHyperlink(scrolledForm.getBody()
        , "Hyperlink.", SWT.WRAP);
```

```
link.addHyperlinkListener(new HyperlinkAdapter() {
  @Override
  public void linkActivated(HyperlinkEvent e) {
    System.out.println(e);
  }
});
```

- The expandable composite control is capable of expanding or collapsing a single child label composite. The composite renders a title that also acts as a hyperlink, and the left and right arrow keys can be used to control the expansion state. Create an expandable composite with a tree node style with the following:

```
ExpandableComposite ec = toolkit.createExpandableComposite( form.getBody()
      , ExpandableComposite.TREE_NODE | ExpandableComposite.CLIENT_INDENT);

ec.setText("Expandable Composite");

Label client = toolkit.createLabel(ec, "Label", SWT.WRAP);
ec.setClient(client);
```

- A section is a variation of the expandable composite with an optional description below the title. Sections provide for logical grouping of information and are often used as basic building blocks in forms.

- The form text control is capable of rendering wrapped text, hyperlinks converted on the fly from text that starts with http://, and formatted XML tags.

- When using formatted XML, the form text control requires the root element <form> to be used.

  - Child tags of <form> can be <p> for paragraphs and <li> for lists.

  - Child tags of <p> and <li> can be <img> for images, <a> for hyperlinks, <b> for bold, <br> for line breaks, <span> for enclosed text, and <control> for custom controls.

- The form text control has limitations. It is not meant to replace the HTML browser. It supports only a subset of HTML tags, and elements cannot be nested. If you need complex formatting capabilities, use the SWT Browser widget instead of a form text control.

CHAPTER 6

▪▪▪

Help Support

Eclipse provides a powerful help system that can be used to add documentation to your RCP applications quickly and with minimal effort. The help system has the following characteristics:

- Browser-based presentation, with full HTML support

- Supported on all of the Eclipse platforms[1]

- Powerful built-in search capabilities

- Localization for additional languages

- Support for context help and a keyword index, provided the appropriate content files are used

- Support for a web-based information center to host the documentation on the Internet

- Programmatic extension points for content producers to generate dynamic help, including the table of contents, keyword index, and content, which can be useful for document format conversion

The help system is a robust, feature-rich, and extensible component, which continues to improve in terms of quality and features. It is the easiest and fastest way to add documentation support to your RCP applications.

This chapter describes the steps required to enable help for your applications, including configuring your products, adding help content, adding context help support, and customizing the help system UI. You'll then put what you've learned into practice by building an information center using the text of this chapter.

Configuring a Product to Use the Help System

Configuring your RCP product to use the help system is a two-step process:

- Add the required help system plug-in dependencies to the product.

- Update the code (the menu bar, for example) to display actions to start the help system.

Let's look at each of these steps in detail.

---

1. A list of all the platforms supported by release build 3.4.1 is available online at http://download. eclipse.org/eclipse/downloads/drops/R-3.4.1-200809111700/index.php.

Adding the Dependency Plug-ins

The help system requires several plug-ins. To add them to your product, open the product editor (.product), click the Configuration tab, and go to the Plug-ins and Fragments section. Choose to add the following plug-ins (see Figure 6-1):

- org.eclipse.help.appserver
- org.eclipse.help.base
- org.eclipse.help.ui
- org.eclipse.help.webapp

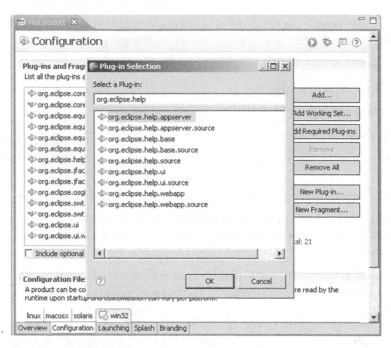

Figure 6-1. *Adding the required help system plug-in through the product editor Configuration tab*

To make sure you've added all the required dependencies, check "Include optional dependencies when computing required plug-ins," and then click Add Required Plug-ins. This will ensure all required plug-ins are included. Missing dependencies will cause the help system to fail at startup.

Updating the Menu Bar

The product should include actions to start the help system from the main menu. Listing 6-1 shows the changes required to the ActionBarAdvisor class from the plug-in product to add the Eclipse factory actions for the help system. The actions are inserted by overriding the method makeActions of the ActionBarAdvisor.

Listing 6-1. *ActionBarAdvisor with Factory Help Menus*

```java
public class ApplicationActionBarAdvisor extends ActionBarAdvisor {
    // ...

    // Help actions
    private IWorkbenchAction showHelpAction;
    private IWorkbenchAction searchHelpAction;
    private IWorkbenchAction dynamicHelpAction;

    // Override this method to insert global menu actions
    protected void makeActions(final IWorkbenchWindow window) {
        // ...

        // Help contents
        showHelpAction = ActionFactory.HELP_CONTENTS.create(window);
        register(showHelpAction);

        // Help search
        searchHelpAction = ActionFactory.HELP_SEARCH.create(window);
        register(searchHelpAction);

        // Dynamic help
        dynamicHelpAction = ActionFactory.DYNAMIC_HELP.create(window);
        register(dynamicHelpAction);

    }


    protected void fillMenuBar(IMenuManager menuBar) {
        // ...

        MenuManager helpMenu = new MenuManager("&Help",
                IWorkbenchActionConstants.M_HELP);


        // Help menu options
        helpMenu.add(showHelpAction);
        helpMenu.add(searchHelpAction);
        helpMenu.add(dynamicHelpAction);
        helpMenu.add(new Separator());

        // ...

    }
}
```

The class `org.eclipse.ui.actions.ActionFactory` gives access to standard actions provided by the workbench. The help system has three factory actions:

- `HELP_CONTENTS`: Opens the help contents in a separate window.

- `HELP_SEARCH`: Opens the help keyword search as a view within the product's main window.

- `DYNAMIC_HELP`: Opens the dynamic help within a view. Dynamic help can change automatically as the user selects a different UI widget. This happens without forcing the user to press F1 again.

The Help menu actions and help view are shown in Figure 6-2.

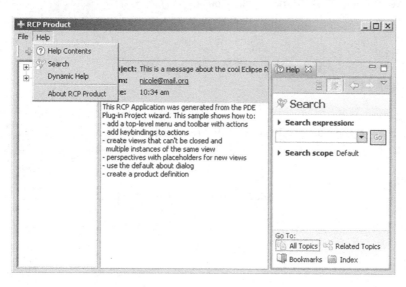

Figure 6-2. *RCP Mail template showing the standard help actions and help view*

Adding Help Content

You should create the help content for your product in its own plug-in project. Fortunately, the Plug-in Project wizard already provides a startup template to build a basic table of contents (TOC). Here is how:

1. From the Eclipse IDE main menu, select File ➤ New ➤ Project ➤ Plug-in Project, and then enter a project name (`MailHelp`, for example).

2. On the Plug-in Content page, uncheck the "Generate an activator" option (as the plug-in will not contribute any code). Make sure the "This plug-in will make contributions to the UI" option is checked, and the "Would you like to create a rich client application?" option is set to No. Figure 6-3 shows these settings. Click Next.

3. On the Templates page, select "Plug-in with sample help content," as shown in Figure 6-4, and then click Next.

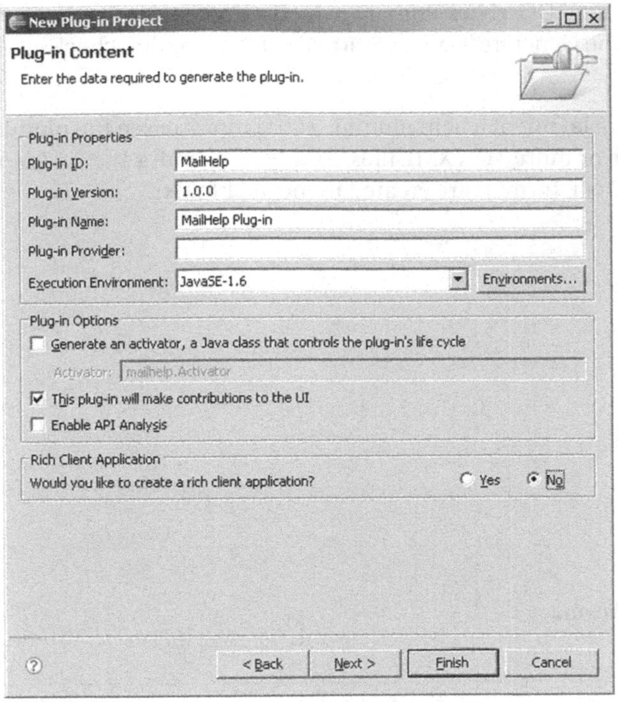

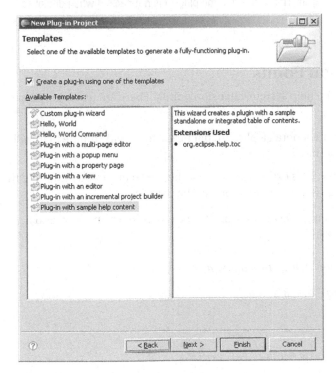

Figure 6-3. *Creating a help plug-in*

Figure 6-4. *Choosing the template for a sample help plug-in*

4. Finally, enter a label for the TOC, check Primary (which will generate a primary, or main, table), and leave the Generate 'Getting Started' category option checked. Click Finish.

Figure 6-5 shows the typical layout of a help plug-in. At the top, you see the plug-in manifest (`plugin.xml`), and one or more TOC XML files, as well as an index file (`index.xml`). The actual help contents (in HTML format) are created in the `html` folder.

Figure 6-5. *Typical help content layout*

Tip As a convenience, to reduce file size, the documentation files can be packed in a ZIP file called `doc.zip` in the root folder of the plug-in. This is useful if the plug-in is not packed when deployed.

Help System Extension Points

The plug-in manifest defines the help system extension points. There are two main help extension points:

- `org.eclipse.help.toc`: In general, a plug-in that needs to provide online help will define one or more TOC files.

- `org.eclipse.help.index`: This extension point defines the name of the index file that contains a list of keywords and related topics of the help content.

Listing 6-2 shows a plug-in manifest with two TOC files—a primary (master) and a secondary—as well as an index file.

Listing 6-2. *Help System Extension Points (in plugin.xml)*

```
<?xml version="1.0" encoding="UTF-8"?>
<?eclipse version="3.2"?>
<plugin>
   <extension
        point="org.eclipse.help.toc">
```

```
<toc
        file="toc.xml"
        primary="true">
</toc>
<toc
        file="tocgettingstarted.xml">
</toc>
</extension>
<extension
    point="org.eclipse.help.index">
<index
        file="index.xml">
</index>
</extension>
</plugin>
```

The `<toc>` element in Listing 6-2 has the `file` and `primary` attributes. The `file` attribute defines the name of the TOC file that contains the TOC or section for the plug-in online help. The `primary` attribute specifies whether the TOC file is a primary TOC and meant to be the master. A nonprimary TOC file is meant to be integrated into another TOC.

Other `<toc>` attributes include `extradir` and `category`. The `extradir` defines a relative path to a directory containing additional documents. All documents in this directory, and all subdirectories, will be indexed and accessible through the documentation search. The `category` attribute defines a unique string used to group related sections together. For example, `chapter 6` would be the category for all of the sections in this chapter.

TOC File

A TOC file consists of a root `<toc>` element with a required `label` attribute. The `topic` attribute provides a link to a documentation file, which is usually an HTML file. The TOC will be shown as a hierarchical navigation tree within the help UI.

The `<topic>` element is the basic element of a TOC file. Topics can be nested within other topics. The most important attributes of a `<topic>` element are `label`, which provides a required label for the topic element, and `href`, which specifies a link to a documentation file, usually in HTML format.

Topics can act as containers for other topics, or they can specify an anchor ID that provides a point where other TOCs can embed their contents. Listing 6-3 shows two XML TOC files (`toc.xml` and `toc1.xml`). The first TOC uses an anchor to define a point that will allow linking other TOC files to this navigation.

Listing 6-3. *Two XML TOC files (toc.xml and toc1.xml) Linked with an Anchor*

```
<?xml version="1.0" encoding="UTF-8"?>
<?NLS TYPE="org.eclipse.help.toc"?>

<toc label="Mail Help" topic="html/toc.html">
   <topic label="Getting Started">
     <anchor id="gettingstarted"/>
```

```
    </topic>
</toc>

<?xml version="1.0" encoding="UTF-8"?>
<?NLS TYPE="org.eclipse.help.toc"?>

<toc label="Getting Started" link_to="toc.xml#gettingstarted">
   <topic label="Welcome to RCP Mail"  href="html/gettingstarted/maintopic.html">
         <topic label="Mail" href="html/gettingstarted/subtopic.html" />
   </topic>
   <topic label="Mail User Interface">
         <topic label="Main Window" href="html/gettingstarted/subtopic2.html" />
   </topic>
</toc>
```

The <link> element allows embedding other TOC files into the parent, similar to the <anchor> element. For example, the following XML includes the TOC file ch01toc.xml within its parent:

```
<topic label="Chapter 1" >
  ...
  <link toc="ch01toc.xml" />
  ...
</topic>
```

Index File

The index file is a keyword index for contributed help content in XML format. It contains a list of keywords and related topics of the content. The XML fragment in Listing 6-4 shows a typical index file.

Listing 6-4. *An Index File (index.xml)*

```
<index>
    <entry keyword="Vehicle">
        <topic href="inventory_of_wheel.html"/>
        <entry keyword="Car">
            <topic href="car.html"/>
        </entry>
        <entry keyword="Ship">
            <topic href="ship.html"/>
        </entry>
        <entry keyword="Airplane">
            <topic href="airplane.html" title="History of aviation"/>
            <topic href="jet.html" title="Jet engine"/>
        </entry>
    </entry>
```

```
    <entry keyword="Engine">
        <entry keyword="Horse">
            <topic href="horse.html"/>
        </entry>
        <entry keyword="Steamer">
            <topic href="steamer.html"/>
        </entry>
        <entry keyword="Wankel engine">
            <topic href="wankel.html"/>
        </entry>
        <entry keyword="Jet engine">
            <topic href="jet.html"/>
        </entry>
    </entry>
    <entry keyword="Electricity">
        <topic href="electricity.html"/>
    </entry>
</index>
```

The index consists of a series of entries. Each entry may contain several links to help topics associated with the keyword. An entry can also be a container for other entries (subentries) to form a hierarchy of keywords. An entry can embed entries or topics simultaneously.

The <topic> element provides reference to help content related to the keyword using the href attribute. To access a file in another plug-in, use the following syntax:

```
<topic label="External Topic" href="../plugin.id/html/other_file.html"/>
```

The title attribute of a topic is used to name the link when multiple topics are contained within an entry. Figure 6-6 shows the index contents displaying within the help view. When a keyword is clicked, the topic contents (from href) will be displayed in the view. The view also implements a powerful search interface.

Figure 6-6. *Help view showing index contents*

Internationalization

The help system supports internationalization for TOC and index files. To do this, the XML files must be translated, and the resulting copies must be placed under a directory named nl/<language>/<country> or nl/<language> within the plug-in root directory. The <language> and <country> are two-letter language and country locale codes.[2] For example, Spanish translations must be placed under nl/es. Figure 6-5, shown earlier in the chapter, includes the folder layout for internationalization. Translated versions of the content documents should be placed here as well.

■Tip The locale search priority order goes as follows (from highest): nl/<language>/<country>, nl/<language>, and then the root directory of the plug-in.

Adding Context Help Support

Context help information is provided when the user presses F1 while a specific widget is active. Figure 6-7 shows an example of context help that appears when the user presses F1 while the mail view from the Mail template is active.

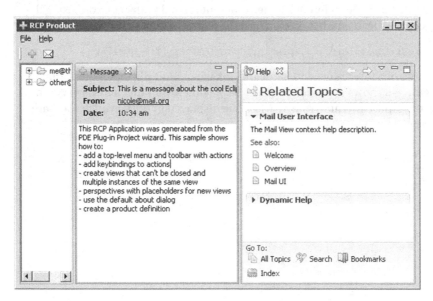

Figure 6-7. *Mail template showing context-sensitive help*

---

2.   ISO language and country codes are available online at http://www.iso.ch/iso/en/prods-services/iso3166ma/02iso-3166-code-lists/list-en1.html.

Adding context-sensitive help to a product is a multistep process that can be a bit confusing the first time. Assuming you have two separate plug-ins (product and help), the following steps are required:

1. In the product plug-in, modify the UI classes to add a help context ID for a given control.

2. In the help plug-in, create a context help file (contexts.xml) using a User Assistance wizard (Context Help), and populate it with some help documentation.

3. Modify the plugin.xml file for the help plug-in to add the org.eclipse.help.contexts extension point for the context help file you created.

Let's take a closer look at each of these steps.

Product Plug-in Modifications

The first step is to set a help context ID on the UI controls. Listing 6-5 adds the context ID Mail.viewer to the Mail view of the Mail template from the "Adding Help Content" section earlier in this chapter.

Listing 6-5. *Adding Context Help Support to a View*

```
public class MailView extends ViewPart {

    public static final String ID = "Mail.view";
    private Composite top;

    public void createPartControl(Composite parent) {
        top = new Composite(parent, SWT.NONE);
        ...

        PlatformUI.getWorkbench().getHelpSystem().setHelp(top, "Mail.viewer");


        ...

    }


    public void setFocus() {
        if (top != null)
            top.setFocus();
    }
}
```

The help context ID of the view in Listing 6-5 should include the plug-in ID and a string identifier by calling getHelpSystem().setHelp(top, "PLUG_IN_ID.CONTEXT_ID"). Otherwise, the help topic may not be found at runtime. This is because a context ID is uniquely identified by pluginID.contextID in memory.

Help Plug-in Modifications

Within the help plug-in project, you need to add a context help file and also add the extension point `org.eclipse.help.contexts` to the `plugin.xml` file.

Creating the Context Help File

Add a `contexts.xml` file to the help plug-in by selecting File ➤ New ➤ Other. On the Select a Wizard page, expand User Assistance and select Context Help, as shown in Figure 6-8. Eclipse provides a powerful editor for help context files, as shown in Figure 6-9.

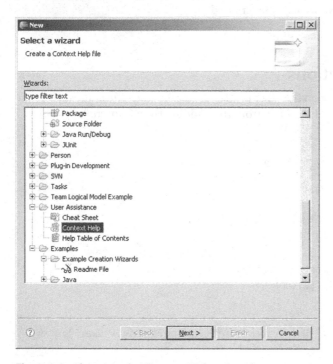

Figure 6-8. *Choosing the Context Help wizard*

Listing 6-6 shows the structure of a `contexts.xml` file.

Listing 6-6. *Structure of a Help Context File (contexts.xml)*

```
<?xml version="1.0" encoding="UTF-8"?>
<contexts>
   <context id="viewer" title="Mail User Interface">
      <description>Context from Help plugin</description>
      <topic href="html/gettingstarted/subtopic2.html" label="Mail UI"/>
   </context>
</contexts>
```

The `id` attribute is passed by the Eclipse Platform runtime to the help system to identify the currently active context.

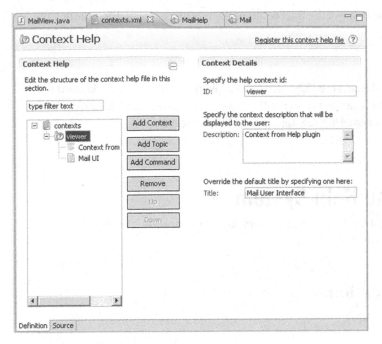

Figure 6-9. *Help context file editor*

■Caution The IDs in the manifest file must not contain the period character, since the IDs are uniquely identified by `pluginID.contextID`.

Adding the Help Contexts Extension Point

The final step is to add the extension point `org.eclipse.help.contexts` to the help plug-in manifest. Listing 6-7 shows an example.

Listing 6-7. *The Help Contexts Extension Point (in plugin.xml)*

```
<extension
        point="org.eclipse.help.contexts">
    <contexts
            file="contexts.xml"
            plugin="Mail">
    </contexts>
</extension>
```

The `file` attribute defines the name of the manifest file that contains the context-sensitive help for this plug-in. The `plugin` attribute defines the plug-in ID to which the context belongs. In this case, the MailHelp plug-in will contribute context to the Mail plug-in.

Figure 6-7, shown earlier, shows the final result of the modifications to the product and help plug-ins.

■Tip The article "Adding Help Support to a Rich Client Platform (RCP) Application," available online at `http://www.eclipse.org/articles/article.php?file=Article-AddingHelpToRCP/index.html`, includes a tutorial that demonstrates adding help support to an RCP application.

Customizing the Help System

You can configure and brand the Eclipse help system to suit your product. Figure 6-10 shows an example of a customized help system.

Figure 6-10. *Customized help for the RCP Mail template*

You can customize help by specifying custom defaults for a number of help preferences. The help preferences are specified in the `plugin_customization.ini` file within the product plug-in. Customizing the help system is a two-step process:

1. Add a property to the plug-in manifest with the plug-in customization file name (`plugin_customization.ini`), as shown in Listing 6-8.

2. Add preferences to `plugin_customization.ini` to customize the help system, as shown in Listing 6-9.

Listing 6-8. *Adding a Property with the Plug-in Customization File Name (in plugin.xml)*

```
<extension
        id="product"
        point="org.eclipse.core.runtime.products">
    <product
        application="Mail.application"
        name="RCP Product">
    ....
    <property
            name="preferenceCustomization"
            value="plugin_customization.ini">
    </property>
    ...
    </product>
</extension>
```

Listing 6-9. *Adding Preferences to Customize the Help System (in plugin_customization.ini)*

```
org.eclipse.help/HELP_DATA = helpData.xml
org.eclipse.help.base/help_home = /MailHelp/html/toc.html
org.eclipse.help.base/banner = /MailHelp/html/banner.html
org.eclipse.help.base/banner_height = 60
```

The HELP_DATA property in plugin_customization.ini allows you to control the order in which contributed parts of the TOC are displayed for your product or to hide parts of the TOC that some of your plug-ins contribute. The helpData.xml file shown in Listing 6-10 sets the TOC display order to toc.xml, followed by toc1.xml. The file toctest.xml will be hidden (this is useful for testing purposes).

Listing 6-10. *Setting the TOC Display Order (in helpData.xml)*

```
<extensions>
 <tocOrder>
  <toc id="/MailHelp/toc.xml"/>
  <toc id="/MailHelp/toc1.xml"/>
 </tocOrder>
 <hidden>
  <toc id="/MailHelp/toctest.xml"/>
 </hidden>
</extensions>
```

The following are other interesting properties that you can set in the `plugin_customization.ini` file (Listing 6-9):

- `org.eclipse.help.base/help_home`: Defines the page to show in the content area when opening help. The format is `/PLUGIN_ID/path/to/file.html`.

- `org.eclipse.help.base/banner`: Defines the location of the banner page to display in the top frame—for example, `org.eclipse.help.base/banner = /MailHelp/html/banner.html`.

- `org.eclipse.help.base/banner_height`: Defines the height of the banner frame.

Now that we have reviewed the basics of providing help information for an RCP application, let's work through an example.

Hands-on Exercise: Create an Infocenter from Custom Documentation

The goal of this exercise is to build a documentation server, known as an *infocenter*, from a set of user-defined documents. The infocenter is meant to be an online documentation repository. In this example, you will use the Word document for this chapter.

The following are the general steps to follow:

1. Split the source documentation into a set of topics in HTML/XHTML format.

2. Create two plug-ins: Content and Infocenter. You will build the Infocenter plug-in as an RCP application to let Eclipse lay the foundation required to start the infocenter from the command line.

3. Add a TOC with references to the topics created in step 1.

4. Configure the plug-ins, including dependencies and extension points.

5. Deploy and start the Infocenter plug-in from the command line.

6. Customize the Infocenter plug-in's look and feel to fit your needs.

Splitting the Documentation into Topic HTML/XHTML Files

Depending on the format of the documentation, a word processor can be used to split this chapter into HTML topic files. Each topic file will represent a section in this chapter. So, you should split this chapter into five topic HTML files (not including this exercise):

- Configuring a Product to Use the Help System

- Adding Help Content

- Adding Context Help Support

- Customizing the Help System

Save the files in a temporary folder. Later on, they will be added to the help content plug-in.

Tip In the real world, documentation writers would work with custom data formats such as DITA, a popular XML-based architecture for authoring, producing, and delivering technical information.

USING CUSTOM HELP AUTHORING TOOLS

You can use third-party tools to generate Eclipse help from your source material (FrameMaker, Microsoft Word, and so on). One such tool is DITA Open Toolkit (http://dita-ot.sourceforge.net/). DITA provides content divided into small, self-contained topics that can be reused in different deliverables. Furthermore, the extensibility of DITA permits organizations to define specific information structures and still use standard tools to work with them. All these features enable DITA to support content reuse and reduce information redundancy.

An example of a commercial authoring tool is Mif2Go (http://www.omsys.com/dcl/omni.htm), which can produce Eclipse help from FrameMaker files.

For example, consider the following Unix script to generate a help plug-in from a set of DITA source files:

```
#!/bin/bash
# *******************************************************************
# Shell script  to create Eclipse Help using DITA-OT1.4.2.1
# *******************************************************************
export ditaroot=/path/to/DITA_TOOLKIT
export input=/path/to/dita/map
export output=/output/folder

ant -Dtranstype=eclipsehelp
    -Ddita.dir=$ditaroot
    -Dargs.input=$input
    -Doutput.dir=$output -f $ditaroot/conductor.xml
```

Creating the Help Contents Plug-in

The Content plug-in will contain the help documentation and TOC files. Use the Plug-in Project wizard to create it. Give it an ID like ch06.help.content. On the Plug-in Content page, uncheck the "Generate an activator" and "This plug-in will make contributions to the UI" options, and set "Would you like to create a rich client application?" to No. Figure 6-11 shows these settings.

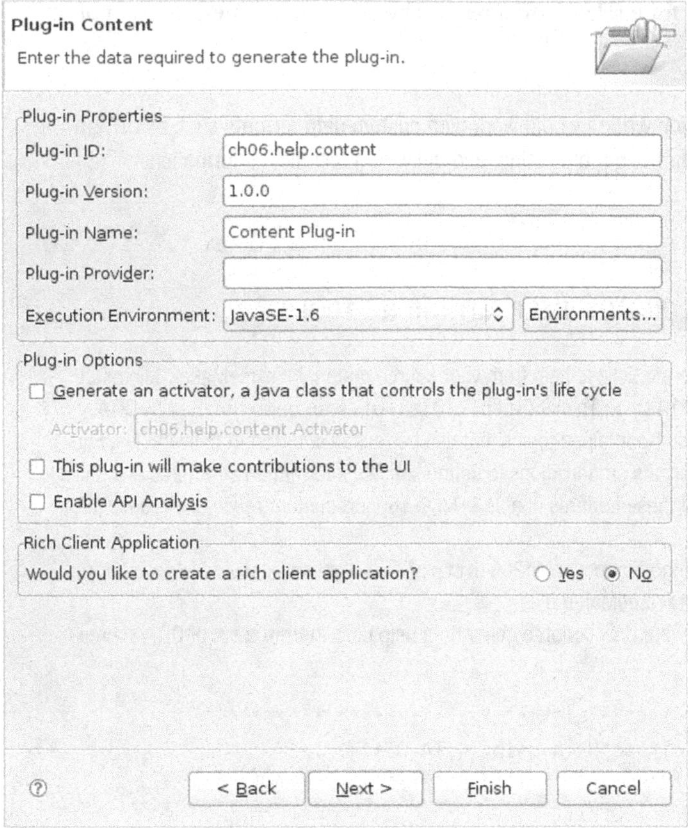

Plug-in Content
Enter the data required to generate the plug-in.

Plug-in Properties

Plug-in ID: ch06.help.content

Plug-in Version: 1.0.0

Plug-in Name: Content Plug-in

Plug-in Provider:

Execution Environment: JavaSE-1.6   Environments...

Plug-in Options

☐ Generate an activator, a Java class that controls the plug-in's life cycle

Activator: ch06.help.content.Activator

☐ This plug-in will make contributions to the UI

☐ Enable API Analysis

Rich Client Application

Would you like to create a rich client application?   ○ Yes ◉ No

⑦   < Back   Next >   Finish   Cancel

Figure 6-11. *Creating the Content plug-in*

Creating the Infocenter Plug-in

The Infocenter plug-in will be an RCP application used to host the help contents and handle the configuration required to resolve the help system dependencies. Again, use the Plug-in Project wizard to create it, giving it an ID like ch06.infocenter, for example. On the Plug-in Content page, check the "Generate an activator" and "This plug-in will make contributions to the UI" options, and set "Would you like to create a rich client application?" to Yes. Figure 6-12 shows these settings. On the Templates page, select the first RCP template.

■Tip The plug-in should be an RCP application so the PDE will create product and application extension points (required by the product configuration file), even though the Infocenter plug-in itself will not have a UI.

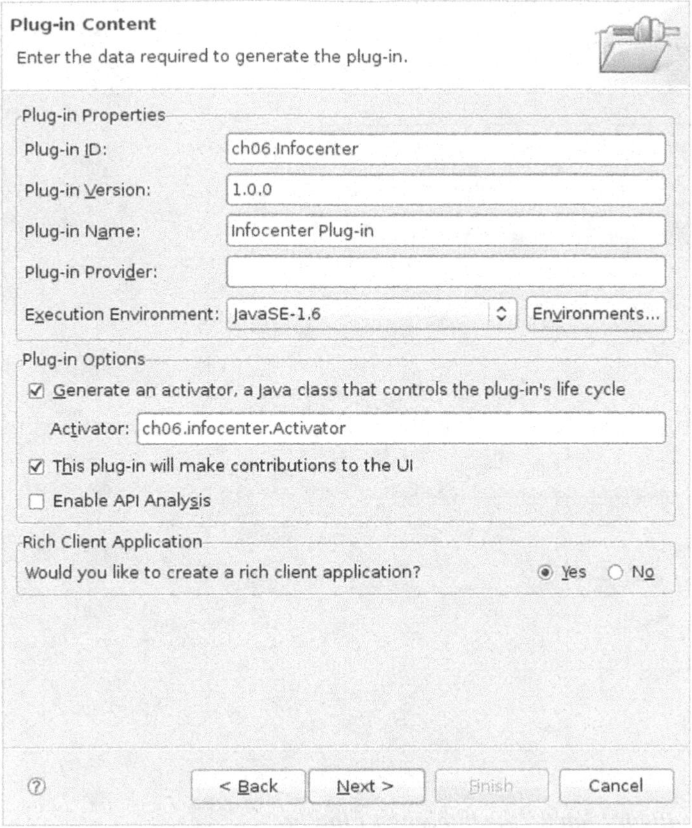

Figure 6-12. *Creating the Infocenter plug-in*

You will be presented with the plug-in manifest editor. Now you can proceed to add a product configuration file.

Adding a Product Configuration File to the Infocenter Plug-in

The product configuration (.product) file is used to build a product around the Infocenter and Content plug-ins. The product will include all of the files necessary to start the Infocenter plug-in from the command line.

To create the product configuration file, from the project navigator, right-click the Infocenter folder, and then select New ➤ Product Configuration. Enter a file name for the product, such as InfoCenter.product. In the "Initialize the file content" section, select to "Use an existing product" and choose ch06.Infocenter.product. Figure 6-13 shows these settings.

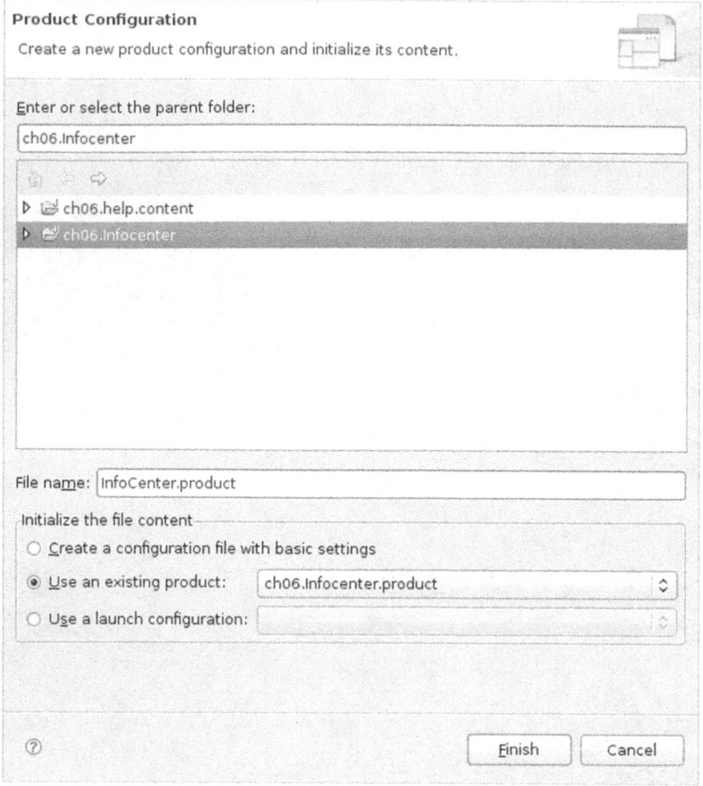

Figure 6-13. *Creating a product configuration for the Infocenter plug-in*

The product editor will open, showing the product information. Close this file and proceed to add a TOC to the Content plug-in.

Adding a TOC to the Help Contents Plug-in

As you've learned, the TOC is an XML file that maps a series of topic names to their respective HTML content files. To create a TOC file, from the project navigator view, follow these steps:

1. Right-click the help content folder (ch06.help.content) and select New ➤ File ➤ Other.

2. On the Select a Wizard page, expand User Assistance and select Help Table of Contents. Then click Next.

3. Enter a file name for the TOC (toc.xml), as shown in Figure 6-14, and then click Finish.

4. Open the TOC file. It will be displayed in the PDE TOC editor, where you can use an intuitive UI to add topics that point to the documentation files, as shown in Figure 6-15. Each topic is described by a label and a content file. Topics can be nested within other topics.

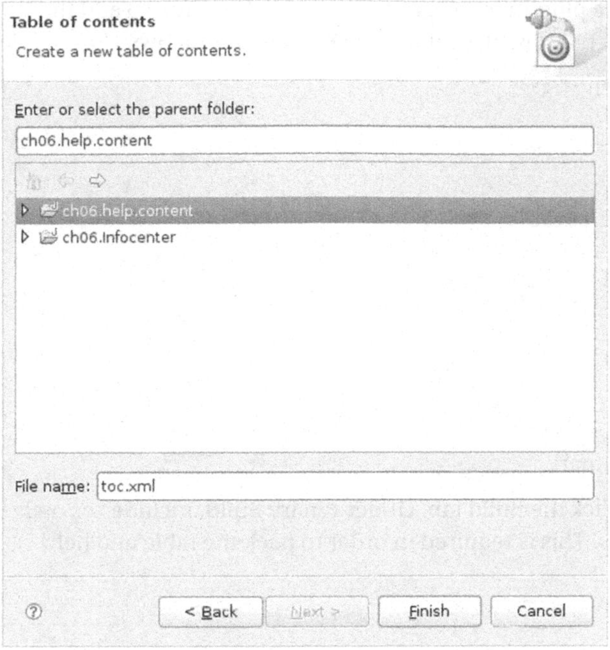

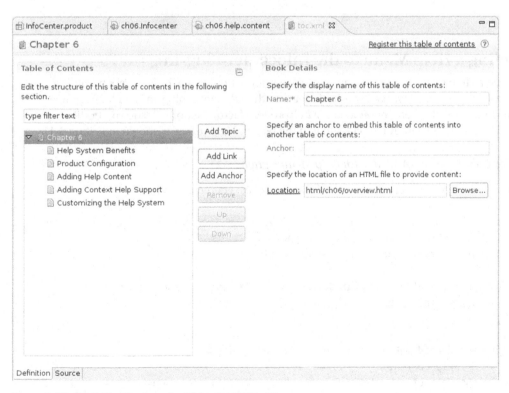

Figure 6-14. *Creating a TOC XML file using the wizard*

Figure 6-15. *TOC file displayed within the PDE editor*

5. Add a TOC extension point to the plug-in manifest. You can use the editor to add the
org.eclipse.help.toc extension point with a child <toc> element, as follows:

```
<?xml version="1.0" encoding="UTF-8"?>
<?eclipse version="3.2"?>
<plugin>
   <extension
         point="org.eclipse.help.toc">
      <toc
            file="toc.xml"
            primary="true">
      </toc>
   </extension>
</plugin>
```

The TOC file should be set as primary.

6. In the plug-in manifest editor, click the Build tab. Under Binary Build, include toc.xml
and the html content directories. This is required in order to pack the table and help
content files for deployment.

■**Caution** If you fail to add toc.xml and help.content in the Binary Build section of the plug-in manifest, the TOC will not display when the Infocenter plug-in is deployed.

Adding a Help Menu to the Infocenter Plug-in

Adding a Help menu to the Infocenter plug-in is an optional step, but it's very helpful to
make sure everything works as desired. Because the Infocenter plug-in is an RCP application, you can add a Help menu with the help system factory actions. To do so, modify the
ApplicationActionBarAdvisor class to add the factory Help menu as shown in Listing 6-11.

Listing 6-11. *ActionBarAdvisor with Help Menu Options*

```
public class ApplicationActionBarAdvisor extends ActionBarAdvisor {
    // Help actions
    private IWorkbenchAction showHelpAction;
    private IWorkbenchAction searchHelpAction;
    private IWorkbenchAction dynamicHelpAction;

    public ApplicationActionBarAdvisor(IActionBarConfigurer configurer) {
        super(configurer);
    }

    protected void makeActions(IWorkbenchWindow window) {
        // Help contents
        showHelpAction = ActionFactory.HELP_CONTENTS.create(window);
        register(showHelpAction);
```

```
        // Help search
        searchHelpAction = ActionFactory.HELP_SEARCH.create(window);
        register(searchHelpAction);

        // Dynamic help
        dynamicHelpAction = ActionFactory.DYNAMIC_HELP.create(window);
        register(dynamicHelpAction);

    }

    protected void fillMenuBar(IMenuManager menuBar) {
        MenuManager helpMenu = new MenuManager("&Help",
                IWorkbenchActionConstants.M_HELP);

        // Help menu options
        helpMenu.add(showHelpAction);
        helpMenu.add(searchHelpAction);
        helpMenu.add(dynamicHelpAction);
        helpMenu.add(new Separator());

        menuBar.add(helpMenu);
    }
}
```

Make sure the help system plug-in dependencies are included in plugin.xml. They are required to start the help system. Open the plug-in manifest editor, and under the Dependencies tab, add the following:

- org.eclipse.help.ui
- org.eclipse.help.webapp

Adding Help System Dependencies to the Product Configuration

The final step is to add all the required dependencies to the product configuration. If you don't do this, the product will fail to start.

Open the product configuration file (Infocenter.product), and click the Configuration tab, as shown in Figure 6-16. Make sure the "Include optional dependencies when computing required plug-ins" option is checked. Add the following plug-ins:

- ch06.help.content
- org.eclipse.help.base
- org.eclipse.help.appserver
- org.eclipse.help.ui
- org.eclipse.help.webapp

Figure 6-16. *Infocenter product configuration showing plug-in dependencies*

Click the Add Required Plug-ins button. The dependencies list should now include all of the required plug-ins.

Caution Missing dependencies can be a major headache for developers. This is actually the most common error in RCP application development.

Testing the Infocenter Plug-in

To test the Infocenter plug-in, open the product configuration (Infocenter.product) file. In the Overview tab, click Synchronize, and then click Launch Eclipse application to run the application. Then from the Help menu, select Help Contents. The Help window should open and display the TOCs.

If the Help window fails to appear, it is probably due to missing plug-in dependencies. The next fragment shows the full dependency list from Infocenter.product.

```xml
<?xml version="1.0" encoding="UTF-8"?>
<?pde version="3.4"?>

<product name="Hello RCP" id="ch06.Infocenter.product"
    application="ch06.Infocenter.application" version="1.0.0" useFeatures="false">
  <configIni use="default">
  </configIni>

  <plugins>
    <plugin id="ch06.Infocenter"/>
    <plugin id="ch06.help.content"/>
    <plugin id="com.ibm.icu"/>
    <plugin id="javax.servlet"/>
    <plugin id="javax.servlet.jsp"/>
    <plugin id="org.apache.ant"/>
    <plugin id="org.apache.commons.el"/>
    <plugin id="org.apache.commons.logging"/>
    <plugin id="org.apache.jasper"/>
    <plugin id="org.apache.lucene"/>
    <plugin id="org.apache.lucene.analysis"/>
    <plugin id="org.eclipse.ant.core"/>
    <plugin id="org.eclipse.core.commands"/>
    <plugin id="org.eclipse.core.contenttype"/>
    <plugin id="org.eclipse.core.databinding"/>
    <plugin id="org.eclipse.core.expressions"/>
    <plugin id="org.eclipse.core.jobs"/>
    <plugin id="org.eclipse.core.runtime"/>
    <plugin id="org.eclipse.core.runtime.compatibility.auth"/>
    <plugin id="org.eclipse.core.runtime.compatibility.registry" fragment="true"/>
    <plugin id="org.eclipse.core.variables"/>
    <plugin id="org.eclipse.equinox.app"/>
    <plugin id="org.eclipse.equinox.common"/>
    <plugin id="org.eclipse.equinox.http.jetty"/>
    <plugin id="org.eclipse.equinox.http.registry"/>
    <plugin id="org.eclipse.equinox.http.servlet"/>
    <plugin id="org.eclipse.equinox.jsp.jasper"/>
    <plugin id="org.eclipse.equinox.jsp.jasper.registry"/>
    <plugin id="org.eclipse.equinox.preferences"/>
    <plugin id="org.eclipse.equinox.registry"/>
    <plugin id="org.eclipse.help"/>
    <plugin id="org.eclipse.help.appserver"/>
    <plugin id="org.eclipse.help.base"/>
    <plugin id="org.eclipse.help.ui"/>
    <plugin id="org.eclipse.help.webapp"/>
```

```
            <plugin id="org.eclipse.jface"/>
            <plugin id="org.eclipse.jface.databinding"/>
            <plugin id="org.eclipse.osgi"/>
            <plugin id="org.eclipse.osgi.services"/>
            <plugin id="org.eclipse.swt"/>
            <plugin id="org.eclipse.swt.gtk.linux.x86" fragment="true"/>
            <plugin id="org.eclipse.ui"/>
            <plugin id="org.eclipse.ui.forms"/>
            <plugin id="org.eclipse.ui.workbench"/>
            <plugin id="org.mortbay.jetty"/>
        </plugins>
</product>
```

If the TOC fails to display, it probably means that you have not included the required extension points in `plugin.xml` for the `ch06.help.contents` project. Also, review the `MANIFEST.MF` file and make sure it points to `toc.xml`. Keep in mind that the TOC must be set to primary.

Deploying the Infocenter Plug-in

Deploying the Infocenter plug-in requires the Eclipse delta pack (for multiplatforms), which is not included in the default Eclipse download. To deploy the plug-in, follow these steps:

1. Install the delta pack from the Eclipse downloads site, if you have not done so already (see Chapter 3 for details on installing and downloading the delta pack).

2. Open the product configuration (`Infocenter.product`) file.

3. Click Eclipse Product export wizard to start the deployment wizard. Enter a destination directory, click Export for multiple platforms, and then click Next.

4. Select your target operating system, and then click Finish.

5. Inspect the destination folder for an Eclipse executable, as well as the plug-ins and features folders.

You can test the Infocenter RCP application by double-clicking the Eclipse binary and opening the Help menu. However, the Infocenter plug-in is meant to be started from the command line and accessed from a web browser.

Tip If the TOC fails to display from the Help menu, that is probably because you forgot to add the help content files in the Build tab of the plug-in manifest editor for `ch06.help.content`.

Starting the Infocenter from the Command Line

Listing 6-11 is a shell script that starts the Infocenter plug-in from the command line. The script runs the help system class `org.eclipse.help.standalone.Infocenter` on port 8080. The version of your Eclipse help system JAR file (org.eclipse.help.base_3.3.100.v20080617.jar) may be different, depending on your installation

Listing 6-11. *Script to Start Infocenter from the Command Line*

```bash
#!/bin/bash

# Eclipse Home is required
ehome=${ECLIPSE_HOME:-$HOME/Documents/InfoCenterApp/eclipse}

if [ -z $ehome ] ; then
     echo "ECLIPSE_HOME is required"
     exit -1
fi

java -classpath $ehome/plugins/org.eclipse.help.base_3.3.100.v20080617.jar \
 org.eclipse.help.standalone.Infocenter \
 -eclipsehome $ehome \
 -port 8080 \
 -data $ehome/workspace \
 -configuration $ehome/configuration \
 -debug -consoleLog -clean \
 -command start
```

The output of Listing 6-11 is as follows:

```
Debugging is on.
Lock obtained.
isApplicationRunning? false
Using workspace /home/vladimirs/Documents/linux.gtk.x86/eclipse/workspace
Ensured old .connection file is deleted.  Launching Eclipse.
isApplicationRunning? false
Launch command is:
  /home/vladimirs/Documents/linux.gtk.x86/eclipse/eclipse
  -vm
  /usr/lib/jvm/jdk1.6.0_06/jre/bin/java
  -nosplash
  -application
  org.eclipse.help.base.infocenterApplication
  -data
  /home/vladimirs/Documents/linux.gtk.x86/eclipse/workspace
  -configuration
  /home/vladimirs/Documents/linux.gtk.x86/eclipse/configuration
  -debug
  -consoleLog
  -clean
  -vmargs
  -Dserver_port=8080
```

```
Configuration location:
    file:/home/vladimirs/Documents/linux.gtk.x86/eclipse/configuration/
Configuration file:
    file:/home/vladimirs/Documents/linux.gtk.x86/eclipse/configuration/config.ini
Install location:
    file:/home/vladimirs/Documents/linux.gtk.x86/eclipse/
Framework located:
    file:/home/vladimirs/Documents/linux.gtk.x86/eclipse/plugins/
        org.eclipse.osgi_3.4.0.v20080605-1900.jar
Framework classpath:
    file:/home/vladimirs/Documents/linux.gtk.x86/eclipse/plugins/
        org.eclipse.osgi_3.4.0.v20080605-1900.jar
isApplicationRunning? false
Debug options:
    file:/home/vladimirs/Documents/linux.gtk.x86/eclipse/.options not found
isApplicationRunning? false
isApplicationRunning? false
Time to load bundles: 267
isApplicationRunning? false
isApplicationRunning? false
Starting application: 1193
isApplicationRunning? false
isApplicationRunning? true
Eclipse launched
Lock released.
```

To access the Infocenter plug-in, open a browser to `http://localhost:8080/help/index.jsp`.

Customizing the Infocenter

The Infocenter can be customized to fit the needs of your organization. For example, you might add a banner to the main web page or specify a configuration XML file to set the ordering of multiple TOCs. As explained earlier in the chapter, you can customize a plug-in's help system by adding a `plugin_customization.ini` file with custom help system properties.

For this example, customize the Infocenter plug-in as follows:

1. Right-click the Infocenter plug-in and select New ➤ File. Name the file `plugin_customization.ini`.

2. Open the Infocenter plug-in manifest editor. On the Extensions tab, expand `org.eclipse.core.runtime.products`.

3. Right-click the RCP product name and select New ➤ Property.

4. Set the name of the property to `preferenceCustomization` and the value to `plugin_customization.ini`.

5. Add custom help system properties to `plugin_customization.ini`. The following properties will add a custom banner to the main page, set the banner height to 60 pixels, and set the main contents page to the chapter overview.

```
org.eclipse.help.base/banner = /ch06.help.content/html/banner.html
org.eclipse.help.base/banner_height = 60
org.eclipse.help.base/help_home = /ch06.help.content/html/ch06/overview.html
```

> **■Note** Be sure to add `plugin_customization.ini` to the Binary Build list of the plug-in manifest editor's Build tab. Otherwise, the customizations won't take effect when you deploy the Infocenter plug-in.

6. Test the customization by redeploying the Infocenter RCP project, restarting the startup script (Listing 6-11), and opening a browser to `http://localhost:8080/help/index.jsp`. The results should look something like Figure 6-17.

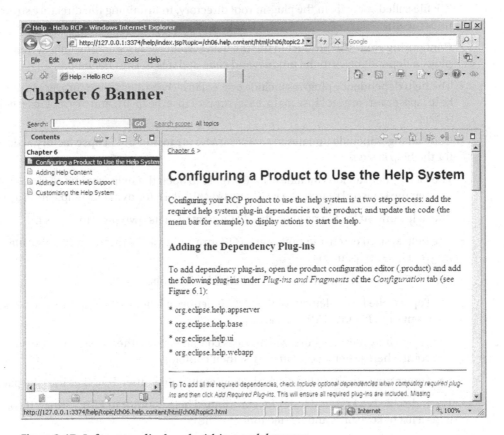

Figure 6-17. *Infocenter displayed within a web browser*

Summary

This chapter explained how to add help support to your RCP applications. The following are the important points to keep in mind:

- The Eclipse help system offers a powerful and easy way to add documentation with full HTML support to your RCP applications.

- The help system includes functionality such as built-in search facilities, localization for additional languages, context help, a keyword index, and a web-based infocenter.

- The help system provides programmatic extension points for content producers to generate dynamic help, including TOCs, keyword indexes, and content.

- The help system uses its own help server to provide web pages from within your documentation plug-in. A help server allows your RCP application to handle a wide variety of web browsers in a browser-independent way, while also providing plug-in–aware support.

- The Eclipse Platform's help server allows the documentation to also be packaged in a ZIP file called doc.zip, in the plug-in root directory, maintaining the directory structure underneath.

- Configuring your RCP product to use the help system requires adding help system plug-in dependencies to the product and code updates to start the help.

- The help dependency plug-ins include org.eclipse.help.appserver, org.eclipse. help.appserver, org.eclipse.help.base, org.eclipse.help.ui, and org.eclipse.help. webapp.

- Code changes include updates to ActionBarAdvisor to add the Eclipse factory actions for the help system.

- The factory help actions include HELP_CONTENTS to open the help window, HELP_SEARCH to open the keyword search as a view, and DYNAMIC_HELP for dynamic help within a view.

- The help content for the product should be created in its own plug-in project.

- The help system extension points are TOC (org.eclipse.help.toc) and index file (org.eclipse.help.index).

- The TOC is an XML file with a set of child topic elements.

  - Topic is the basic element of the TOC. It defines a label and a link (href) to a documentation file in HTML format.

  - Topics may have anchors, which act as containers for other topics and provide a point where other TOCs can embed their contents.

  - Topics may also have links, which allow embedding other TOC files into the parent.

- The index file is a keyword index for contributed help content in XML format. It contains a list of keywords and related topics of the content.

- Context help is provided when a user requests context-sensitive help by pressing F1 when a widget is active.

- Adding context help requires making changes to the UI classes to add a help context ID for a given control, creating a help context XML file with documentation, and adding the extension point `org.eclipse.help.contexts` to `plugin.xml`.

- The Eclipse help system can be configured and branded to suit your product by specifying custom defaults for a number of help preferences.

  - To customize the help system, add custom properties to `plugin_customization.ini` within the product.

  - Some custom properties include `HELP_DATA`, `help_home`, `banner`, and `banner_height`.

  - The `HELP_DATA` property allows you to control the order in which contributed parts of the TOC are displayed for your product or to hide parts of the TOC.

CHAPTER 7

■ ■ ■

2D Graphics with GEF and Zest

The Eclipse Graphical Editing Framework (GEF) is a powerful 2D graphics framework for building rich GUIs. GEF provides a layer of abstraction for native 2D graphics on the Eclipse Platform. Most of the operations provided by GEF can be extended by developers, thus reducing development time and maximizing reusability.

The 2D framework is made of two components (plug-ins): Draw2d, which provides a layout and rendering toolkit for displaying 2D graphics, and GEF, which is an intuitive MVC framework built on top of Draw2d. The MVC architecture separates the UI from the underlying structure (model), so that implementation changes in one part of the application do not require changes to another part. This means you can more easily prototype your work. For example, you might create a prototype application, change the application in response to user feedback, and then implement production-level programs on the same or other operating systems. Outside the work you do on the programs themselves, your only adjustments are to the presentation layer, leaving the model layer intact. Along with ease of modification and maintenance (due to the cleaner separation of tasks), the MVC architecture better supports scalability for bigger applications.

This chapter covers Draw2d and GEF, as well as the Zest visualization toolkit for Eclipse, which is designed to make graph-based programming easy. In the exercise at the end of the chapter, you will build an advanced graph editor using GEF and Zest.

Draw2d—The Big Picture

Draw2d (also known as `org.eclipse.draw2d`) is a neat component that allows developers to create all kinds of 2D graphs. These graphs are usually accompanied by a tools palette. Behind the scenes, Draw2d provides the core interfaces for this purpose.

A fundamental concept in Draw2d is the *figure*. A figure is a low-footprint Java object (an object that does not use any operating system resources). Here are some facts about figures:

- Figures can have children.

- Each figure, and its children, is painted within a bounding rectangle.

- A layout manager can place figures within a bounding rectangle based on an index.

- Figures can be connected with lines (and arrowheads) displayed above their drawing surface. A connection always has a router (the connection line), and at least two points on the connection: the source and target endpoints. The endpoints are anchored to a specific figure.

Consider Figure 7-1, which shows a shapes graph from the GEF/Draw2d `org.eclipse.gef.examples.shapes` plug-in, available from Eclipse. On the left side is a palette that offers two shapes (Ellipse and Rectangle), which can be dragged to the canvas on the right and manipulated as desired. We'll take a closer look at the `org.eclipse.gef.examples.shapes` plug-in in the "Exploring the GEF Shapes Example" section, later in this chapter.

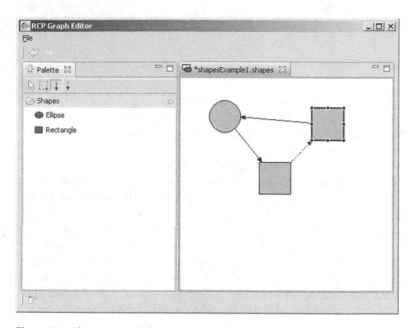

Figure 7-1. *Shapes graph from the org.eclipse.gef.examples plug-in*

Figures can be composed to create complex graphics. They are encapsulated by the interface `org.eclipse.draw2d.IFigure` and must obey the following rules:

Use the SWT Graphics Context (GC): Figures must be painted using the GC for extended functionality and to optimize performance. This makes perfect sense, since SWT is the foundation that provides access to the native hardware. The GC encapsulates all of the drawing API, including how to draw lines shapes, text, images, and fill shapes.

Follow the layout manager's layout process: Figures must follow a layout process that is delegated to a layout manager. The layout is a top-down process done in two steps. In the first step, a collection of figures (or images) is invalidated. In the second step, the branches of figures that are invalid are validated. This process is performed by the layout manager, which will call a `validate()` method for each figure. The figure then will mark itself as valid and perform its layout. After this, the figure will validate its children.

Use the Draw2d coordinate system: Figures must obey a coordinate system used for adjustments required when painting children, such as when panning or zooming a figure. Draw2d defines two coordinate systems:

- In an *absolute coordinate system*, all figures paint in the same coordinates. It is mostly used when determining the bounds of a parent based on the bounds of the children.

- In a *relative coordinate system*, the bounds of children are relative to the client area of their parent. When figure with relative coordinates is moved, the children come along automatically. It is mostly used when translating or moving a figure, or when only the figure's bounds must be updated, and the children should move as well.

The painting process of a figure can be overridden by the developer using the following methods of the IFigure interface:

- paint(): This starts the painting process by setting a set of graphics properties, including the font, background, and foreground color. These properties are inherited by the children.

- paintFigure(): Using this method, the figure paints itself. This is an optional method, as figures are not required to paint themselves. For example, you might use it to draw a bounding rectangle filled with a background color.

- paintClientArea(): This paints the client area where the figure appears. This method applies changes, such as coordinate system modifications, to the children's graphics. This method also clips the graphics region where children will appear.

- paintChildren(): This paints the children. This method does not override the inherited graphics settings from the parent.

- paintBorder(): This paints decorations that should appear on top of the children, including the border if set on the figure.

To check for figure collisions, Draw2d performs *hit testing*. Hit testing is used to figure out when figures overlap each other and perform appropriate actions. The IFigure interface provides the following methods for hit testing:

- findFigureAt(x, y): Finds the topmost figure at x, y coordinates.

- findFigureAt(Point p): Finds the topmost figure at Point p.

- findFigureAtExcluding(int x, int y, Collection exclude): Finds the topmost figure for the given coordinates that is not in the exclusion set or contained by a figure in the exclusion set. This is used for ignoring a figure being dragged, or for ignoring transparent layers or figures that are not involved in an interaction.

- findFigureAt(int x, int y, TreeSearch): All of the previous methods call this method. TreeSearch is a helper that is used to quickly prune branches that should not be searched, and to accept the final candidate figure.

Using GEF

GEF (refers to both Draw2d and GEF) is the MVC wrapper around Draw2d that ensures a clean separation of the presentation from the model layer. While Draw2d focuses on efficient painting and layout of figures, GEF adds editing capabilities on top. It provides for the display of any model graphically using Draw2d figures, as well as for interactions with the mouse, keyboard, and workbench. A GEF-enabled widget consists of the following components:[1]

Model: The model is any data that is persisted and has some sort of notification mechanism. Commands are commonly used to modify the model in a way that can be undone and redone by the user. As a rule of thumb, commands should work only on the model itself.

View: The view consists of elements visible to the user, including figures and tree items.

Controller: The controller is responsible for maintaining the view, and for interpreting UI events and turning them into operations on the model. The controller is also called an *EditPart*. The EditPart is responsible for editing using *EditPolicies*, which handle much of the editing task.

Viewer: The viewer, also called the *EditPartViewer*, is where EditParts display their view. GEF provides two types of viewers: a graphical viewer, which hosts figures, and a tree viewer, which displays native tree items.

Displaying Figures

Displaying a graphical view of figures involves creating a series of EditParts to piece the model and figures together. EditParts associate their view and model, but they also form their own structure. An EditPart maintains children. Usually, this corresponds to a similar containment found in the model.

A graphical view consists of one or more of the following EditParts:

Root EditPart: The root is not part of the model. Its purpose is to set up the viewer and provide a uniform context for all of the application's real EditParts.

Content EditPart: Content refers to the base model object that seeds the viewer with the graphical diagram being displayed. The viewer's *EditPart factory* is responsible for taking the contents and constructing the appropriate EditPart, which is then set on the root EditPart. At that point, the content EditPart will construct its children, reusing the viewer's factory, which in turn creates their children and/or connections, and so on. The process repeats until all of the EditParts and their views have been created.

Child EditPart: The children display information to the user, such as a figure or a composition of multiple figures. For example, a child may be a `ShapeEditPart` that creates instances for `EllipticalShape` or `RectangularShape` figures.

Connection EditPart: A connection simply connects any two EditParts in a diagram.

Exploring the GEF Shapes Example

Earlier, you saw a shapes graph from the GEF/Draw2d `org.eclipse.gef.examples.shapes` plug-in (Figure 7-1). Now, let's look at this plug-in in more detail. (To follow along with the

---

1. From GEF Programmer's Guide, "Overview," at http://help.eclipse.org/stable/index.jsp?topic=/ org.eclipse.draw2d.doc.isv/guide/guide.html.

discussion, download this plug-in from the Eclipse repository, following the instructions in the "Downloading GEF Samples from the Eclipse Repository" section of the hands-on exercise later in this chapter.)

The org.eclipse.gef.examples.shapes plug-in has the following major components:

Shapes EditPart factory: The role of this factory is to construct the appropriate EditPart based on the model element.

Shape EditPart: This EditPart encapsulates common behavior for all shape EditParts.

Connection EditPart: This EditPart encapsulates connections between two shapes.

EditPolicies: These define the types of operations that can be performed on shapes, such as copy, paste, and delete.

Palette factory: This factory creates an instance of the palette used by the application. It contains tools to draw the shapes on the canvas.

Figures 7-2 and 7-3 show a UML class diagram depicting partial relationships between the major shape EditParts of the sample. The model (or data of the sample) consists of two shape classes: RectangularShape and EllipticalShape. These classes, in turn, inherit from the abstract class Shape, which provides a prototype for the model.

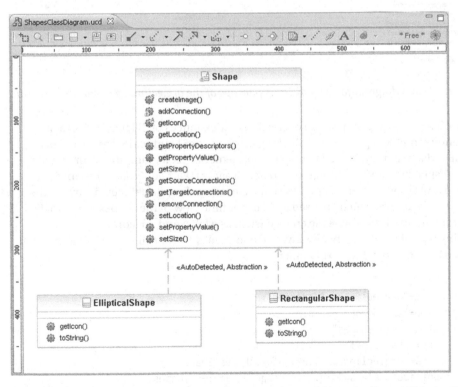

Figure 7-2. *Partial class diagram for the Shapes package of the org.eclipse.gef.examples plug-in*

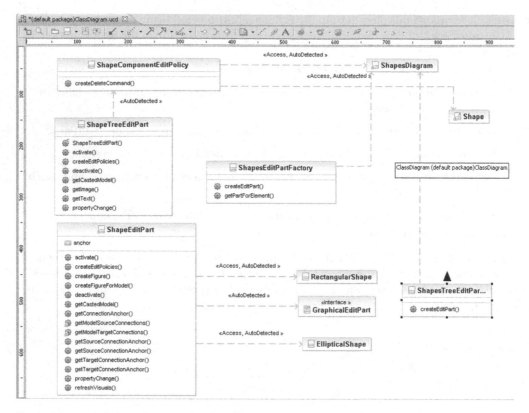

Figure 7-3. *Partial class diagram for the EditParts package of the org.eclipse.gef.examples plug-in*

The class ShapeEditPart is in charge of creating new instances of Ellipse or Rectangle figures, depending on the type of model (RectangularShape or EllipticalShape). A factory class, ShapesEditPartFactory, is used to map model elements (a diagram, shape, or connection) to their respective EditParts (DiagramEditPart, ShapeEditPart, or ConnectionEditPart). ShapeEditPart and ShapeEditPartFactory have the corresponding ShapeTreeEditPart and ShapeTreeEditPartFactory, which are used by in the outline view of the shapes editor to display information about the shape being created (such as a label and an icon).

Everything is finally put together by a wizard and shapes editor extension points (defined in plug-in.xml), as shown in the next fragment.

```
<plugin>
  <extension point="org.eclipse.ui.editors">
    <editor name="GEF Shapes Example"
            extensions="shapes"
            icon="shapes.gif"
            class="org.eclipse.gef.examples.shapes.ShapesEditor"
            contributorClass="org.eclipse.gef.examples.shapes.
                ShapesEditorActionBarContributor"
        id="GEF Shapes Editor">
    </editor>
  </extension>
</plugin>
```

```
    <extension point="org.eclipse.ui.newWizards">
        <category name="Examples"
                parentCategory="org.eclipse.ui.Examples"
                id="org.eclipse.gef.examples"/>
          <wizard name="Shapes Diagram"
                icon="shapes.gif"
                category="org.eclipse.ui.Examples/org.eclipse.gef.examples"
                class="org.eclipse.gef.examples.shapes.ShapesCreationWizard"
                id="org.eclipse.gef.examples.shapes.ShapesCreationWizard">
              <selection class="org.eclipse.core.resources.IResource"/>
          </wizard>
    </extension>
</plugin>
```

The first extension point defines the editor named GEF Shapes Example. The `extensions` attribute specifies that files with the extension `.shapes` will be automatically opened with this editor. Its implementation is defined by the class `org.eclipse.gef.examples.shapes.` `ShapesEditor`, and it also contributes actions to a toolbar (defined by `contributorClass`). The `id` attribute uniquely identifies the editor.

The `wizard` extension point is used to create a new shapes diagram from the File ➤ New main menu of the workbench or the context menu of the project, navigator, or package explorer views (which are built-in workbench views). The wizard is grouped by the category `Examples` and implemented by the class `ShapesCreationWizard`. The `<selection>` element indicates the wizard is capable of selecting workbench resources such as files or directories. The `id` attribute uniquely identifies this wizard.

The next sections explain some of the major components of this shapes editor, starting with the Shapes EditPart factory.

Shapes EditPart Factory

The Shapes EditPart factory recognizes the contents model and constructs its EditPart. This factory doesn't need to paint, but you still need to choose the layout manager and the figure type based on the root EditPart. Listing 7-1 shows an example of an EditPart factory for a Shapes model.

Listing 7-1. *EditPart Factory for a Shapes Model (from org.eclipse.gef.examples)*

```
/**
 * Factory that maps model elements to EditParts.
 */
public class ShapesEditPartFactory implements EditPartFactory {

    public EditPart createEditPart(EditPart context, Object modelElement) {
        // Get EditPart for model element
        EditPart part = getPartForElement(modelElement);
        // Store model element in EditPart
        part.setModel(modelElement);
        return part;
    }
```

```
/**
 * Map an object to an EditPart.
 *
 * @throws RuntimeException
 *                 if no match was found (programming error)
 */
private EditPart getPartForElement(Object modelElement) {
    if (modelElement instanceof ShapesDiagram) {
        return new DiagramEditPart();
    }
    if (modelElement instanceof Shape) {
        return new ShapeEditPart();
    }
    if (modelElement instanceof Connection) {
        return new ConnectionEditPart();
    }
    throw new RuntimeException("Can't create part for model element: "
            + ((modelElement != null) ? modelElement.getClass()
                    .getName() : "null"));
}
}
```

The getPartForElement() constructs the appropriate EditPart—ShapesDiagram, Shape, or Connection—based on the root EditPart object type.

Shape EditParts

As noted, the children's role is to display some information to the user. They may use one of the provided figures, a custom figure, or a composition of multiple figures.

When the viewer is populated, the refreshVisuals() method is called for each EditPart to show the model's properties in the view. EditParts must override this method based on the model and figure with which they work. Listing 7-2 shows an example of a class to create rectangular or elliptical EditParts for a Shapes model factory.

Listing 7-2. *Base Class to Create Rectangular or Elliptical Shape EditParts for the Shapes Model Factory (from org.eclipse.gef.examples)*

```
class ShapeEditPart extends AbstractGraphicalEditPart implements
        PropertyChangeListener, NodeEditPart {

    private ConnectionAnchor anchor;

    /**
     * Upon activation, attach to the model element as a property change
     * listener.
     */
```

```java
public void activate() {
    if (!isActive()) {
        super.activate();
        ((ModelElement) getModel()).addPropertyChangeListener(this);
    }
}

protected void createEditPolicies() {
    // Allow removal of the associated model element
    installEditPolicy(EditPolicy.COMPONENT_ROLE,
            new ShapeComponentEditPolicy());

    // Add EditPolicies here
    // They allow the creation of connections and
    // the reconnection of connections between Shape instances
}

protected IFigure createFigure() {
    IFigure f = createFigureForModel();
    f.setOpaque(true); // non-transparent figure
    f.setBackgroundColor(ColorConstants.green);
    return f;
}

/**
 * Return an IFigure depending on the instance of the current model
 * element. This allows this EditPart to be used for both subclasses of
 * Shape.
 */
private IFigure createFigureForModel() {
    if (getModel() instanceof EllipticalShape) {
        return new Ellipse();
    } else if (getModel() instanceof RectangularShape) {
        return new RectangleFigure();
    } else {
        // If Shapes gets extended, the conditions above must be updated
        throw new IllegalArgumentException();
    }
}

/**
 * Upon deactivation, detach from the model element as a property
 * change listener.
 */
```

```java
    public void deactivate() {
        if (isActive()) {
            super.deactivate();
            ((ModelElement) getModel()).removePropertyChangeListener(this);
        }
    }

    private Shape getCastedModel() {
        return (Shape) getModel();
    }

    protected ConnectionAnchor getConnectionAnchor() {
        if (anchor == null) {
            if (getModel() instanceof EllipticalShape)
                anchor = new EllipseAnchor(getFigure());
            else if (getModel() instanceof RectangularShape)
                anchor = new ChopboxAnchor(getFigure());
            else
                // If Shapes gets extended, the conditions above must be
                // updated
                throw new IllegalArgumentException("unexpected model");
        }
        return anchor;
    }

    /*
     * getModelSourceConnections()
     */
    protected List getModelSourceConnections() {
        return getCastedModel().getSourceConnections();
    }

    /*
     * Methods deleted for simplicity:getModelTargetConnections()
     *   getSourceConnectionAnchor
     * getSourceConnectionAnchor(Request request)
     *   getTargetConnectionAnchor
     * propertyChange(PropertyChangeEvent evt)
     */

    protected void refreshVisuals() {
        Rectangle bounds = new Rectangle(getCastedModel().getLocation(),
                getCastedModel().getSize());
        ((GraphicalEditPart) getParent()).setLayoutConstraint(this,
                getFigure(), bounds);
    }

}
```

ShapeEditPart is the parent class used for Shape instances (EllipticalShape or RectangularShape in this example). Figure 7-4 shows sample elliptical and rectangular shapes that inherit from ShapeEditPart.

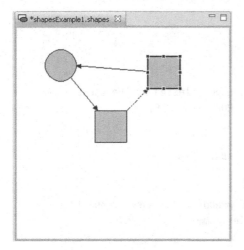

Figure 7-4. *Custom edit view showing circle and rectangle EditParts*

ShapeEditPart implements the PropertyChangeListener interface, so it can be notified of property changes in the corresponding model element. Upon activation, the model element is attached as a property change. The method refreshVisuals() is overridden to notify the parent container of the changed position and location. Otherwise, the XYLayoutManager used by the parent container will not know the bounds of this figure and will not draw it correctly.

Connection EditParts

Connections are special EditParts that connect any two EditParts in a diagram. The connections are created and managed in a shared way by the source and target nodes. Each node in the diagram must override getModelSourceConnections() and getModelTargetConnections() to return the model object representing the connection, as shown in Listing 7-3. GEF then checks to see if the connection EditPart has already been created (by the other node at the other end), and if not, it asks the factory to create the connection EditPart. The source node is responsible for activating and adding the connection figure to the diagram.

Listing 7-3. *Connection EditPart for the Shapes Model (from org.eclipse.gef.examples)*

```
class ConnectionEditPart extends AbstractConnectionEditPart implements
        PropertyChangeListener {

    /**
     * Upon activation, attach to the model element as a property change
     * listener.
     */
```

```java
public void activate() {
    if (!isActive()) {
        super.activate();
        ((ModelElement) getModel()).addPropertyChangeListener(this);
    }
}

protected void createEditPolicies() {
    // Selection handle edit policy.
    // Makes the connection show a feedback, when selected by the user.
    installEditPolicy(EditPolicy.CONNECTION_ENDPOINTS_ROLE,
            new ConnectionEndpointEditPolicy());

    // Allows the removal of the connection model element
    installEditPolicy(EditPolicy.CONNECTION_ROLE,
            new ConnectionEditPolicy() {
                protected Command getDeleteCommand(GroupRequest request) {
                    return new ConnectionDeleteCommand(
                            getCastedModel());
                }
            });
}

protected IFigure createFigure() {
    PolylineConnection connection = (PolylineConnection) super
            .createFigure();

    // Arrow at target endpoint
    connection.setTargetDecoration(new PolygonDecoration());

    // Line drawing style
    connection.setLineStyle(getCastedModel().getLineStyle());
    return connection;
}

/**
 * Upon deactivation, detach from the model element as a property
 * change listener.
 */
public void deactivate() {
    if (isActive()) {
        super.deactivate();
        ((ModelElement) getModel()).removePropertyChangeListener(this);
    }
}
```

```
private Connection getCastedModel() {
    return (Connection) getModel();
}

public void propertyChange(PropertyChangeEvent event) {
    String property = event.getPropertyName();
    if (Connection.LINESTYLE_PROP.equals(property)) {
        ((PolylineConnection) getFigure())
                .setLineStyle(getCastedModel().getLineStyle());
    }
}

}
```

Adding EditPolicies

Editing is the most complex task for an EditPart and involves making changes to the model, as well as showing graphical feedback during interactions with the view. Editing is done by creating requests and then calling the various API methods on EditPart based on the interaction. Editing also involves the manipulation of EditPolicies and commands.

EditParts handle editing through EditPolicies. This allows editing behavior to be reused across different implementations. Also, behavior can change dynamically, such as when the layouts or routing methods change. Each EditPolicy is able to focus on a single editing task or group of related tasks.

Commands are used to encapsulate and combine changes to the application's model. Commands are grouped and executed by applications in stacks, which dictate the order in which commends are executed. Stacks process elements in a last-in/first-out (LIFO) sequence.

Listing 7-4 defines ConnectionCreateCommand.java, a command to create a connection between two shapes. The command supports undo/redo and is designed to be used together with a GraphicalNodeEditPolicy.

Listing 7-4. *Command to Create Connections Between Shapes*

```
public class ConnectionCreateCommand extends Command {
    /** The connection instance. */
    private Connection connection;
    /** The desired line style for the connection (dashed or solid). */
    private final int lineStyle;

    /** Start endpoint for the connection. */
    private final Shape source;
    /** Target endpoint for the connection. */
    private Shape target;

    /**
     * Instantiate a command that can create a connection between two
     * shapes.
     *
```

```
 * @param source
 *              the source endpoint (a non-null Shape instance)
 * @param lineStyle
 *              the desired line style. See Connection#setLineStyle(int)
 *              for details
 * @throws IllegalArgumentException
 *               if source is null
 * @see Connection#setLineStyle(int)
 */
public ConnectionCreateCommand(Shape source, int lineStyle) {
    if (source == null) {
        throw new IllegalArgumentException();
    }
    setLabel("connection creation");
    this.source = source;
    this.lineStyle = lineStyle;
}

public boolean canExecute() {
    // Disallow source -> source connections
    if (source.equals(target)) {
        return false;
    }
    // Return false, if the source -> target connection exists already
    for (Iterator iter = source.getSourceConnections().iterator(); iter
            .hasNext();) {
        Connection conn = (Connection) iter.next();
        if (conn.getTarget().equals(target)) {
            return false;
        }
    }
    return true;
}

public void execute() {
    // Create a new connection between source and target
    connection = new Connection(source, target);
    // Use the supplied line style
    connection.setLineStyle(lineStyle);
}

public void redo() {
    connection.reconnect();
}
```

```
/**
 * Set the target endpoint for the connection.
 *
 * @param target
 *             that target endpoint (a non-null Shape instance)
 * @throws IllegalArgumentException
 *             if target is null
 */
public void setTarget(Shape target) {
    if (target == null) {
        throw new IllegalArgumentException();
    }
    this.target = target;
}

public void undo() {
    connection.disconnect();
}
}
```

To use the command in Listing 7-4 properly, the following steps are necessary:

1. Create a subclass of `GraphicalNodeEditPolicy`.

2. Override the `getConnectionCreateCommand()` method to create a new instance of this class and put it into the `CreateConnectionRequest`.

3. Override the `getConnectionCompleteCommand()` method to obtain the command from the `ConnectionRequest`, call `setTarget()` to set the target endpoint of the connection, and return this command instance.

Adding a Palette

GEF provides a selection tool and a palette for your custom figures (EditParts). The selection tool is the primary tool used in GEF and is often the default for an application. Ironically, the selection tool doesn't select EditParts, but rather delegates drag events to a class called `DragTracker`. All mouse clicks are handled as drags.

The palette is an SWT control that allows the user to select which tool is active. It can also be a drag source for dragging objects from the palette directly into the diagram. The palette can be placed anywhere, including inside the editor. GEF provides a workbench view for hosting the palette.

Tip The palette provides several display modes, such as icon-only. You can also provide a customizer to allow the user to modify or create palette content. For more information about this topic, see the GEF Tools and Palette Guide at `http://help.eclipse.org/stable/index.jsp?topic=/org.eclipse.draw2d.doc.isv/guide/guide.html`.

Listing 7-5 creates a GEF palette with a shapes drawer. A drawer is a container for tools that perform a common function. In this case, we have a drawer for an elliptical and rectangular shapes, as shown in Figure 7-5.

Listing 7-5. *Palette for the Shapes Model*

```
final class ShapesEditorPaletteFactory {

    /** Create the "Shapes" drawer. */
    private static PaletteContainer createShapesDrawer() {
        // Shapes drawer
        PaletteDrawer componentsDrawer = new PaletteDrawer("Shapes");

        // Add elliptical shape to the drawer
        CombinedTemplateCreationEntry component =
            new CombinedTemplateCreationEntry(
                "Ellipse", "Create an elliptical shape",
                EllipticalShape.class, new SimpleFactory(
                        EllipticalShape.class), ImageDescriptor
                    .createFromFile(ShapesPlugin.class,
                            "icons/ellipse16.gif"), ImageDescriptor
                    .createFromFile(ShapesPlugin.class,
                            "icons/ellipse24.gif"));
        componentsDrawer.add(component);

        // Add rectangular shape
        component = new CombinedTemplateCreationEntry("Rectangle",
                "Create a rectangular shape", RectangularShape.class,
                new SimpleFactory(RectangularShape.class), ImageDescriptor
                    .createFromFile(ShapesPlugin.class,
                            "icons/rectangle16.gif"), ImageDescriptor
                    .createFromFile(ShapesPlugin.class,
                            "icons/rectangle24.gif"));
        componentsDrawer.add(component);

        return componentsDrawer;
    }

    /**
     * Creates the PaletteRoot and adds all palette elements. Use this
     * factory method to create a new palette for your graphical editor.
     */
    static PaletteRoot createPalette() {
        PaletteRoot palette = new PaletteRoot();
        palette.add(createToolsGroup(palette));
        palette.add(createShapesDrawer());
        return palette;
    }
```

```java
/** Create the "Tools" group. */
private static PaletteContainer createToolsGroup(PaletteRoot palette) {
    PaletteToolbar toolbar = new PaletteToolbar("Tools");

    // Add a selection tool to the group
    ToolEntry tool = new PanningSelectionToolEntry();
    toolbar.add(tool);
    palette.setDefaultEntry(tool);

    // Add a marquee tool to the group
    toolbar.add(new MarqueeToolEntry());

    // Add (solid-line) connection tool
    tool = new ConnectionCreationToolEntry("Solid connection",
            "Create a solid-line connection", new CreationFactory() {
                public Object getNewObject() {
                    return null;
                }

                // See ShapeEditPart#createEditPolicies()
                // This is used to transmit the desired line style
                public Object getObjectType() {
                    return Connection.SOLID_CONNECTION;
                }
            }, ImageDescriptor.createFromFile(ShapesPlugin.class,
                    "icons/connection_s16.gif"), ImageDescriptor
                    .createFromFile(ShapesPlugin.class,
                            "icons/connection_s24.gif"));
    toolbar.add(tool);

    // Add (dashed-line) connection tool
    tool = new ConnectionCreationToolEntry("Dashed connection",
            "Create a dashed-line connection", new CreationFactory() {
                public Object getNewObject() {
                    return null;
                }

                // See ShapeEditPart#createEditPolicies()
                // This is used to transmit the desired line style
                public Object getObjectType() {
                    return Connection.DASHED_CONNECTION;
                }
            }, ImageDescriptor.createFromFile(ShapesPlugin.class,
                    "icons/connection_d16.gif"), ImageDescriptor
                    .createFromFile(ShapesPlugin.class,
                            "icons/connection_d24.gif"));
    toolbar.add(tool);
```

```
        return toolbar;
    }

    /** Utility class. */
    private ShapesEditorPaletteFactory() {
    }
}
```

Figure 7-5. *Shapes palette*

The createPalette() method creates a new palette (with all palette elements) for your graphical editor. The class also creates the tools group with solid and dashed connections.

Note Check out the Eclipse GEF Project page at http://www.eclipse.org/gef/overview.html for more examples and tips on using GEF.

Using Zest

Zest is a visualization toolkit for Eclipse,[2] designed to facilitate graph-based programming. It provides the following benefits:

- Zest was developed using SWT/Draw2d, and it integrates seamlessly within Eclipse.

- Graphs in Zest are SWT components that have been wrapped using JFace viewers. This allows developers to use Zest the same way they use JFace tables, trees, and lists.

---

2. The Zest visualization toolkit is available online at http://www.eclipse.org/gef/zest/.

- Zest integrates well with Eclipse views. This means that providers, actions, and listeners used within existing applications can be leveraged within Zest.

- Zest includes an independent graph layout package that can be used within existing Java applications (SWT or AWT).

Zest Components

Zest has the following basic components:

- Graph: Extends FigureCanvas (a canvas that contains figures) and holds the nodes and connections for the graph.

- GraphNode: Simple node class that has properties such as color, size, location, and a label. It also has a list of connections and anchors.

- GraphConnection: The graph connection model that stores the source and destination nodes and the properties of this connection (color, line width, and so on).

Listing 7-6 shows an example of using these Zest components to display a hierarchical tree graph. The result is shown in Figure 7-6.

Listing 7-6. *Sample Tree Graph Using Zest*

```
public class TreeGraph {

    /**
     * @param args
     */
    public static void main(String[] args) {
        Display display = new Display();

        Image imgInfo = Display.getDefault().getSystemImage(
                SWT.ICON_INFORMATION);

        Shell shell = new Shell(display);
        shell.setText("Tree Graph");

        shell.setLayout(new FillLayout());
        shell.setSize(400, 400);

        final Graph graph = new Graph(shell, SWT.NONE);

        GraphNode a = new GraphNode(graph, SWT.NONE, "Root", imgInfo);
        GraphNode b = new GraphNode(graph, SWT.NONE, "B");
        GraphNode c = new GraphNode(graph, SWT.NONE, "C");
        GraphNode d = new GraphNode(graph, SWT.NONE, "D");
        // Code removed for simplicity...
```

```
GraphConnection connection = new GraphConnection(graph, SWT.NONE,
        a, b);
connection.setData(Boolean.FALSE);

connection = new GraphConnection(graph, SWT.NONE, a, c);
connection.setData(Boolean.FALSE);

connection = new GraphConnection(graph, SWT.NONE, a, d);
connection.setData(Boolean.FALSE);

connection = new GraphConnection(graph, SWT.NONE, b, e);
connection.setData(Boolean.FALSE);

// Code removed for simplicity...

connection = new GraphConnection(graph,
        ZestStyles.CONNECTIONS_DIRECTED, b, c);
connection.setLineColor(ColorConstants.red);
connection.setLineWidth(3);

connection = new GraphConnection(graph,
        ZestStyles.CONNECTIONS_DIRECTED, c, d);
connection.setLineColor(ColorConstants.red);
connection.setLineWidth(3);


TreeLayoutAlgorithm treeLayoutAlgorithm = new TreeLayoutAlgorithm(
        LayoutStyles.NO_LAYOUT_NODE_RESIZING);
Filter filter = new Filter() {
    public boolean isObjectFiltered(LayoutItem item) {

        // Get the "Connection" from the Layout Item
        // and use this connection to get the "Graph Data"
        Object object = item.getGraphData();
        if (object instanceof GraphConnection) {
            GraphConnection connection = (GraphConnection) object;
            if (connection.getData() != null
                    && connection.getData() instanceof Boolean) {
                // If the data is false, don't filter, otherwise,
                // filter.
                return ((Boolean) connection.getData())
                        .booleanValue();
            }
            return true;
        }
        return false;
    }
```

```
    };
    treeLayoutAlgorithm.setFilter(filter);
    graph.setLayoutAlgorithm(treeLayoutAlgorithm, true);

    shell.open();
    while (!shell.isDisposed()) {
        while (!display.readAndDispatch()) {
            display.sleep();
        }
    }
  }
}
```

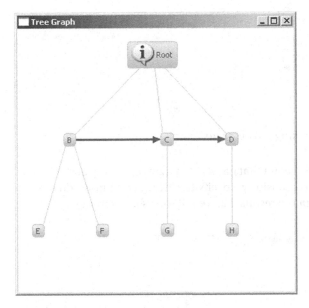

Figure 7-6. *Tree graph from Listing 7-6*

Zest Layouts

Zest lays out objects using an AbstractLayoutAlgorithm, which handles common elements in all layout algorithms. The following are some of the most interesting layouts:

- TreeLayoutAlgorithm: Arranges graph nodes in a layered vertical tree-like layout (see Figure 7-6).

- GridLayoutAlgorithm: Arranges graph nodes in a column/row-based grid (see Figure 7-7).

- HorizontalTreeLayoutAlgorithm: Arranges graph nodes in a layered horizontal tree-like layout.

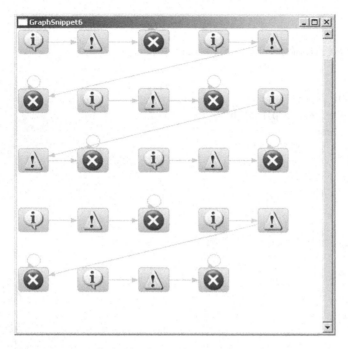

Figure 7-7. *Graph displaying nodes using a grid layout*

- SpringLayoutAlgorithm: A complex layout that has its own data repository and relation repository. A user can populate the repository, specify the layout conditions, do the computation, and query the computed results. Figure 7-8 shows an example.

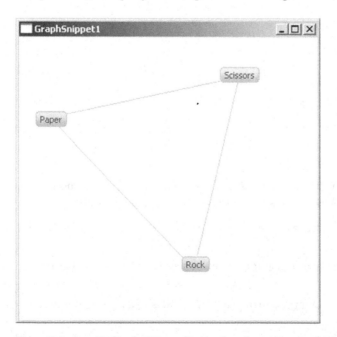

Figure 7-8. *Graph displaying undirected nodes using the Spring layout*

Note The `SpringLayoutAlgorithm` has no relationship to the Spring Framework.

Using the `SpringLayoutAlgorithm` involves the following steps:

1. Instantiate a `SpringLayout` object.

2. Populate the data repository using `addEntity()`.

3. Populate the relation repository using `addRelationship()`.

4. Execute `compute()`.

5. Execute `fitWithinBounds()`.

6. Query the computed results (node size and node position).

Tip The layout should be chosen based on the requirements of your graph. Some applications may need to display objects in a grid or tree. Complex layouts like the `SpringLayout` are useful for visualizing undirected networks.

Hands-on Exercise: Build Your Own Advanced 2D Graphics Editor

The goal of this exercise is to build an advanced graphics editor using some GEF examples provided by Eclipse, plus some brand-new Zest code. The editor will be capable of creating four types of 2D graphs:

- An electronics logic diagram, complete with flow containers, gates, circuits, connectors, and other parts

- A shapes diagram, with rectangular and elliptical shapes plus a palette

- An activity flow diagram, with sequential or parallel activities and a palette

- A Zest hierarchical tree diagram, with nodes, icons, and connectors

Each graph type may be saved into a file. The application will also feature a wizard to create graphs and a navigator to browse or create projects or graph files. The graph files may be saved on disk for later use.

This exercise will use the following extension points:

- `org.eclipse.core.runtime.products`: Defines the plug-in product.

- `org.eclipse.core.runtime.applications`: Defines the main entry point for the platform runtime.

- `org.eclipse.ui.perspectives`: Defines a default workbench perspective.

- `org.eclipse.ui.views`: Defines workbench views (visual components) for the work-bench.

- `org.eclipse.ui.navigator.viewer`: Defines the configuration for a project and diagram common viewer.

- `org.eclipse.ui.newWizards`: Defines custom wizards for all graph types.

The application will use a project navigator view, which includes a custom pop-up menu to add projects and open wizards.

Additionally, the example will use the following plug-ins:

- `org.eclipse.gef.examples.flow`: GEF example plug-in for creating flow diagrams.

- `org.eclipse.gef.examples.logic`: GEF example plug-in for creating logic diagrams.

- `org.eclipse.gef.examples.shapes`: GEF example plug-in for creating shape (ellipse and rectangle) diagrams.

- `org.eclipse.zest.examples`: Custom plug-in to create a tree or icon graph.

Creating the RCP Product

The first task is to create an RCP product to host the GEF and Zest plug-ins.

1. From the Eclipse IDE main menu, select File ➤ New ➤ Project ➤ Plug-in Project. Name the new plug-in project `GraphEditor`.

2. On the Plug-in Content page, make sure the "This plug-in will make contributions to the UI" option is checked, and the "Would you like to create a rich client application?" option is set to Yes. Click Next.

3. On the Templates page, select the Hello RCP template, and then click Next.

4. Check Add branding, and then click Finish.

5. Right-click the plug-in project and select New ➤ Other.

6. Select Product Configuration under Plug-in Development. Click Next.

7. Enter a product file name. Make sure `GraphEditor.product` is selected under "Initialize the file content." Click Finish.

8. Test the application from the product editor by clicking Synchronize, then Launch Eclipse application.

Downloading GEF Samples from the Eclipse Repository

Now you need some plug-ins for your graph editor. The fastest way to get things going is to download the GEF samples from the Eclipse CVS repository. These examples provide an excellent starting point for understanding GEF's capabilities and building your own graphics editors.

1. Open the CVS Repositories view. To do this, select Window ➤ Show View ➤ Other, type CVS in the text box, and select CVS Repositories, as shown in Figure 7-9. Then click OK.

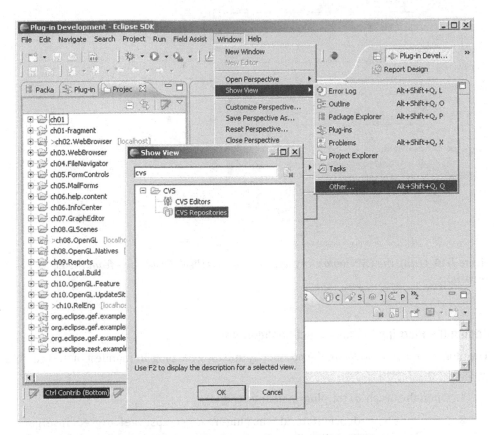

Figure 7-9. *Accessing the CVS Repositories view from the Eclipse IDE*

2. Add a new repository by right-clicking the view and selecting New ➤ Repository Location.

3. For the CVS repository host, enter dev.eclipse.org. For the path, enter /cvsroot/tools. For the user, enter anonymous, as shown in Figure 7-10. Check Save password, and then click Finish.

4. Under org.eclipse.gef/examples, check out the projects org.eclipse.gef.examples. flow, org.eclipse.gef.examples.logic, and org.eclipse.gef.examples.shapes.

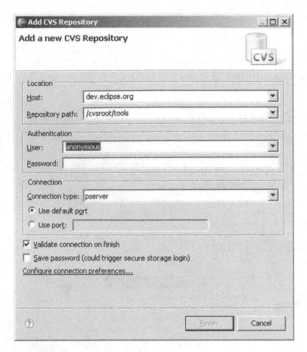

Figure 7-10. *Using the CVS Repository wizard to access the GEF samples from the Eclipse tools repository*

Adding the Plug-ins to the Product Configuration

The plug-ins must be added to the product by updating the plug-in manifest of the `GraphEditor` project.

1. Open the `GraphEditor` plug-in manifest editor.

2. From the Dependencies tab, add the plug-ins `orgeclipse.gef`, `org.eclipse.gef.examples.flow`, `org.eclipse.gef.examples.logic`, and `org.eclipse.gef.examples.shapes`.

3. Add a Common Navigator extension point to create graph editor projects or open the graph wizards provided by the plug-ins. Listing 7-7 shows this extension point.

Listing 7-7. *Extension Points for the Eclipse Common Navigator View (in plugin.xml)*

```
<extension
        point="org.eclipse.ui.views">
    <view
        class="org.eclipse.ui.navigator.CommonNavigator"
        icon="icons/alt_window_16.gif"
        id="eclipse.navigator.view"
        name="Project Navigator">
    </view>
</extension>
```

```
<extension
        point="org.eclipse.ui.navigator.viewer">
    <viewerActionBinding
        viewerId="eclipse.navigator.view">
      <includes>
          <actionExtension pattern="org.eclipse.ui.navigator.resources.*" />
      </includes>
    </viewerActionBinding>
    <viewerContentBinding
        viewerId="eclipse.navigator.view">
      <includes>
        <contentExtension pattern="org.eclipse.ui.navigator.resourceContent" />
        <contentExtension
            pattern="org.eclipse.ui.navigator.resources.filters.*"/>
        <contentExtension
            pattern="org.eclipse.ui.navigator.resources.linkHelper"/>
        <contentExtension \
            pattern="org.eclipse.ui.navigator.resources.workingSets"/>
      </includes>
    </viewerContentBinding>
</extension>
```

4. Add org.eclipse.ui.navigator and org.eclipse.ui.navigator.resources to the Dependencies tab. These are required for the Common Navigator view to display properly.

Creating a Default Perspective

The last thing you need to do before testing the GEF samples is to create a default perspective. The perspective will show the Common Navigator and the palette views, which are needed when working with graphs. Listing 7-8 shows this perspective.

Listing 7-8. *Default Perspective for the GEF Samples Project*

```
public class Perspective implements IPerspectiveFactory {

    public void createInitialLayout(IPageLayout layout) {
        String editorArea = layout.getEditorArea();
        layout.setEditorAreaVisible(false);

        IFolderLayout topLeft = layout.createFolder("topLeft",
                IPageLayout.LEFT, 0.5f, editorArea);
        topLeft.addView("eclipse.navigator.view");

        IFolderLayout botLeft = layout.createFolder("bottomLeft",
                IPageLayout.BOTTOM, 0.5f, "topLeft");
        botLeft.addView(PaletteView.ID);

    }
}
```

Testing the Product

Open the product configuration file and click Synchronize, then Launch Eclipse application. Your RCP Graph Editor window should look similar to Figure 7-1.

To create a graph, right-click in the project navigator and select New ➤ Other. You should see a list of examples defined by the plug-ins, as shown in Figure 7-11. Select a graph type, and then click Finish.

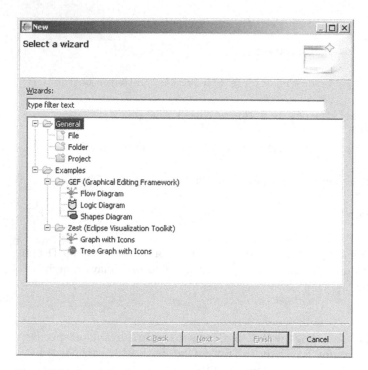

Figure 7-11. *Sample plug-in wizard pages*

Building a Zest Plug-in

You are making good progress so far. You have a product with some graph editors, but let's go further and build a Zest sample plug-in with some graphs.

Create a new plug-in project with the ID org.eclipse.zest.examples. Make sure the "This plug-in will make contributions to the UI" is checked and "Would you like to create a rich client application?" is set to No.

The plug-in will define two graph-creation wizards and their corresponding views, as shown in Listing 7-9.

Listing 7-9. *Extension Points for the Graph Wizards and Views*

```
<?xml version="1.0" encoding="UTF-8"?>
<?eclipse version="3.2"?>
<plugin>
    <extension
```

```
            point="org.eclipse.ui.newWizards">
        <category
            name="Zest (Eclipse Visualization Toolkit)"
            parentCategory="org.eclipse.ui.Examples"
            id="org.eclipse.zest.examples">
        </category>
        <wizard
            canFinishEarly="true"
            category="org.eclipse.ui.Examples/org.eclipse.zest.examples"
            class="org.eclipse.zest.examples.ui.GraphCreationWizard"
            hasPages="false"
            icon="view.gif"
            id="org.eclipse.gef.examples.flow.wizard.new.file"
            name="Graph with Icons">
        </wizard>
        <wizard
            canFinishEarly="true"
            category="org.eclipse.ui.Examples/org.eclipse.zest.examples"
            class="org.eclipse.zest.examples.ui.TreeGraphCreationWizard"
            hasPages="false"
            icon="icons/sample.gif"
            id="org.eclipse.gef.examples.flow.wizard.new.file"
            name="Tree Graph with Icons">
        </wizard>

    </extension>
    <extension
            point="org.eclipse.ui.views">
        <category
            id="org.eclipse.zest.examples"
            name="Zest">
        </category>
        <view
            allowMultiple="true"
            category="org.eclipse.zest.examples"
            class="org.eclipse.zest.examples.views.Graph1View"
            icon="view.gif"
            id="org.eclipse.zest.examples.views.Graph1View"
            name="Zest Graph with Icons">
        </view>
        <view
            allowMultiple="true"
            category="org.eclipse.zest.examples"
            class="org.eclipse.zest.examples.views.TreeGraphView"
            icon="icons/sample.gif"
            id="org.eclipse.zest.examples.views.TreeGraphView"
            name="Tree Graph with Icons"
```

```
            restorable="true">
      </view>
   </extension>
</plugin>
```

Listing 7-9 defines two wizards, Graph with Icons and Tree Graph with Icons, with their corresponding views, Graph1View and TreeGraphView. Each wizard node points to a graph-creation class, which in turn shows the corresponding view, as shown in Listing 7-10.

Listing 7-10. *Wizard Class to Create a Tree Graph*

```
public class TreeGraphCreationWizard extends Wizard implements INewWizard {

    private static int fileCount = 1;
    private IWorkbench workbench;

    public void init(IWorkbench workbench, IStructuredSelection selection) {
        this.workbench = workbench;
    }

    @Override
    public boolean canFinish() {
        return true;
    }

    @Override
    public boolean performFinish() {
        // Create a new file, result != null if successful
        fileCount++;

        // Open newly created file in the editor
        IWorkbenchPage page = workbench.getActiveWorkbenchWindow()
                .getActivePage();
        try {
            page.showView(TreeGraphView.ID, "treeView" + fileCount,
                    IWorkbenchPage.VIEW_CREATE);

        } catch (PartInitException e) {
            e.printStackTrace();
            return false;
        }
        return true;
    }
}
```

Listing 7-10 creates multiple instances of TreeGraphView, which in turn displays the graph in the workbench by making this call:

```
showView(TreeGraphView.ID, "treeView" + fileCount, IWorkbenchPage.VIEW_CREATE)
```

The class TreeGraphView, which draws the actual tree graph, is shown in Listing 7-11.

Listing 7-11. *View to Display the Tree Graph*

```
public class TreeGraphView extends ViewPart {
    public static final String ID = TreeGraphView.class.getName();

    public TreeGraphView() {
        // TODO Auto-generated constructor stub
    }

    @Override
    public void createPartControl(Composite parent) {
        Image imgInfo = Display.getDefault().getSystemImage(
                SWT.ICON_INFORMATION);

        parent.setLayout(new FillLayout());

        Graph graph = new Graph(parent, SWT.NONE);
        graph.setConnectionStyle(ZestStyles.CONNECTIONS_DIRECTED);

        GraphNode a = new GraphNode(graph, SWT.NONE, "Root", imgInfo);
        GraphNode b = new GraphNode(graph, SWT.NONE, "B");
        GraphNode c = new GraphNode(graph, SWT.NONE, "C");
        GraphNode d = new GraphNode(graph, SWT.NONE, "D");
        GraphNode e = new GraphNode(graph, SWT.NONE, "E");
        GraphNode f = new GraphNode(graph, SWT.NONE, "F");
        GraphNode g = new GraphNode(graph, SWT.NONE, "G");
        GraphNode h = new GraphNode(graph, SWT.NONE, "H");

        GraphConnection connection = new GraphConnection(graph, SWT.NONE,
                a, b);
        connection.setData(Boolean.FALSE);

        connection = new GraphConnection(graph, SWT.NONE, a, c);
        connection.setData(Boolean.FALSE);

        connection = new GraphConnection(graph, SWT.NONE, a, c);
        connection.setData(Boolean.FALSE);

        connection = new GraphConnection(graph, SWT.NONE, a, d);
        connection.setData(Boolean.FALSE);

        connection = new GraphConnection(graph, SWT.NONE, b, e);
        connection.setData(Boolean.FALSE);

        connection = new GraphConnection(graph, SWT.NONE, b, f);
        connection.setData(Boolean.FALSE);
```

```
        TreeLayoutAlgorithm treeLayoutAlgorithm = new TreeLayoutAlgorithm(
                LayoutStyles.NO_LAYOUT_NODE_RESIZING);
        Filter filter = new Filter() {
            public boolean isObjectFiltered(LayoutItem item) {

                // Get the "Connection" from the Layout Item
                // and use this connection to get the "Graph Data"
                Object object = item.getGraphData();
                if (object instanceof GraphConnection) {
                    GraphConnection connection = (GraphConnection) object;
                    if (connection.getData() != null
                            && connection.getData() instanceof Boolean) {
                        // If the data is false, don't filter; otherwise,
                        // filter.
                        return ((Boolean) connection.getData())
                                .booleanValue();
                    }
                    return true;
                }
                return false;
            }

        };
        treeLayoutAlgorithm.setFilter(filter);
        graph.setLayoutAlgorithm(treeLayoutAlgorithm, true);

    }

    @Override
    public void setFocus() {
    }

}
```

Listing 7-11 starts by setting a fill layout of the parent widget:

```
parent.setLayout(new FillLayout())
```

Next, a Graph object (to host the actual graph) is created:

```
Graph graph = new Graph(parent, SWT.NONE)
```

The Graph object allows you to set many graph properties, such as the connection style.

■**Tip** To inspect all methods available in the Graph class within the Eclipse IDE, simply place the cursor in the Graph class and press F3 to open its source code.

Now, it is simply a matter of adding nodes to the tree, with a call such as the following:

```
GraphNode Node1 = new GraphNode(graph, SWT.NONE, "Root")
```

If the nodes are to be connected, then each connection must be created, as follows:

```
GraphConnection connection = new GraphConnection(graph, SWT.NONE, Node1, Node2)
```

Note that a graph, a source, and target nodes are required for each connection. Finally, lay out the graph in a tree mode:

```
graph.setLayoutAlgorithm(
        new TreeLayoutAlgorithm(LayoutStyles.NO_LAYOUT_NODE_RESIZING)
        , true)
```

The layout constant NO_LAYOUT_NODE_RESIZING indicates that the layout algorithm should not resize any of the nodes. The TreeLayoutAlgorithm class arranges graph nodes in a layered, vertical tree-like layout. Note that Listing 7-11 uses a filter to separate nodes from connections:

```
connection = new GraphConnection(graph, SWT.NONE, a, c);
connection.setData(Boolean.FALSE);
...

Filter filter = new Filter() {

    public boolean isObjectFiltered(LayoutItem item) {

        // Get the "Connection" from the Layout Item
        // and use this connection to get the "Graph Data"
        Object object = item.getGraphData();

        // If a connection is detected
        if (object instanceof GraphConnection) {
            GraphConnection connection = (GraphConnection) object;

            if (connection.getData() != null
                    && connection.getData() instanceof Boolean) {
                // If the data is false, don't filter, otherwise,
                // filter.
                return ((Boolean) connection.getData())
                        .booleanValue();
            }
            return true;
        }
        return false;
    }
};

treeLayoutAlgorithm.setFilter(filter);
```

Once the filter is implemented, interested parties can ask this filter whether a specific object is filtered, with this callback:

```
public boolean isObjectFiltered(LayoutItem item)
```

For example, in a visualization tool, only unfiltered objects should be displayed. Before displaying an object, the display can ask this filter if the object is filtered. In this case, removing the filter will line up all the nodes vertically in the same line (the default behavior), as opposed to aligning them in a neat, evenly spaced tree style.

Testing the Final Product

At this point, you should have a graph editor with some neat GEF and Zest functionality. Before testing the final product, do the following:

1. Open the Graph Editor product file (`GraphEditor.product`). Click the Configuration tab and check "Include optional dependencies . . . ." Click the Add button and enter the name of the recently created Zest plug-in (`org.eclipse.zest.examples`). Then click Add Required Plug-ins. This will ensure all dependencies are included.

2. Click the Overview tab of the product editor. Click Synchronize to refresh the changes, and then click Launch an Eclipse application.

Run the product and test the different graph types and wizards. The final application is shown in Figure 7-12.

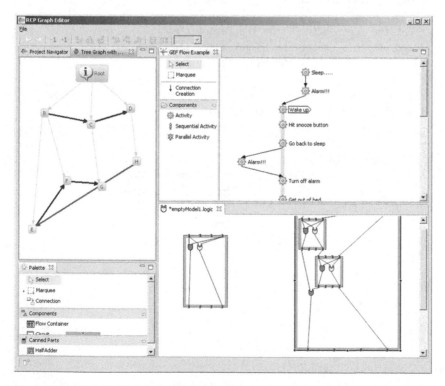

Figure 7-12. *Final RCP Graph Editor product*

Summary

This chapter covered creating 2D graphics with Eclipse GEF. Here are the main points:

- Draw2d is a set of lightweight Java objects called *figures*, which are painted using the SWT GC.

- Draw2d uses a deferred layout strategy integrated with native painting to determine the locations of figures in a drawing.

- Hit testing is the process of finding a figure in a mouse location (for example, dragging a figure on the canvas) and is done in exactly the same way as painting.

- Connections are used to display a line between two points. The source and target endpoints of a connection are each defined using a ConnectionAnchor. A connection always has a router that sets at least two points on the connection: the source and target.

- Coordinate systems are used by certain optimizations and features provided by Draw2d (usually when translating or zooming graphics). Coordinate systems can be absolute or relative (local).

  - In an absolute coordinate system, all figures paint in the same coordinates. Use an absolute coordinate system when determining the bounds of a parent based on the bounds of the children.

  - In a relative coordinate system, the bounds of children are relative to the client area of their parent. When a figure is moved, the children come along automatically, without any changes to their bounds. Use a relative coordinate system when translating or moving a figure and the figure's bounds must be updated.

- GEF is a powerful framework designed for building rich GUIs using native 2D graphics (Draw2d). It is application-neutral and provides the foundation for building many types of applications, such as activity diagrams, GUI builders, class diagram editors, state machines, and WYSIWYG editors.

- GEF is an MVC wrapper on top of Draw2d. GEF is extensible and uses MVC architecture to provide separation of the presentation and logic layers.

- GEF can be used anywhere where an SWT control can be used: an editor, a view, a wizard page, and so on. GEF requires the Eclipse RCP and the views plug-in (org.eclipse. ui.views), which provides property sheet support.

- GEF viewers are similar to JFace viewers in that they manage an SWT control.

- GEF graphical views use EditParts to piece the model and figures together. An EditPart performs the following functions:

  - Creates and maintains a view (figure or tree item) listening directly to the model object(s) with which it is associated

  - Creates and maintains children EditParts

  - Creates and maintains connection EditParts

  - Provides support for model editing

- Graphical views extend `AbstractGraphicalEditPart` and override the following methods based on each part's model:

  - `createFigure()`: This method creates the EditPart's view, or figure. This method does not reflect the model's state in the figure. That is done in `refreshVisuals()`.

  - `refreshVisuals()`: This method reflects model attributes in the view. Complex EditParts may further decompose this method into several helper methods.

  - `getModelChildren()`: This method is called to determine if there are model elements for which children EditParts should be created.

- EditParts can be content, children, and connection EditParts.

  - Content EditParts use an EditPartFactory for constructing the appropriate EditPart (content or connection).

  - Children EditParts display information to the user, such as figures or a composition of multiple figures.

  - Connection EditParts connect any two EditParts in a diagram.

- EditParts handle editing through EditPolicies and commands. EditPolicies allow for editing behavior to be reused across different implementations. Commands are used to encapsulate and combine changes to the application's model.

- Zest is a visualization toolkit for Eclipse. Its goal is to make graph-based programming easy.

- In Zest, graphs are considered SWT components that have been wrapped using standard JFace viewers. This allows developers to use Zest in the same way that they use JFace tables, trees, and lists.

- The main objects in Zest are `Graph`, `GraphNode`, and `GraphConnection`.

  - `Graph` extends `FigureCanvas` (a canvas that contains figures) and holds the nodes and connections for the graph.

  - `GraphNode` has properties such as color, size, location, and a label. It also has a list of connections and anchors.

  - `GraphConnection` stores the source and destination nodes and the properties of this connection such as color, line width, and so on.

- Zest lays out objects using an `AbstractLayoutAlgorithm`, which handles common elements. The most interesting layouts are `GridLayoutAlgorithm` (a column/row-based grid) `TreeLayoutAlgorithm` (a layered vertical tree), `HorizontalTreeLayoutAlgorithm` (a layered horizontal tree), and `SpringLayoutAlgorithm` (a complex layout with its own data repository and relation repository).

CHAPTER 8

■ ■ ■

3D Graphics for RCP with OpenGL

OpenGL is the de facto standard environment for developing portable, interactive 3D graphics applications. OpenGL has become one of the most widely used and supported 3D graphics APIs, bringing thousands of applications to a wide variety of computer platforms.

This chapter introduces OpenGL development for Eclipse, without going into much detail about the intricacies of OpenGL itself. The goal is to give you a taste of the power of OpenGL targeted to the RCP platform.

We will start with an overview of how RCP interacts with OpenGL. Then we'll move on to some scene development—first, a simple 3D scene to render basic shapes, and then a more complex scene that draws a 3D chart and demonstrates some advanced concepts. Finally, the exercise at the end of the chapter shows how easy it is to build a powerful 3D Earth navigator with Eclipse and OpenGL.

OpenGL and SWT

Before we dig into the 3D scenes, you should understand how RCP interacts with OpenGL. This interaction is done through SWT with two fundamental APIs:

A device-independent package: The org.eclipse.swt.opengl package provides platform-independent OpenGL support with two basic classes: GLCanvas and GLData. It also provides the integration between SWT applications and OpenGL graphics.

An OpenGL binding: This is the layer that implements the OpenGL specification and interacts with the machine hardware. The binding uses the Java Native Interface (JNI) to perform native calls, and it is in charge of accessing the hardware, such as the graphics card.

Let's take a closer look at the device-independent package and the OpenGL bindings that SWT supports.

The Device-Independent Package

The org.eclipse.swt.opengl package integrates SWT and OpenGL graphics by providing platform-independent OpenGL support through the following classes:

- org.eclipse.opengl.GLCanvas: A widget to display OpenGL content.

- org.eclipse.opengl.GLData: A device-independent description of the pixel format attributes of a GL drawable. A GL drawable is simply a 3D rendering surface. Pixel format attributes are a set of properties that define the OpenGL state in preparation for drawing. The most useful pixel attributes are listed in Table 8-1. For a complete list of attributes, see the org.eclipse.swt.opengl.GLData class reference.[1]

Table 8-1. *Some Pixel Attributes Used to Configure the OpenGL State*

Property	Description
boolean doubleBuffer	Specifies a double-buffered surface. Graphics operations that require multiple complex painting operations can cause the rendered images to appear to flicker or have an otherwise unacceptable appearance. Double-buffering uses a memory buffer to address the flicker problems associated with multiple paint operations. When double-buffering is enabled, all paint operations are first rendered to a memory buffer, instead of to the drawing surface on the screen. After all paint operations are completed, the memory buffer is copied directly to the drawing surface associated with it. Because only one graphics operation is performed on the screen, the image flickering is eliminated.
boolean stereo	Specifies a stereo surface. A stereo surface provides the visual perception of depth.
int redSize	Specifies the minimum number of bits per pixel to use for the red channel. The default value is 0. Red, green, and blue channels are used to describe the RGB color model with extra information, and have an effect on the color resolution.
int greenSize	Specifies the minimum number of bits per pixel to use for the green channel. The default value is 0.
int blueSize	Specifies the minimum number of bits per pixel to use for the blue channel. The default value is 0.
int alphaSize	Specifies the minimum number of bits per pixel to use for the alpha channel. The default value is 0. The alpha channel is useful for alpha compositing, which is the process of combining an image with a background to create the appearance of partial transparency.
int stencilSize	Specifies the desired number of stencil bit planes. A stencil buffer is used to limit the area of rendering (stenciling). In more advanced uses, the stencil buffer interacts with the depth buffer in the rendering pipeline to make a vast number of effects possible (shadows, outline drawing, and highlighting). The quintessential application of the stencil and depth buffers is to add shadows or planar reflections to 3D applications. Note that they often require several rendering passes, which can put a heavy load on the graphics hardware.

---

1. The GLData class reference is available from http://help.eclipse.org/stable/index.jsp?topic=/org.eclipse.platform.doc.isv/reference/api/org/eclipse/swt/opengl/GLData.html.

OpenGL Bindings for SWT

SWT 3.2 and later provide a thin layer above the window-system specific API (WGL for windows; GLX for Unix). This enables applications to use their Java OpenGL binding of choice. SWT supports three popular OpenGL bindings:

Lightweight Java Game Library (LWJGL): LWJGL is targeted to commercial games.[2] It provides access to the Open Audio Library (OpenAL) for state-of-the-art 3D games and sound.

Java OpenGL (JOGL): JOGL is a binding designed to provide hardware-supported access to the OpenGL 2.0 specification, as well as nearly all vendor extensions.[3] JOGL integrates with the Abstract Window Toolkit (AWT) and Swing widget sets. This becomes an issue when developing for SWT, but as you'll see in this chapter's hands-on exercise, SWT has created a clever solution.

gljava: gljava is specifically aimed at game development.[4] Its design goal is to be as simple and thin as possible. gljava does not force you to use a widget toolkit such as AWT or Swing.

All of the code in this chapter has been written for JOGL.

Creating OpenGL Scenes with JOGL and SWT

Now it's time to get our feet wet with two OpenGL scenes. First, we'll create the wire cubes scene, which simply draws three wire cubes (red, green, and blue) on top of a white rectangle. Then we'll create the more complex 3D chart scene, which draws a series of cylinders (bar values) over two planar axes (x and y). The scene uses some GL tricks (such as display lists) to increase performance, as well as a GL utility library to draw quadrics (cylinders). Both scenes allow for user interaction by using mouse and keyboard listeners for panning, zooming, and tilting. The scenes will be displayed within two RCP views.

The following classes will be created for the scenes:

- GLScene: This is the base class for both scenes and encapsulates common functionality. Its role is to bind a GL canvas with an SWT component for drawing. It also initializes the GL drawing attributes (pixel format attributes) and parent control listeners to resize or dispose of the canvas when the parent requests.

- CubeScene: This is the class that actually draws the wire cubes. It inherits from GLScene.

- ChartScene: This is the class that draws a 3D chart, and it also inherits from GLScene. It is more complex than CubeScene. This class uses OpenGL display lists for fast drawing of a series of cylinders (BarValue) and planar x and y axes.

The following utility classes will also be created:

- SceneGrip: This class is used to rotate and move the scene by using mouse and keyboard listeners.

- Refresher: This is a thread that renders the scene in the background many times per second. Its job is to refresh the scene whenever the user changes something.

---

2. LWJGL is available from http://lwjgl.org/index.php.
3. JOGL binding for OpenGL is available from https://jogl.dev.java.net/.
4. gljava is available from http://gljava.sourceforge.net/.

- GLUT: This is a simple helper class to draw a wire cube. It is used by CubeScene.

- CompiledShape: This class provides the OpenGL display lists used to increase performance whenever the same object must be rendered multiple times. It is used to draw the cylinders and axis planes from ChartScene.

- BarValue: This class represents a bar value (cylinder) in the chart. It extends CompiledShape for performance. It also uses the OpenGL Utility Library (GLU) to draw the cylinder shapes.

Setting Up for the OpenGL Scenes

Before we get started on the scenes, we need to do some setup. We will create an RCP application with two views, and add the JOGL dependencies.

Creating the RCP Application

Follow these steps to create the RCP application for the scenes:

1. From the main Eclipse menu, select File ➤ New ➤ Project ➤ Plug-in Development ➤ Plug-in Project, as shown in Figure 8-1. Click Next.

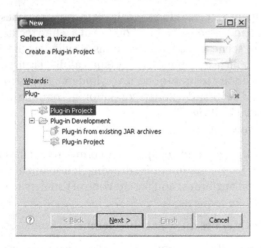

Figure 8-1. *Choosing to create a new plug-in project*

Tip Use the filter text box on the Select a Wizard page for fast access to the wizard. Simply type a few characters, such as "plug-."

---

2. Enter a project name (such as ch08.GLScenes), as shown in Figure 8-2. Click Next.

3. On the Plug-in Content page, make sure "This plug-in will make contributions to the UI" is selected and "Would you like to create a rich client application?" is set to Yes, as shown in Figure 8-3. Then click Next.

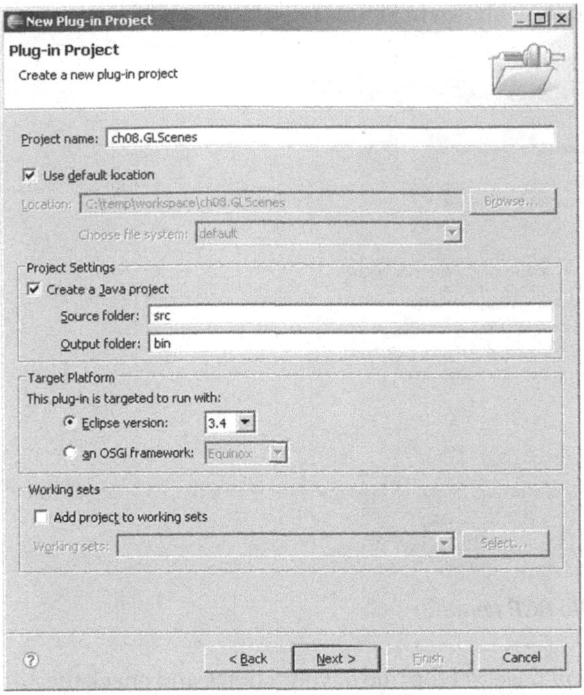

Figure 8-2. *Naming the new plug-in project*

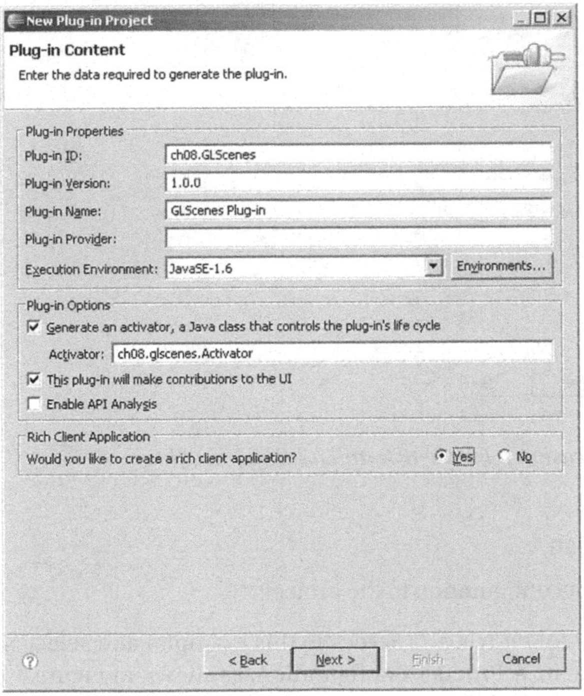

Figure 8-3. *Filling in the Plug-in Content page*

4. Select the Hello RCP template, as shown in Figure 8-4, and then click Next.

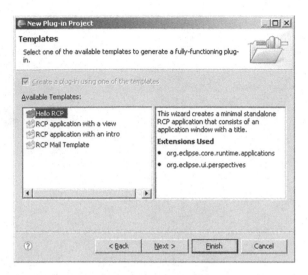

Figure 8-4. *Choosing the Hello RCP template*

5. On the Basic RCP Application page, set the title of your choice and check the Add branding option (this is required to create a product extension point), as shown in Figure 8-5. Click Finish.

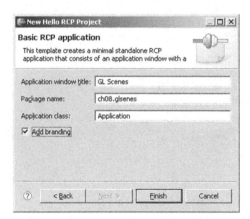

Figure 8-5. *Setting the application window title and adding branding*

Creating a Production Configuration

Follow these steps to add a product configuration to the project:

1. Right-click the new project folder (ch08.GLScenes in this example) and select New ➤ Other ➤ Plug-in Development ➤ Product Configuration, as shown in Figure 8-6. Click Next.

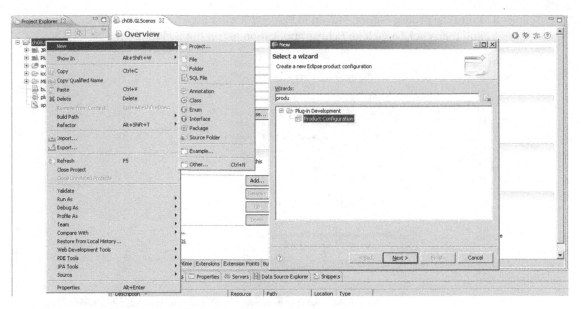

Figure 8-6. *Choosing to add a product configuration*

2. Enter a name for the product file (GLScenes.product in this example). Make sure the correct product is selected under "Use an existing product," as shown in Figure 8-7. Click Finish.

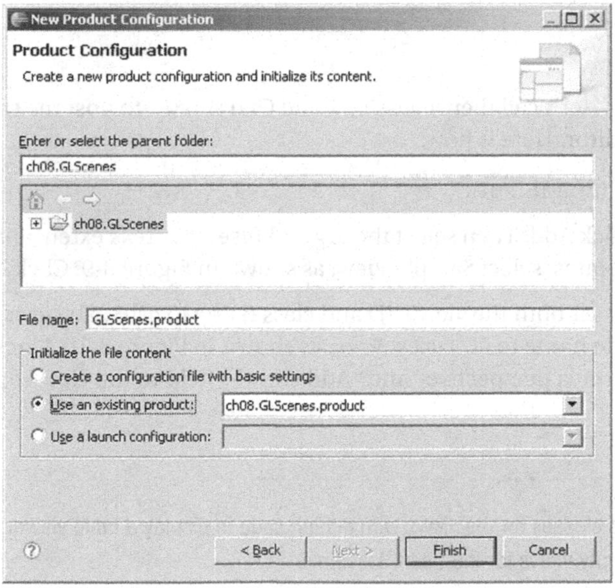

Figure 8-7. *Configuring a new product*

3. From the product editor, shown in Figure 8-8, click Synchronize to publish changes, and then click Launch an Eclipse application to test the skeleton.

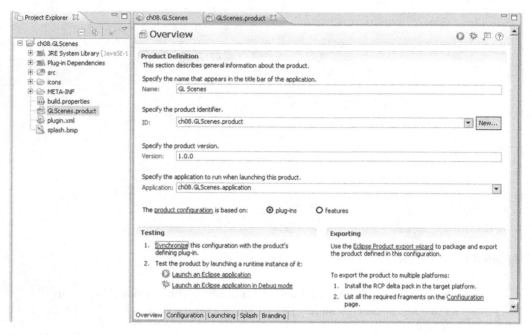

Figure 8-8. *The GLScenes product editor*

Creating the Views

You must also create two views—let's call them CubesView and ChartView—to host the scenes. This is easy using the plug-in editor. Here is how:

1. Open the plug-in editor (plugin.xml).

2. In the Extensions tab, click Add. Then select the org.eclipse.ui.views extension point. From the available templates, select Sample View, as shown in Figure 8-9. Click Next.

3. In the next wizard page, set both the view's ID and class name to ch08.glscenes. views.CubesView, and the name to GL Cubes View, as shown in Figure 8-10. Uncheck the "Add the view to the java perspective" and "Add context help to the view" options. Click Finish.

Note The wizard will create Java classes for the views with default code to display a table viewer. Make sure you remove this code to get empty views for the OpenGL scenes.

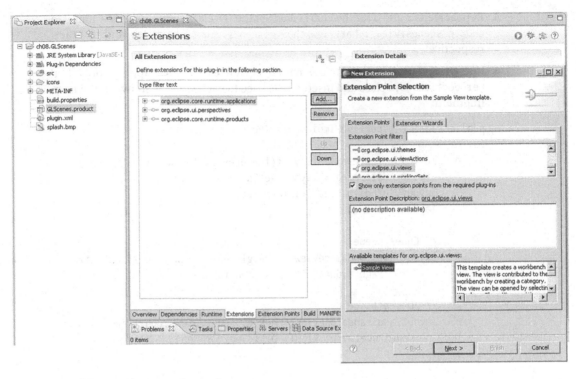

Figure 8-9. *Adding a view extension point*

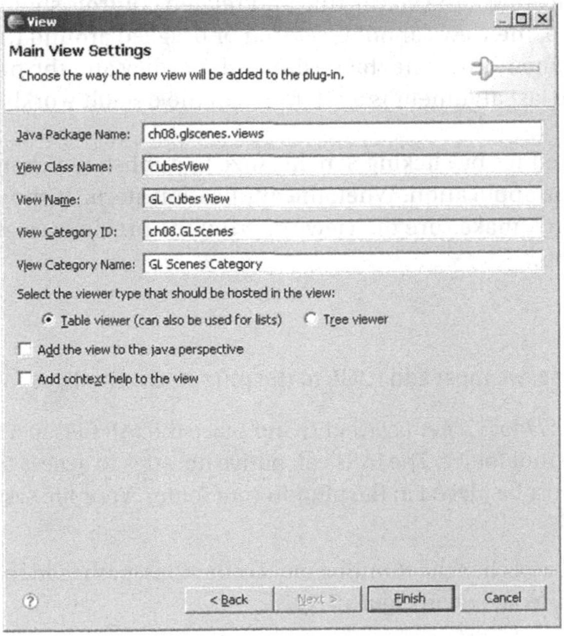

Figure 8-10. *Specifying the main view settings*

4. Repeat steps 2 and 3 for the chart view. Set the ID, class name, and view name to ch08.glscenes.views.ChartView, ch08.glscenes.views.ChartView, and 3D Chart, respectively.

5. Both views must be added to the main perspective of the RCP application. Edit the Perspective.java class and insert a reference to each view, as shown in the next fragment:

```
public class Perspective implements IPerspectiveFactory {

    public void createInitialLayout(IPageLayout layout) {
        String editorArea = layout.getEditorArea();
        layout.setEditorAreaVisible(false);
        layout.setFixed(true);

        // Cubes scene
        layout.addStandaloneView("ch08.glscenes.views.CubesView", true,
                IPageLayout.LEFT, 0.5f, editorArea);

        // 3D chart scene
        layout.addStandaloneView("ch08.glscenes.views.ChartView", true,
                IPageLayout.RIGHT, 0.5f, editorArea);
    }
}
```

This method hides the default editor area of the main window. It then adds both views. The first argument to addStandaloneView is the view's ID (as defined in steps 3 and 4). The second argument is a Boolean indicating if the view's title and related controls should be shown. If you set this value to false, the view cannot be closed or dragged around the main window. The third and fourth arguments indicate the position of the view and the percentage of real estate they use. The last argument is a reference to the default workbench editor.

Test the RCP from the plug-in editor by clicking Synchronize to publish the changes, and then clicking Launch an Eclipse application. When the application starts, it should display two empty views. If it doesn't, make sure the view IDs from the previous fragment match the IDs defined in plugin.xml.

Adding JOGL Dependencies

Before we start writing the scene code, we must add JOGL to the plug-in classpath, as follows:

1. Download JOGL (from https://jogl.dev.java.net/) and place the JAR files in a folder called lib within the plug-in root folder. The JARs call native libraries to access the graphics hardware, which must be placed in the plug-in root folder. Your file system should look like Figure 8-11.

2. Open the project plugin.xml and click the Runtime tab. Under Classpath, add the JOGL JARs to the plug-in classpath, as shown in Figure 8-12.

Figure 8-11. *GLScenes file system*

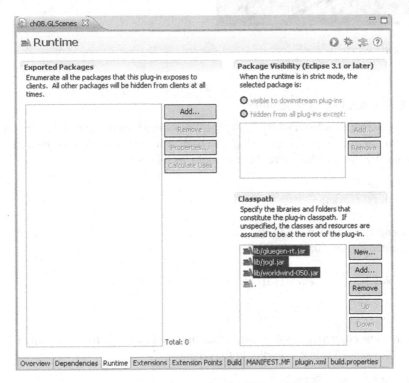

Figure 8-12. *Classpath dependencies for the GLScenes project*

Creating the Wire Cubes Scene

Our first example is the simple wire cubes scene shown in Figure 8-13. This requires a base class (GLScene), which encapsulates common behavior, and a child scene class (CubeScene), which draws the actual wire cubes.

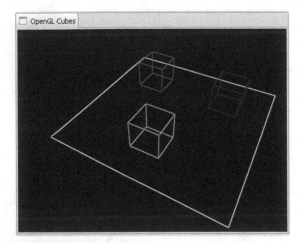

Figure 8-13. *Wire cubes scene*

Creating the Base Scene Class (GLScene)

GLScene is the base scene class from which both OpenGL scenes inherit. Its role is to encapsulate common behavior and to get things rolling with basic initialization. We first need to create a new scene owned by the specified parent component, as follows:

```
public class GLScene {
    private GLCanvas canvas;

    public GLScene(Composite parent) {
        GLData data = new GLData();
          ...
        this.canvas = new GLCanvas(parent, SWT.NO_BACKGROUND, data);
    }
}
```

Within the GLScene constructor, we first initialize the pixel format attributes of the GL drawable using GLData (see Table 8-1, earlier in the chapter).

```
        GLData data = new GLData();
        data.depthSize = 1;
        data.doubleBuffer = true;
```

Next, we add a listener to receive notifications when the control is resized or moved by using the GLCanvas addControlListener method:

```
this.canvas.addControlListener(new ControlAdapter() {
    public void controlResized(ControlEvent e) {
        resizeScene();
    }
});
```

We also add a listener to receive notifications when the control is disposed of, using the GLCanvas addDisposeListener method:

```
this.canvas.addDisposeListener(new DisposeListener() {
    public void widgetDisposed(DisposeEvent e) {
        dispose();
    }
});
```

Next, we initialize the scene by calling the methods initGLContext and initGL:

```
protected void initGLContext() {
    this.canvas.setCurrent(); // Activate the rendering context
    context = GLDrawableFactory.getFactory().createExternalGLContext();
}

protected void initGL() {
    GL gl = context.getGL ();
    // Black background
    gl.glClearColor(0.0f, 0.0f, 0.0f, 0.0f);
    gl.glClearDepth(1.0f);
    gl.glDepthFunc(GL.GL_LESS);

    // Enable depth test and shading model
    gl.glEnable(GL.GL_DEPTH_TEST);
    gl.glShadeModel(GL.GL_SMOOTH);
}
```

The initGLContext method creates a drawing context, GLContext, which is an abstraction for all drawing operations. It is the critical object that provides access to the entire OpenGL specification. To create a GLContext, we use GLDrawableFactory.getFactory.createExternalGLContext(), which provides a virtual machine and a mechanism for creating GL drawables that is independent of the operating system.

The initGL method initializes OpenGL. It is commonly used to set a background color and shading model.

Note that all OpenGL functions use the following naming convention:

<library><function name><number of arguments><type of arguments>

For example, the previous snippet includes the function to set the GL canvas background:

```
gl.glClearColor(0.0f, 0.0f, 0.0f, 0.0f);
```

Here, gl refers to an OpenGL function. OpenGL Utility Toolkit (GLUT) functions will be prefixed with glut, and GLU functions are prefixed with glu. The function name is ClearColor. Following the name are the number and types of arguments. The complete scene class is shown in Listing 8-1.

Listing 8-1. *OpenGL Scene Base Class*

```java
public class GLScene {

    private GLCanvas canvas;
    private GLContext context;

    /**
     * Creates a new scene owned by the specified parent component.
     */
    public GLScene(Composite parent) {
        GLData data = new GLData();
        data.depthSize = 1;
        data.doubleBuffer = true;
        this.canvas = new GLCanvas(parent, SWT.NO_BACKGROUND, data);

        this.canvas.addControlListener(new ControlAdapter() {
            public void controlResized(ControlEvent e) {
                resizeScene();
            }
        });
        this.canvas.addDisposeListener(new DisposeListener() {
            public void widgetDisposed(DisposeEvent e) {
                dispose();
            }
        });
        this.init();
        Rectangle clientArea = parent.getClientArea();
        this.canvas.setSize(clientArea.width, clientArea.height);
    }

    /**
     * Initializes this scene, by calling the initGLContext
     * and initGL methods.
     */
    protected void init() {
        this.initGLContext();
        this.initGL();
    }
```

```
/**
 * Disposes of the GLContext. This method is called when the canvas is
 * disposed.
 */
protected void dispose() {
}


/**
 * Returns whether or not this scene is disposed.
 */
public boolean isDisposed() {
    return this.canvas.isDisposed();
}


/**
 * Causes the receiver to have the keyboard focus.
 */
public boolean setFocus() {
    return this.canvas.setFocus();
}


/**
 * Provides direct access to this GLContext.
 */
public GLContext getGLContext() {
    return this.context;
}


/**
 * Returns the drawable used by the GLContext to render GL scenes.
 */
protected Canvas getCanvas() {
    return this.canvas;
}

public Display getDisplay() {
    return this.canvas.getDisplay();
}


/**
 * Renders the next scene.
 */
public void render() {
    if (!this.canvas.isCurrent()) {
        this.canvas.setCurrent();
    }
```

```
        this.drawScene();
        this.canvas.swapBuffers();
    }

    protected void initGLContext() {
        this.canvas.setCurrent(); // Activate the rendering context
        context = GLDrawableFactory.getFactory().createExternalGLContext();
    }

    /**
     * Initializes OpenGL by creating a context, setting background,
     * shading model, and such.
     */
    protected void initGL() {
        GL gl = context.getGL();
        gl.glClearColor(0.0f, 0.0f, 0.0f, 0.0f);
        gl.glClearDepth(1.0f);
        gl.glDepthFunc(GL.GL_LESS);
        gl.glEnable(GL.GL_DEPTH_TEST);
        gl.glShadeModel(GL.GL_SMOOTH);
        gl.glHint(GL.GL_PERSPECTIVE_CORRECTION_HINT, GL.GL_NICEST);
    }

    /**
     * Corrects the size of the GL scene.
     */
    protected void resizeScene() {
        Rectangle rect = this.canvas.getClientArea();
        context.makeCurrent();
        GL gl = context.getGL();

        gl.glViewport(0, 0, rect.width, rect.height);
        gl.glMatrixMode(GL.GL_PROJECTION);
        gl.glLoadIdentity();
        GLU glu = new GLU();
        glu.gluPerspective(45.0f,
                (float) rect.width / (float) rect.height, 0.1f, 100.0f);
        gl.glMatrixMode(GL.GL_MODELVIEW);
        gl.glLoadIdentity();

        context.release();
    }

    /**
     * Draws the GL scene. The default implementation clears the scene and
     * resets the view.
     */
```

```
    protected void drawScene() {
        GL gl = context.getGL();

        gl.glClear(GL.GL_COLOR_BUFFER_BIT | GL.GL_DEPTH_BUFFER_BIT);
        gl.glLoadIdentity();


    }
}
```

Creating the Wire Cubes Scene Class

Listing 8-2 shows the actual wire cube scene (CubeScene). This scene inherits from GLScene and overrides the method drawScene() to create three wire cubes (red, green, and blue) over a white line loop floor (see Figure 8-13). CubeScene also overrides initGL() to define a line type and blending operations.

Listing 8-2. *Wire Cube OpenGL Scene Class*

```
public class CubeScene extends GLScene {
    private SceneGrip grip;

    public CubeScene(Composite parent) {
        super(parent);

        this.grip = new SceneGrip(context);
        this.grip.setOffsets(0.0f, 0.0f, -15.0f);
        this.grip.setRotation(45.0f, -30.0f);

        // Listen for mouse and keyboard events
        this.getCanvas().addMouseListener(this.grip);
        this.getCanvas().addMouseMoveListener(this.grip);
        this.getCanvas().addListener(SWT.MouseWheel, this.grip);
        this.getCanvas().addKeyListener(this.grip);
    }

    protected void initGL() {
        super.initGL();
        context.makeCurrent();
        GL gl = context.getGL();

        // Specify implementation specific hints
        // GL_LINE_SMOOTH_HINT: Indicates the sampling quality of lines.
        // GL_NICEST: highest quality option.
        gl.glEnable(GL.GL_LINE_SMOOTH);
        gl.glHint(GL.GL_LINE_SMOOTH_HINT, GL.GL_NICEST);
        gl.glEnable(GL.GL_BLEND);
```

```
        // Define the operation of blending when it is enabled
        gl.glBlendFunc(GL.GL_SRC_ALPHA, GL.GL_ONE_MINUS_SRC_ALPHA);

        context.release();
    }

    protected void drawScene() {
        context.makeCurrent();
        GL gl = context.getGL();

        super.drawScene();
        this.grip.adjust();

        // Draw a white floor square
        gl.glColor3f(1.0f, 1.0f, 1.0f);

        gl.glBegin(GL.GL_LINE_LOOP);
        gl.glVertex3f(-6.0f, -1.0f, -9.0f);
        gl.glVertex3f(6.0f, -1.0f, -9.0f);
        gl.glVertex3f(6.0f, -1.0f, 3.0f);
        gl.glVertex3f(-6.0f, -1.0f, 3.0f);
        gl.glEnd();

        // Red wire cube
        gl.glTranslatef(-3.0f, 0.0f, -6.0f);
        gl.glColor3f(1.0f, 0.0f, 0.0f);
        GLUT.wireCube(gl, 2.0f);

        // Green wire cube
        gl.glTranslatef(3.0f, 0.0f, 6.0f);
        gl.glColor3f(0.0f, 1.0f, 0.0f);
        GLUT.wireCube(gl, 2.0f);

        // Blue wire cube
        gl.glTranslatef(3.0f, 0.0f, -6.0f);
        gl.glColor3f(0.0f, 0.0f, 1.0f);
        GLUT.wireCube(gl, 2.0f);

        context.release();
    }
}
```

Look at the constructor carefully. The first line initializes the base class GLScene, which in turn creates a GLCanvas (using the parent composite) and a GLContext. The helper class SceneGrip is used to move the scene around using the keyboard or mouse (see the "Rotating and Moving the Scene" section later in this chapter for details). Finally, listeners for the keyboard and mouse are added with SceneGrip.

To draw the actual wire cubes, the helper class GLUT.wireCube() uses a series of line loops to draw the front and back faces plus four connecting lines, as shown in Listing 8-3. (Note that GLUT.wireCube has nothing to do with the GL GLUT library; it simply defines a class with a similar name.)

Note GLUT is the OpenGL Utility Toolkit and provides support for: multiple windows for OpenGL rendering, callback-driven events, input devices, timers, and utility routines to generate various solid and wire frame objects. GLUT is not used in the sample scenes of this chapter.

Listing 8-3. *Helper Class to Draw a Wire Cube*

```java
public class GLUT {
    public static final void wireCube(GL gl, float size) {
        float neg = -0.5f * size;
        float pos = 0.5f * size;

        // Front face
        gl.glBegin(GL.GL_LINE_LOOP);
        gl.glVertex3f(neg, neg, neg);
        gl.glVertex3f(pos, neg, neg);
        gl.glVertex3f(pos, pos, neg);
        gl.glVertex3f(neg, pos, neg);
        gl.glEnd();

        // Back face
        gl.glBegin(GL.GL_LINE_LOOP);
        gl.glVertex3f(neg, neg, pos);
        gl.glVertex3f(pos, neg, pos);
        gl.glVertex3f(pos, pos, pos);
        gl.glVertex3f(neg, pos, pos);
        gl.glEnd();

        gl.glBegin(GL.GL_LINES);
        gl.glVertex3f(neg, neg, neg);
        gl.glVertex3f(neg, neg, pos);

        gl.glVertex3f(pos, neg, neg);
        gl.glVertex3f(pos, neg, pos);

        gl.glVertex3f(pos, pos, neg);
        gl.glVertex3f(pos, pos, pos);

        gl.glVertex3f(neg, pos, neg);
        gl.glVertex3f(neg, pos, pos);
        gl.glEnd();
    }
}
```

The wire cube is created by drawing front and back squares using a line loop (GL.GL_LINE_LOOP). Then both squares are joined by lines through the vertices. A size factor is used to compute the positions of the vertices.

Creating the 3D Chart Scene

Next, let's create a more complex scene to draw a 3D chart with a series of cylinder bars and axis panels, as shown in Figure 8-14. For the 3D chart scene, we will use display lists and GLU functions.

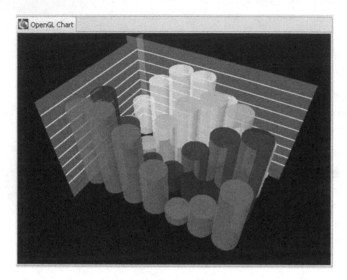

Figure 8-14. *3D chart OpenGL scene*

Increasing Performance with Display Lists

Display lists are all about performance. They provide a simple way of enhancing your OpenGL application to make it run faster. Similar to an ordinary function in a computer program, a display list is defined once, and then you can use it as many times as you want. A display list stores a group of OpenGL commands so that they can be used repeatedly just by calling the display list.

Display lists are created with glNewList. All subsequent commands are placed in the display list, in the order issued, until glEndList is called. glNewList has two arguments:

- list: A positive integer that becomes the unique name for the display list. Names can be created and reserved with glGenLists and tested for uniqueness with glIsList.

- mode: A symbolic constant that can assume one of two values: GL_COMPILE, so commands are merely compiled, or GL_COMPILE_AND_EXECUTE, so commands are executed as they are compiled into the display list.

The 3D chart scene uses display lists to increase performance by creating a CompiledShape class to encapsulate a display list, as shown in Listing 8-4. This compiled shape will make rendering much faster the next time it is requested.

Listing 8-4. *The CompiledShape Class Using Display Lists for Better Performance*

```
public abstract class CompiledShape {
    private int listIndex;
    private GL gl;

    public CompiledShape(GL gl) {
        this.listIndex = gl.glGenLists(1);
        this.gl = gl;
    }

    public int getListIndex() {
        return this.listIndex;
    }

    public void draw() {
        gl.glCallList(this.getListIndex());
    }

    public void dispose() {
        gl.glDeleteLists(this.getListIndex(), 1);
    }
}
```

When the display list needs to be called, the draw() method is invoked. To delete the display list, invoke dispose(). Listing 8-5 shows the Axis class, and Figure 8-15 shows the rendered image.

Listing 8-5. *3D Chart Axis Class*

```
private static class Axis extends CompiledShape {
        private static float[] COLOR1 = new float[] { 0.6f, 0.6f, 0.6f,
                0.3f };
        private static float[] COLOR2 = new float[] { 1.0f, 1.0f, 1.0f,
                1.0f };
        private static float[] COLOR3 = new float[] { 0.6f, 0.0f, 0.0f,
                1.0f };

        public Axis(GL gl, float x, float y, float z) {
            super(gl);
```

```
            // New display list
            gl.glNewList(this.getListIndex(), GL.GL_COMPILE);

            gl.glBegin(GL.GL_QUADS);
            gl.glColor4fv(FloatBuffer.wrap(COLOR1));

            // Two intersecting four-sided polygons (GRAY)
            gl.glVertex3f(0.0f, y, z);
            gl.glVertex3f(0.0f, -1.0f, z);
            gl.glVertex3f(0.0f, -1.0f, -1.0f);
            gl.glVertex3f(0.0f, y, -1.0f);

            // Second polygon
            gl.glVertex3f(-1.0f, y, 0.0f);
            gl.glVertex3f(-1.0f, -1.0f, 0.0f);
            gl.glVertex3f(x, -1.0f, 0.0f);
            gl.glVertex3f(x, y, 0.0f);
            gl.glEnd();

            // Polygon panel divider lines (WHITE)
            gl.glColor4fv(FloatBuffer.wrap(COLOR2));
            for (float a = 1.0f; a < y; a += 1.0f) {
                gl.glBegin(GL.GL_LINE_STRIP);
                gl.glVertex3f(0.1f, a, z);
                gl.glVertex3f(0.1f, a, 0.1f);
                gl.glVertex3f(x, a, 0.1f);
                gl.glEnd();
            }

            // X, Y, Z axis lines (RED)
            gl.glColor4fv(FloatBuffer.wrap(COLOR3));
            gl.glBegin(GL.GL_LINE_STRIP);
            gl.glVertex3f(0.1f, 0.0f, z);
            gl.glVertex3f(0.1f, 0.0f, 0.1f);
            gl.glVertex3f(x, 0.0f, 0.1f);
            gl.glEnd();

            gl.glBegin(GL.GL_LINES);
            gl.glVertex3f(0.1f, -1.0f, 0.1f);
            gl.glVertex3f(0.1f, y, 0.1f);
            gl.glEnd();
            gl.glEndList();
        }
    }
```

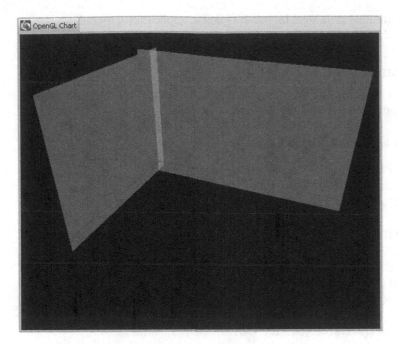

Figure 8-15. *Axis panels for the 3D chart*

Using GLU

GLU consists of a number of functions that use the base OpenGL library to provide higher-level drawing routines than the more primitive routines that OpenGL provides, generally in more human-friendly terms than the routines supplied by OpenGL. GLU is usually distributed with the base OpenGL package. It includes functions to perform the following:

- Map between screen and world coordinates

- Generate texture *mipmaps*, which are precalculated, optimized collections of bitmap images that accompany a main texture, and are intended to increase rendering speed

- Draw *quadrics*, which are *n*-dimensional surfaces described by a polynomial such as a cylinder, sphere, or paraboloid

- NURBS, which stands for nonuniform rational basis spline and is a mathematical model used in graphics for generating and representing curves and surfaces

- Tessellate polygonal primitives

- Interpret OpenGL error codes

- Extend transformation routines

■**Note** In GLU, these functions can be easily recognized because they all have `glu` as a prefix.

GLU also provides additional primitives for use in OpenGL applications, including spheres, cylinders, and disks.

Creating the BarValue Class

The BarValue class, shown in Listing 8-6, represents an element in the 3D chart. It uses the display list functionality provided by CompiledShape and utilities from GLU.

Listing 8-6. *The BarValue Class for the 3D Chart Scene*

```
private static class BarValue extends CompiledShape {
        public static final float RADIUS = 1.0f;
        public static GLUquadric QUADRIC;

        public BarValue(GL gl, float value) {
            super(gl);

            gl.glNewList(this.getListIndex(), GL.GL_COMPILE);
            gl.glRotatef(-90.0f, 1.0f, 0.0f, 0.0f);

            glu.gluCylinder(BarValue.QUADRIC, RADIUS, RADIUS, value,
                        32, 1);
            glu.gluDisk(BarValue.QUADRIC, 0.0, RADIUS, 32, 32);

            gl.glTranslatef(0.0f, 0.0f, value);
            glu.gluDisk(BarValue.QUADRIC, 0.0, RADIUS, 32, 32);

            gl.glTranslatef(0.0f, 0.0f, -value);
            gl.glRotatef(90.0f, 1.0f, 0.0f, 0.0f);
            gl.glEndList();
        }
}
```

Each bar value is a 3D cylinder along the z axis drawn using gluCylinder. The base of the cylinder is placed at z = 0, and the top at z = height. Like a sphere, a cylinder is subdivided around the z axis into slices, and along the z axis into stacks. The parameters of gluCylinder are as follows:

- quad: Specifies the quadrics object (GLUquadric).

- base: Specifies the radius of the cylinder at z = 0.

- top: Specifies the radius of the cylinder at z = height.

- height: Specifies the height of the cylinder.

- slices: Specifies the number of subdivisions around the z axis.

- stacks: Specifies the number of subdivisions along the z axis.

Creating the ChartScene Class

The ChartScene class is shown in Listing 8-7. Its job is to draw the axis and the bar values.

Listing 8-7. *The ChartScene Class for the 3D Chart Scene*

```
/**
 * A 3D cylinder chart.
 */
public class ChartScene extends GLScene {
    public static final int ROW_LENGTH = 6;
    public static final int CHART_COUNT = 4;

    private static final float[][] COLOR = { { 1.0f, 1.0f, 0.0f, 0.7f },
            { 0.0f, 1.0f, 0.0f, 0.7f }, { 0.0f, 0.0f, 1.0f, 0.7f },
            { 1.0f, 0.0f, 1.0f, 0.7f }, };

    private BarValue[][] chart;
    private Axis axis;
    private SceneGrip grip;

    static GLU glu = new GLU();

    public ChartScene(Composite parent) {
        super(parent);

        this.grip = new SceneGrip(context);
        this.grip.setOffsets(-3.25f, 3.25f, -30.5f);
        this.grip.setRotation(45.0f, -30.0f);

        this.getCanvas().addMouseListener(this.grip);
        this.getCanvas().addMouseMoveListener(this.grip);
        this.getCanvas().addListener(SWT.MouseWheel, this.grip);
        this.getCanvas().addKeyListener(this.grip);
    }

    protected void initGL() {
        super.initGL();

        context.makeCurrent();
        GL gl = context.getGL();

        BarValue.QUADRIC = glu.gluNewQuadric();
        gl.glBlendFunc(GL.GL_SRC_ALPHA, GL.GL_ONE_MINUS_SRC_ALPHA);
        gl.glEnable(GL.GL_BLEND);
        gl.glEnable(GL.GL_LINE_SMOOTH);
        glu.gluQuadricNormals(BarValue.QUADRIC, GLU.GLU_SMOOTH);
```

```
        gl.glLightfv(GL.GL_LIGHT1, GL.GL_DIFFUSE, new float[] { 1.0f,
                1.0f, 1.0f, 1.0f }, 0);
        gl.glLightfv(GL.GL_LIGHT1, GL.GL_AMBIENT, new float[] { 0.5f,
                0.5f, 0.5f, 1.0f }, 0);
        gl.glLightfv(GL.GL_LIGHT1, GL.GL_POSITION, new float[] { -50.f,
                50.0f, 100.0f, 1.0f }, 0);

        gl.glEnable(GL.GL_LIGHT1);
        gl.glEnable(GL.GL_LIGHTING);
        gl.glEnable(GL.GL_COLOR_MATERIAL);
        gl.glColorMaterial(GL.GL_FRONT, GL.GL_AMBIENT_AND_DIFFUSE);

        this.axis = new Axis(context.getGL(), 15.0f, 9.0f, 11.0f);

        this.chart = new BarValue[CHART_COUNT][ROW_LENGTH];

        double slice = Math.PI / ROW_LENGTH;

        // Initialize chart values
        for (int i = 0; i < this.chart.length; ++i) {
            BarValue[] value = this.chart[i];
            double shift = i * Math.PI / 4.0;

            for (int j = 1; j <= value.length; ++j) {
                value[j - 1] = new BarValue(context.getGL(),
                        (float)(8.0 * Math.abs(
                                Math.sin(slice * j - shift))));
            }
        }
        context.release();
    }

    protected void drawScene() {
        context.makeCurrent();
        GL gl = context.getGL();

        super.drawScene();
        this.grip.adjust();

        gl.glLineWidth(1.0f);

        // Draw axis
        this.axis.draw();
```

```
        gl.glTranslatef(BarValue.RADIUS, 0.0f, BarValue.RADIUS);

        // Draw bar values
        for (int i = 0; i < this.chart.length; ++i) {
            BarValue[] value = this.chart[i];
            gl.glColor4fv(COLOR[i % COLOR.length], 0);

            for (int j = 0; j < value.length; ++j) {
                value[j].draw();
                gl.glTranslatef(2.0f * BarValue.RADIUS, 0.0f, 0.0f);
            }

            gl.glTranslatef(-2.0f * BarValue.RADIUS * value.length
                    , 0.0f ,2.0f * BarValue.RADIUS + 0.5f);
        }

        context.release();
    }

    public void dispose() {
        glu.gluDeleteQuadric(BarValue.QUADRIC);

        for (int i = 0; i < this.chart.length; ++i) {
            BarValue[] value = this.chart[i];

            for (int j = 0; j < value.length; ++j) {
                value[j].dispose();
                value[j] = null;
            }
        }

        this.axis.dispose();
        super.dispose();
    }
}
```

ChartScene extends GLScene to perform the following tasks:

- Create a quadrics object using gluNewQuadric.

- Define the operation of blending glBlendFunc.

- Specify what kind of normals are desired for quadrics rendered with gluQuadricNormals. GLU_SMOOTH is the default; one normal is generated for every vertex of a quadric.

- Set light source parameters with glLightfv, which has the parameters of light number and light name. Lights are identified by symbolic names of the form GL_LIGHTn, where n ranges from 0 to the value of GL_MAX_LIGHTS – 1. The light name specifies a light source parameter. The following are common values:

  - GL_AMBIENT: Used to define four integer or floating-point values that specify the ambient RGBA intensity of the light.

  - GL_DIFFUSE: Used to define four integer or floating-point values that specify the diffuse RGBA intensity of the light.

  - GL_POSITION: Used to define four integer or floating-point values that specify the position of the light in homogeneous object coordinates.

Tip Lighting is initially disabled. To enable and disable lighting calculation, call glEnable and glDisable with the argument GL_LIGHTING.

- Specify which material parameters track the current color using glColorMaterial.

The final 3D chart scene is shown in Figure 8-16.

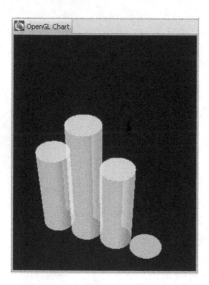

Figure 8-16. *3D cylinders drawn using gluQuadric*

Rotating and Moving the Scene

With the scene created, the next step is to allow some user interaction—moving and rotating the scene with the mouse or keyboard. This is accomplished with the SceneGrip class. SceneGrip extends org.eclipse.swt.events.MouseAdapter to deal with MouseEvents, and override the methods mouseDown and mouseUp to deal with the events generated as mouse buttons are pressed. SceneGrip also implements the following listeners:

- MouseMoveListener: Provides the method mouseMove to deal with the events that are generated as the mouse pointer moves.

- KeyListener: Provides the methods keyPressed and keyReleased to deal with the events that are generated as keys on the keyboard are pressed.

The next fragment is taken from the CubeScene class in Listing 8-7 and demonstrates how to add mouse and key listeners. ChartScene starts by creating an instance of SceneGrip with a GL context as an argument. Because ChartScene inherits from GLScene (which initializes the GLContext and creates a GLCanvas), it can get the GLCanvas instance, which in turn is used to add mouse and key listeners with a SceneGrip as an argument.

```
public ChartScene(Composite parent) {
    super(parent);

    this.grip = new SceneGrip(context);
    this.grip.setOffsets(-3.25f, 3.25f, -30.5f);
    this.grip.setRotation(45.0f, -30.0f);

    this.getCanvas().addMouseListener(this.grip);
    this.getCanvas().addMouseMoveListener(this.grip);
    this.getCanvas().addListener(SWT.MouseWheel, this.grip);
    this.getCanvas().addKeyListener(this.grip);
}
```

As the mouse moves, the mouseMove() method in SceneGrip will be invoked, and when a key is pressed or released, the appropriate method will be invoked.

Note SceneGrip also listens for mouse wheel events using addListener(SWT.MouseWheel, Listener) and implements the Listener.handleEvent(Event) method to deal with the mouse and key events.

Listing 8-8 shows a SceneGrip class capable of moving or rotating the scene with the mouse or keyboard.

Listing 8-8. *SceneGrip.java, to Control Mouse and Keyboard Movement of a GL Scene*

```
public class SceneGrip extends MouseAdapter
        implements MouseMoveListener, Listener, KeyListener {
    private float xrot;
    private float yrot;
    private float zoff;
    private float xoff;
    private float yoff;
    private float xcpy;
```

```java
private float ycpy;
private boolean move;
private int xdown;
private int ydown;
private int mouseDown;

private GLContext context;

public SceneGrip(final GLContext context) {
    this.init();
    this.context = context;
}

protected void init() {
    this.xrot = this.yrot = 0.0f;
    this.xoff = this.yoff = 0.0f;
    this.zoff = -8.0f;
}

public void mouseDown(MouseEvent e) {
    if (++this.mouseDown == 1) {
        if ((this.move = e.button == 3)) {
            this.xcpy = xoff;
            this.ycpy = yoff;
            ((Control) e.widget).setCursor(e.widget.getDisplay()
                    .getSystemCursor(SWT.CURSOR_HAND));
        } else {
            this.xcpy = xrot;
            this.ycpy = yrot;
            ((Control) e.widget).setCursor(e.widget.getDisplay()
                    .getSystemCursor(SWT.CURSOR_SIZEALL));
        }

        this.xdown = e.x;
        this.ydown = e.y;
    }
}

public void mouseUp(MouseEvent e) {
    if (--this.mouseDown == 0) {
        ((Control) e.widget).setCursor(e.widget.getDisplay()
                .getSystemCursor(SWT.CURSOR_ARROW));
    }
}

public void mouseMove(MouseEvent e) {
    Point p = ((Control) e.widget).getSize();
```

```java
    if (this.mouseDown > 0) {
        int dx = e.x - this.xdown;
        int dy = e.y - this.ydown;

        if (this.move) {
            yoff = this.ycpy + ((zoff + 1.0f) * dy) / (2.0f * p.y);
            xoff = this.xcpy - ((zoff + 1.0f) * dx) / (2.0f * p.x);
        } else {
            xrot = this.xcpy + dy / 2.0f;
            yrot = this.ycpy + dx / 2.0f;
        }
    }
}

public void handleEvent(Event event) {
    this.zoff += event.count / 6.0f;
}

public void keyPressed(KeyEvent e) {
    switch (e.keyCode) {
    case SWT.ARROW_UP:
        if ((e.stateMask & SWT.CTRL) != 0) {
            this.xrot -= 0.5f;
        } else {
            this.yoff += 0.05f;
        }
        break;
    case SWT.ARROW_DOWN:
        if ((e.stateMask & SWT.CTRL) != 0) {
            this.xrot += 0.5f;
        } else {
            this.yoff -= 0.05f;
        }
        break;
    case SWT.ARROW_LEFT:
        if ((e.stateMask & SWT.CTRL) != 0) {
            this.yrot -= 0.5f;
        } else {
            this.xoff -= 0.05f;
        }
        break;
    case SWT.ARROW_RIGHT:
        if ((e.stateMask & SWT.CTRL) != 0) {
            this.yrot += 0.5f;
        } else {
            this.xoff += 0.05f;
        }
```

```
                    break;
                case SWT.PAGE_UP:
                    this.zoff += 0.05f;
                    break;
                case SWT.PAGE_DOWN:
                    this.zoff -= 0.05f;
                    break;
                case SWT.HOME:
                    this.init();
                    break;
            }
        }

        public void keyReleased(KeyEvent e) {
        }

        public void adjust() {
            GL gl = context.getGL();
            gl.glTranslatef(this.xoff, this.yoff, this.zoff);
            gl.glRotatef(this.xrot, 1.0f, 0.0f, 0.0f);
            gl.glRotatef(this.yrot, 0.0f, 1.0f, 0.0f);
        }

        public void setOffsets(float x, float y, float z) {
            this.xoff = x;
            this.yoff = y;
            this.zoff = z;
        }

        public void setRotation(float x, float y) {
            this.xrot = x;
            this.yrot = y;
        }
    }
```

Let's look at the public methods of SceneGrip in more detail:

- adjust: Translates the scene to its initial x, y, z offsets, thus centering it when the program starts. It also rotates the scene to the x, y values. The adjust method will be called many times by the scene refresher to update the scene's coordinates.

- keyPressed: Listens for the arrow keys and updates the x, y offsets of the scene. It also updates the z offset when the PageUp and PageDown keys are pressed. When Home is pressed, the scene is reinitialized.

- mouseDown: Changes the mouse cursor to a hand and saves the x, y coordinates for the next refresh.

- mouseMove: Updates the x, y, z coordinates based on the pointer position.

- mouseUp: Returns the cursor shape to the arrow.

Refreshing the Scene

The last piece of this puzzle is a class used to refresh the scene. Refresher is a thread that renders the scene in the background based on a delay interval. Refresher takes a GLScene in its constructor and calls render() within its run() method, as shown in Listing 8-9.

Listing 8-9. *The Scene Refresher Class*

```
public class Refresher implements Runnable {
    public static final int DELAY = 100;

    private GLScene scene;

    public Refresher(GLScene canvas) {
        this.scene = canvas;
    }

    public void run() {
        if (this.scene != null && !this.scene.isDisposed()) {
            this.scene.render();
            this.scene.getDisplay().timerExec(DELAY, this);
        }
    }
}
```

Within the run() method, Refresher fires a timer interval to call itself, thus effectively refreshing the scene at the specified times—every 100 milliseconds in this example.

Putting the Scene into an RCP View

To render a GLScene in RCP, you need to use a view. As you saw in the previous section, GLScene takes an SWT composite as the parent control. Thus, you just need to override the createPartControl() method of the View class to add the GLScene, as shown in Listing 8-10.

Listing 8-10. *Adding GLScene to an RCP View*

```
public class GLCubesView extends ViewPart {
    public static final String ID = GLCubesView.class.getName();

    private GLScene scene;

    /**
     * This is a callback that will allow us to create the viewer and
     * initialize it.
     */
    public void createPartControl(Composite parent) {
        this.scene = new CubeScene(parent);
        new Refresher(this.scene).run();
    }
```

```
/**
 * Passing the focus request to the viewer's control.
 */
public void setFocus() {
    this.scene.setFocus();
}
}
```

Notice how the Refresher thread fits into the big picture. Without it, the scene won't be repainted, and nothing will work as expected.

So far, I have attempted to explain in the simplest terms the complexities of OpenGL without going into too much detail. The next section puts some of these concepts to the test with a real-life application.

Note OpenGL can be a daunting subject. Check out the tutorials at http://opengl.j3d.org/tutorials/index.html for both beginner and seasoned developers.

Hands-on Exercise: Build a Powerful 3D Earth Navigator

In this exercise, you will build a powerful, real-life application using JOGL and the National Aeronautics and Space Administration (NASA) World Wind SDK. The application is a 3D Earth navigator, similar to Google Earth. It uses the following components:

- The World Wind Java (WWJ) SDK, which allows developers to embed World Wind's geospatial visualization technology (which uses NASA's geospatial data) in their own applications[5]

- The Yahoo! Geocoding API, which allows you to find the specific latitude and longitude for an address[6]

Before we start building the application, we need to review some WWJ basics.

WWJ Basics

The WWJ SDK is a 3D graphics globe built on top of JOGL. WWJ uses a map tiling system and a Cartesian coordinate system to divide the sphere in rectangular sections and display textures (images) on top.[7] Each section has a latitude/longitude bounding box.

---

5. The World Wind Java SDK is available from http://worldwind.arc.nasa.gov/java/index.html.
6. Yahoo! Maps Web Services – Geocoding API is available from http://developer.yahoo.com/maps/rest/V1/geocode.html.
7. For more information about the World Wind tiling system, see http://www.worldwindcentral.com/wiki/Tiling_System. For more information about the WWJ coordinate system, see http://www.worldwindcentral.com/wiki/Coordinate_System.

Behind the scenes, WWJ fetches images from NASA dataset servers and projects them onto the sphere. When the user zooms in, the number of tiles quadruples based on a computed zoom level. Because the number of tiles at high resolutions can be huge, each tile is cached on disk for performance.

The most important dataset in WWJ is called the Blue Marble, which displays NASA's imagery of the Earth as a whole, provided by the Earth Observatory (with a resolution of 1 kilometer per pixel). Figure 8-17 shows an example of a World Wind Earth view image. Other datasets include the following:

- I-cubed Landsat 7, a global land cover facility from the University of Maryland, Institute for Advanced Computer Studies (resolution of 15 meters per pixel)

- U.S. place names from the USGS Geographic Names Information System (GNIS)

- World place names from the National Geospatial-Intelligence Agency

Figure 8-17. *World Wind Earth view*

World Wind System Architecture

The World Wind API is defined primarily by interfaces. This allows third-party developers to selectively replace components with alternative components. At the core of the WWJ class hierarchy is WorldWindowGLCanvas, which is a subclass of GLCanvas, an AWT component. The following are the major interfaces:

- WorldWindow: Represents the highest level interface with the OpenGL canvas provided for Swing/AWT.

- Globe: Represents a planet's shape and terrain.

- Layer: Applies imagery or information to a globe.

- Model: Aggregates a globe and the layers to apply to it. The application typically interacts with the model to create a globe of the Earth, Mars, or whatever the model needs to be. It can even be the universe.

- SceneController: Controls the rendering of a model. It is also responsible for giving the scene update, timing, and events, as well as for mapping user actions.

- View: Controls the user's view of the model.

In a typical usage, a developer would associate a Globe object and several custom Layer objects with a Model object. The Model object is then passed to a SceneController object, which displays the globe and its layers in a WorldWindow. The SceneController subsequently manages the display of the globe and its layers in conjunction with an interactive View interface that defines the user's view of the planet. The next fragment demonstrates this technique:

```
private static final WorldWindowGLCanvas world =
    new WorldWindowGLCanvas();

/**
 * Initialize the default WW layers
 */
static {
  Model m = (Model) WorldWind
      .createConfigurationComponent(AVKey.MODEL_CLASS_NAME);

  m.setShowWireframeExterior(false);
  m.setShowWireframeInterior(false);
  m.setShowTessellationBoundingVolumes(false);

  world.setModel(m);

  // Add Terrain Profiler Layer
  TerrainProfileLayer tp = new TerrainProfileLayer();

  tp.setEventSource(world);
  tp.setStartLatLon(LatLon.fromDegrees(0, -10));
  tp.setEndLatLon(LatLon.fromDegrees(0, 65));
  tp.setFollow(TerrainProfileLayer.FOLLOW_CURSOR);

  world.getModel().getLayers().add(tp);
}
```

All data is persisted to the local computer by the file cache. The file cache manages multiple disk storage locations and is accessible through the World Wind singleton.

Embedding WWJ into Eclipse

As noted earlier, WWJ's `WorldWindowGLCanvas` is a subclass of `GLCanvas`, which is an AWT component. The Swing/AWT nature of WWJ is a problem for Eclipse applications because Eclipse uses the SWT, which is incompatible with AWT. Furthermore, AWT and JOGL are tightly integrated, making a port of the AWT interfaces to SWT very difficult.

To overcome this problem, the folks at the Eclipse foundation developed the SWT/AWT Bridge, which allows you to embed AWT/Swing components into SWT. The bridge has been part of SWT since version 3.0, and it is a very simple API located in the package `org.eclipse.swt.awt`.

The SWT/AWT Bridge is the key component required to embed the AWT-based World Wind 3D globe into an Eclipse application via SWT.

Setting Up the Earth Navigator Project

We're now ready to start building our 3D Earth navigator. The first thing we need is an RCP application and product skeleton to host the following views:

- Navigator (`NavView`) contains a list of available WWJ layers and a simple UI to perform location searches using the Yahoo Geocoding interface.

- Earth (`GlobeView`) displays the WWJ 3D Earth.

These views can be seen in Figure 8-18.

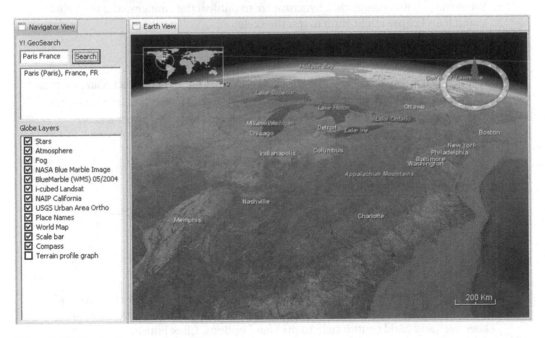

Figure 8-18. *Navigator and globe views*

Creating the RCP Application

Follow these steps to create the skeleton project:

1. From the main Eclipse menu, select File ➤ New ➤ Project ➤ Plug-in Development ➤ Plug-in Project. Click Next.

2. Enter a project name (ch08.OpenGL). Click Next.

3. On the Plug-in Content page, make sure "This plug-in will make contributions to the UI" is selected and "Would you like to create a rich client application?" is set to Yes.

4. Select the Hello RCP template, and then click Next.

5. On the Basic RCP Application page, set the title to Earth navigator and check the Add branding option. Then click Finish.

Creating a Production Configuration

Now create a product configuration to launch the RCP application:

1. Right-click the new project folder (ch08.OpenGL) and select New ➤ Other ➤ Plug-in Development ➤ Product Configuration. Click Next.

2. Enter a file name for the product file (OpenGL). Make sure the correct product is selected under "Use an existing product." Click Finish.

3. From the product editor, click Synchronize to publish the changes, and then click Launch an Eclipse application to test the skeleton.

Tip When you launch an Eclipse application created with the wizard from the product editor, the default, the window size will be 400 by 400 pixels. You can remove the line configurer.setInitialSize(new Point(400, 300)) in the ApplicationWorkbenchWindowAdvisor class for a bigger window.

Creating the Navigator and Earth View Skeletons

The layer navigator and Earth views must be created using extension points, as follows:

1. Open the plug-in editor (plugin.xml).

2. On the Extensions tab, click Add. Then select the org.eclipse.ui.views extension point. From the available templates, select Sample View. Click Next.

3. Set the view's ID to ch08.opengl.views.GlobeView, the class name to ch08.opengl.views.GlobeView, and the name to Earth. Uncheck the "Add the view to the java perspective" and "Add context help to the view" options. Click Finish.

4. Repeat steps 2 and 3 for the navigator view. Set the ID to ch08.opengl.views.NavView, class to ch08.opengl.views.NavView, and view name to Layer Navigator.

With the skeleton views created, the default perspective must be updated to display them. Edit the class ch08.opengl.Perspective to insert the views, as shown in the next fragment.

```
public class Perspective implements IPerspectiveFactory {

    public void createInitialLayout(IPageLayout layout) {
        String editorArea = layout.getEditorArea();
        layout.setEditorAreaVisible(false);
        layout.setFixed(true);

        IFolderLayout topLeft = layout.createFolder("topLeft",
                IPageLayout.LEFT, 0.22f, editorArea);

        topLeft.addView("ch08.opengl.views.NavView");


        IFolderLayout topRight = layout.createFolder("topRight",
                IPageLayout.RIGHT, 0.3f, editorArea);
        topRight.addView("ch08.opengl.views.GlobeView");
    }
}
```

Refresh the product configuration and launch the application. You should now have an RCP with two views to host the WWJ layers and 3D Earth. Before we create these views, we need to include the WWJ dependencies in the project.

Adding WWJ Dependencies

World Wind JARs and native libraries must be added to the project so the 3D globes can be used. First, add the JARs to the classpath, as follows:

1. Create a folder called lib within the main project folder to host the WWJ JAR archives. To do this, right-click the main folder and select New ➤ Folder. Enter lib as the name, and then click Finish.

2. Download the World Wind Java SDK from NASA (http://worldwind.arc.nasa.gov/ java/index.htm). Unzip the SDK and copy the JARs (gluegen-rt.jar, jogl.jar, and worldwind.jar) to the lib folder you just created.

3. Open the project plugin.xml. Click the Runtime tab. Under Classpath, add the JARs you downloaded to the classpath. This is required so the plug-in will be able to see the WWJ archives.

This will add WWJ to the classpath of the plug-in. However, WWJ includes native libraries, which must be included to the plug-in classpath via a fragment, as follows:

1. Create a fragment project to host WWJ native libraries. To do this, from the main Eclipse menu, select File ➤ New ➤ Project ➤ Plug-in Development ➤ Plug-in Project. Click Next.

2. Enter a name (ch08.OpenGL.Natives). Click Next.

3. On the Fragment Content page, set the host plug-in ID to ch08.OpenGL. Click Finish.

4. Copy all the native libraries (DLLs in windows; SOs in Linux) to the fragment folder.

Tip The host plug-in ID indicates the plug-in to which the fragment will attach its classpath at runtime. Thus, the fragment native libraries will be included to the ch08.OpenGL plug-in classpath at runtime.

At this point, all the required WWJ dependencies should be in place for the RCP application.

Creating the Earth Navigator View

With the SWT/AWT Bridge already in SWT, embedding a WWJ 3D Earth globe within your view is a snap. Listing 8-11 demonstrates a basic Eclipse view to perform this task.

Listing 8-11. *Eclipse View for the WWJ Earth Globe*

```
public class GlobeView extends ViewPart {
    public static final String ID = GlobeView.class.getName();

    private static final WorldWindowGLCanvas world = new WorldWindowGLCanvas();

    /**
     * Initialize the default WW layers
     */
    static {
        initWorldWindLayerModel();
    }


    /**
     * This is a callback that will allow us to create the viewer and
     * initialize it.
     */
    public void createPartControl(Composite parent) {
        // Build GUI:
        // top(SWT)->Frame(AWT)->Panel(AWT)->WorldWindowGLCanvas(AWT)
        Composite top = new Composite(parent, SWT.EMBEDDED);
        top.setLayoutData(new GridData(GridData.FILL_BOTH));

        java.awt.Frame worldFrame = SWT_AWT.new_Frame(top);
        java.awt.Panel panel = new java.awt.Panel(
                new java.awt.BorderLayout());
```

```java
        worldFrame.add(panel);
        panel.add(world, BorderLayout.CENTER);

        // Max parent widget
        parent.setLayoutData(new GridData(GridData.FILL_BOTH));
    }

    /*
     * Initialize WW model with default layers
     */
    static void initWorldWindLayerModel() {
        Model m = (Model) WorldWind
                .createConfigurationComponent(AVKey.MODEL_CLASS_NAME);

        m.setShowWireframeExterior(false);
        m.setShowWireframeInterior(false);
        m.setShowTessellationBoundingVolumes(false);

        world.setModel(m);

        // Add Terrain Profiler
        TerrainProfileLayer tp = new TerrainProfileLayer();

        tp.setEventSource(world);
        tp.setStartLatLon(LatLon.fromDegrees(0, -10));
        tp.setEndLatLon(LatLon.fromDegrees(0, 65));
        tp.setFollow(TerrainProfileLayer.FOLLOW_CURSOR);

        world.getModel().getLayers().add(tp);
    }

    /**
     * Passing the focus request to the viewer's control.
     */
    public void setFocus() {
    }

    public void repaint() {
        world.repaint();
    }

    @Override
    public void dispose() {
        super.dispose();
    }
```

```
public void flyTo(LatLon latlon) {
    View view = world.getView();
    Globe globe = world.getModel().getGlobe();

    view.applyStateIterator(FlyToOrbitViewStateIterator
            .createPanToIterator((OrbitView) view, globe,
                    new Position(latlon, 0) // bbox
                    , Angle.ZERO // Heading
                    , Angle.ZERO // Pitch
                    , 3e3) // Altitude/Zoom (m) Angle.ZERO.degrees)
        );
}

public LayerList getLayers() {
    return world.getModel().getLayers();
}
}
```

The createPartControl() method starts by creating a top SWT component, which will use the bridge to embed the WWJ Swing OpenGL canvas:

```
Composite top = new Composite(parent, SWT.EMBEDDED);
top.setLayoutData(new GridData(GridData.FILL_BOTH));
```

Next, within the top SWT component, a child AWT frame is created, using the bridge, to host the Swing Panel required by the WWJ OpenGL canvas:

```
java.awt.Frame worldFrame = SWT_AWT.new_Frame(top);
java.awt.Panel panel = new java.awt.Panel(new java.awt.BorderLayout());
```

Finally, the WWJ GLCanvas is added to the Swing Panel:

```
WorldWindowGLCanvas world = new WorldWindowGLCanvas();
panel.add(world, BorderLayout.CENTER);
```

Flying to a Location Within a Globe

To fly to specific latitude/longitude, three objects are required:

- A View that provides a coordinate transformation from model coordinates to eye coordinates, following the OpenGL convention of a left-handed coordinate system. (Note that this View object is not related to the RCP concept of a view.)

- A Globe representing the 3D ellipsoidal sphere of the world you are viewing.

- The latitude/longitude coordinates of the point you wish to reach. Optional information includes angles for heading and pitch, and altitude in meters.

Listing 8-12 shows the flyTo() method.

Listing 8-12. *The flyTo Method to Fly to a Specific Latitude/Longitude Point on the Globe*

```
public void flyTo (LatLon latlon)
{
   View view = world.getView();
   Globe globe = world.getModel().getGlobe();

   view.applyStateIterator(FlyToOrbitViewStateIterator.createPanToIterator(
       (OrbitView)view
       , globe
       , latlon          // Bounding box
       , Angle.ZERO      // Heading
       , Angle.ZERO      // Pitch
       , 3e3 )           // Altitude/Zoom (m)
       );
}
```

The applyStateIterator() method of the View class pans or zooms the globe, producing a smooth "fly to" or an instantaneous "zoom" effect on the globe's target coordinates.

To make good use of the flyTo() method, we need the means to find locations by latitude and longitude. The Yahoo Geocoding API can help.

Finding Latitude and Longitude with the Yahoo Geocoding API

The Yahoo Geocoding API is a great way to find the specific latitude and longitude for a specific address. This service works by sending an HTTP GET request to the URL http://local. yahooapis.com/MapsService/V1/geocode. The following are the most important parameters of the request:

- appid: The application ID.

- street: Street name. The number is optional.

- city: City name.

- state: The U.S. state. You can spell out the full state name or use the two-letter abbreviation.

- zip: The five-digit ZIP code or the five-digit code plus four-digit extension. If this location contradicts the city and state specified, the ZIP code will be used for determining the location, and the city and state will be ignored.

- location: A free-form field that lets users enter just the ZIP code or combinations of the other location information, such as the street, city, and state.

- output: The format for the output, either xml or php. If php is requested, the results will be returned in serialized PHP format.

For example, enter the following URL in your browser to find the latitude and longitude of Paris, France:

```
http://local.yahooapis.com/MapsService/V1/geocode?appid=YD-f7BUYpg_JX25g8v
.EmGtMxpfMhpX2XIz17DeSzXV&location=Paris+France
```

You should see the following:

```
<Result precision="zip">
<Latitude>48.856925</Latitude>
<Longitude>2.341210</Longitude>
<Address/>
<City>Paris (Paris)</City>
<State>France</State>
<Zip/>
<Country>FR</Country>
</Result>
</ResultSet>
```

Try typing any address, place, or ZIP code for the location parameter. You'll see that this API is very powerful, and it will provide what we need for the Earth navigator example. All we need now is a class to send the request and parse the response XML. Listing 8-13 shows the class YGeoSearch to perform this task.

Listing 8-13. *YGeoSearch, to Find the Latitude and Longitude for a Given Location Using the Yahoo Geocoding API*

```
public class YGeoSearch {

    private String location;

    /**
     * Yahoo search result object
     */
    public static class YResult {
        public double latitude, longitude;
        public String address, city, state, zip, country;
        public String warning;

        public String debug() {
            return "Y! lat= " + latitude + " lon=" + longitude + " city="
                    + city + " st=" + state + " zip=" + zip + " c="
                    + country;
        }

        @Override
        public String toString() {
            return (warning != null ? warning + ", " : "")
                    + (address != null ? address + ", " : "")
                    + (city != null ? city + ", " : "")
                    + (state != null ? state + ", " : "")
                    + (zip != null ? zip + ", " : "")
                    + (country != null ? country : "");
        }
    }
}
```

```
/**
 * Search for a place using Yahoo
 *
 * @param location
 */
public YGeoSearch(String location) {
    if (location == null)
        throw new IllegalArgumentException("Invalid location");

    this.location = location.replaceAll(" ", "+");
}


/**
 * Get search locations
 *
 * @return array of {@link YResult} objects
 * @throws Exception
 */
public YResult[] getLocations() throws Exception {

    final String url = "http://local.yahooapis.com/MapsService/V1/geocode"
        + "?appid=YD-f7BUYpg_JX25g8v.EmGtMxpfMhpX2XIz17DeSzXV&location="
        + location;

    SimpleHTTPClient client = new SimpleHTTPClient(new URL(url));
    final String xml = client.doGet();

    if (client.getStatus() == HttpURLConnection.HTTP_OK) {
        client.close();
        return parseYahooXml(xml);
    }

    // Handle error
    throw new IOException("HTTP request failed " + client.getStatus()
            + " " + url);
}


/**
 * Parse Y! results XML
 * @param xml
 * @throws Exception
 */
private YResult[] parseYahooXml(String xml) throws Exception {
    Document doc = parse(new ByteArrayInputStream(xml.getBytes()));

    // KML Doc
    NodeList results = doc.getElementsByTagName("Result");
```

```java
        YResult[] Yresults = new YResult[results.getLength()];

        for (int i = 0; i < results.getLength(); i++) {
            final Element e = (Element) results.item(i);

            YResult Yres = new YResult();

            Yres.warning = getAttributeValue(e, "warning");
            Yres.address = getNodeValue(e, "Address");
            Yres.latitude = Double
                    .parseDouble(getNodeValue(e, "Latitude"));
            Yres.longitude = Double.parseDouble(getNodeValue(e,
                    "Longitude"));
            Yres.city = getNodeValue(e, "City");
            Yres.state = getNodeValue(e, "State");
            Yres.country = getNodeValue(e, "Country");
            Yres.zip = getNodeValue(e, "Zip");

            Yresults[i] = Yres;
        }
        return Yresults;
    }

    /*
     * XML Document Utilities
     */
    public static Document parse(InputStream is) throws SAXException,
            IOException, ParserConfigurationException {
        DocumentBuilderFactory docBuilderFactory = DocumentBuilderFactory
                .newInstance();
        docBuilderFactory.setNamespaceAware(true);
        DocumentBuilder docBuilder = docBuilderFactory
                .newDocumentBuilder();
        return docBuilder.parse(is);
    }

    /**
     * Extract the value of an XML element
     * @param e Document element
     * @param name Element name
     * @return Value
     */
    static public String getNodeValue(Element e, String name) {
        NodeList nl = e.getElementsByTagName(name);
```

```
        try {
            return (nl != null && nl.getLength() > 0) ? nl.item(0)
                    .getFirstChild().getNodeValue().trim() : null;

        } catch (NullPointerException ex) {
            return null;
        }
    }

    static public String getTextContent(Element e, String name) {
        NodeList nl = e.getElementsByTagName(name);

        try {
            return (nl != null && nl.getLength() > 0) ? nl.item(0)
                    .getTextContent().trim() : null;

        } catch (NullPointerException ex) {
            return null;
        }
    }

    /**
     * Get an attribute value
     * @return Attribute value or null
     */
    static public String getAttributeValue(Element e, String name) {
        Node n = e.getAttributes().getNamedItem(name);
        return (n != null) ? n.getNodeValue() : null;

    }
}
```

To fetch the latitude/longitude of a given location, simply use this fragment:

```
YGeoSearch search = new YGeoSearch("My home address");

YResult[] results =  search.getLocations();

for ( int i = 0 ; i < results.length ; i++ ) {
    System.out.println("Address+" results[i].address
        + " Lat:" + results[i].latitude
        + " Lon:" + results[i].longitude);
}
```

The Earth navigator will wrap this search logic in a navigator view.

Creating the Layer Navigator View with Geocoding

The navigator view for the Earth navigator will do two things:

- Provide a GUI to find a location on the globe and fly to it when selected
- Display the globe's built-in layers, allowing the user to enable or disable them

The navigator has two table viewers: one for the search results and one for the globe layers, as shown in Listing 8-14.

Listing 8-14. *Navigator View Skeleton*

```
public class NavView extends ViewPart implements Listener {
    public static final String ID = NavView.class.getName();

    private TableViewer viewer;
    private Text searchText;

    private CheckboxTableViewer layers;

    /**
     * This is a callback that will allow us to create the viewer and
     * initialize it.
     */
    public void createPartControl(Composite parent) {
        parent.setLayout(new GridLayout(2, true));

        Label l1 = new Label(parent, SWT.NONE);
        l1.setText("Y! GeoSearch");
        l1.setLayoutData(new GridData(SWT.FILL, SWT.FILL, true, false, 2,
                1));

        // Search box
        searchText = new Text(parent, SWT.BORDER);
        searchText.setLayoutData(new GridData(SWT.FILL, SWT.FILL, true,
                false));

        // Search button
        Button b1 = new Button(parent, SWT.PUSH);

        b1.setText("Search");
        b1.addListener(SWT.Selection, this);
        b1.addListener(SWT.DefaultSelection, this);

        // Results table viewer
        viewer = new TableViewer(parent, SWT.BORDER | SWT.H_SCROLL
                | SWT.V_SCROLL);
```

```
viewer.getTable().setLayoutData(
        new GridData(SWT.FILL, SWT.FILL, true, false, 2, 1));
viewer.getTable().addListener(SWT.Selection, this);

// Layers label
Label l2 = new Label(parent, SWT.NONE);
l2.setText("Globe Layers");
l2.setLayoutData(new GridData(SWT.FILL, SWT.FILL, true, false, 2,
        1));

Table tableLayers = new Table(parent, SWT.CHECK | SWT.BORDER
        | SWT.H_SCROLL | SWT.V_SCROLL);

// Layers table viewer
layers = new CheckboxTableViewer(tableLayers);
layers.getTable().setLayoutData(
        new GridData(SWT.FILL, SWT.FILL, true, true, 2, 1));

// Fires when a layer on the table viewer is checked.
layers.addCheckStateListener(new ICheckStateListener() {
    @Override
    public void checkStateChanged(CheckStateChangedEvent event) {
        // Enable/disable globe layer based on the check status
        // of the table
        Layer layer = (Layer) event.getElement();
        layer.setEnabled(event.getChecked());

        // Repaint globe
        GlobeView view = (GlobeView) Activator.getView(
                getViewSite().getWorkbenchWindow(), GlobeView.ID);
        view.repaint();
    }
});

    init();
}
...
}
```

When the view initializes, it loads the World Wind layers from the globe view, and adds them to the layers table viewer. To get a reference to the globe view, you use the Eclipse view registry, as shown in Listing 8-15.

Listing 8-15. *Loading World Wind Layers from the Globe View*

```
/**
 * Load layers from the globe and add them to the table viewer
 */
private void init() {
        GlobeView view = (GlobeView) Activator.getView(getViewSite()
                .getWorkbenchWindow(), GlobeView.ID);
        if (view != null) {
            LayerList list = view.getLayers();

            for (Layer layer : list) {
                layers.add(layer);
                layers.setChecked(layer, layer.isEnabled());
            }
        }
}

public static IViewPart getView (IWorkbenchWindow window,  String ViewID)
{
        IViewReference[] refs = window.getActivePage().getViewReferences();

        for (IViewReference viewReference : refs) {
            if ( viewReference.getId().equals(ViewID) )
                return viewReference.getView(true);
        }
        return null;
}
```

Our cool Earth navigator is now complete. As you've seen, World Wind is a Java technology component that you can integrate into your applications to incorporate 3D Earth modeling. More data on the planets, moons, stars, weather, satellites, and time series is becoming available all the time. Soon more data formats will be natively supported. The useful components coming are a layer manager, animation player, drag-and-drop functionality, and UI helpers. Additionally, World Wind will include RSS feed support and APIs for scripting extensions.

Summary

This chapter covered developing 3D graphics applications with OpenGL. Here are the important points to keep in mind:

- OpenGL is the de facto environment for developing portable, interactive 3D graphics applications. Java provides a wealth of tools and APIs to abstract the complexities of OpenGL.

- The OpenGL coordinate system uses x, y, and z axes, where 0, 0, 0 is the middle of the screen. It is called a left-handed coordinate system.

- SWT supports three OpenGL bindings: Lightweight Java Game Library (LWGL), Java OpenGL (JOGL), and gljava.

- The platform-independent OpenGL classes provided by SWT are `GLCanvas` and `GLData`. `GLCanvas` is a widget capable of displaying OpenGL content. `GLData` is a device-independent description of the pixel format attributes of a GL drawable.

- An OpenGL binding that wishes to interact with SWT should implement the class `javax.media.opengl.GLContext`. This class is abstraction for an OpenGL rendering context.

- OpenGL display lists are a simple way of enhancing your OpenGL application to make it run faster. A display list stores a group of OpenGL commands so that they can be used repeatedly just by calling the display list.

- GLU is the OpenGL Utility Library. It consists of a number of functions that use the base OpenGL library to provide higher-level drawing routines than the more primitive routines that OpenGL provides. GLU also provides additional primitives for use in OpenGL applications, including spheres, cylinders, and disks.

CHAPTER 9

■ ■ ■

Professional Reports with the Business Intelligence and Report Toolkit

The Business Intelligence and Report Toolkit (BIRT) is a powerful open source reporting system for RCP, stand-alone, or web applications. You can use it to create a variety of report types, including the following:

- Data lists grouped or ordered with totals, averages, and other summaries

- Interactive 2D and 3D charts

- Various types of documents, such as textual documents, letters, notices, and spreadsheets

- Compound reports that combine all of the other types

BIRT can be used in two ways. One way is as a full-fledged application, using the BIRT designer (within the Eclipse IDE) or RCP designer (which is a stand-alone application). The other is as a web application, by deploying the BIRT viewer into a Java EE container.

At its core, BIRT consists of three main components:

- Report Designer, which is the Eclipse UI for creating reports

- Runtime, which is a set of APIs to use BIRT within your own Java or Java EE application

- Chart engine, which allows developers to create custom chart types

In this chapter, we'll look at the various ways to use BIRT, beginning with creating reports with the Report Designer in the Eclipse IDE.

Using the Report Designer Within the Eclipse IDE

Using the Report Designer, you can create professional-looking reports. For example, Figure 9-1 shows a compound report that uses data from the sample database that comes with BIRT.

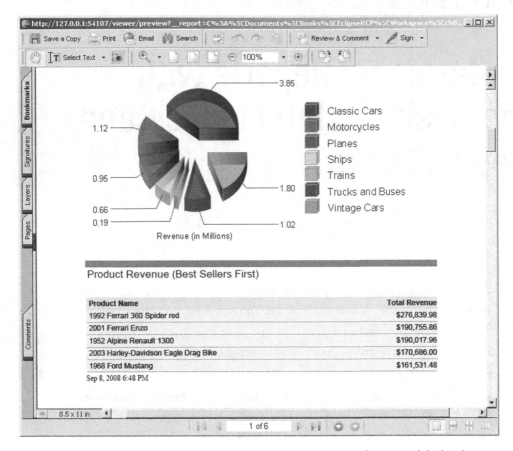

Figure 9-1. *Compound report of car revenue sales from the BIRT Classic Models database*

The easiest way to start learning BIRT is to use the Report Designer to create a basic report. However, depending on your Eclipse installation, the Report Designer may not be installed by default. To see if BIRT is installed, from the Eclipse IDE main menu, select Window ➤ Open Perspective ➤ Other. If the Report Design perspective is present, then you are in good shape. Otherwise, you'll need to install BIRT using the Software Updates Manager, as described next.

Installing BIRT Using the Software Updates Manager

BIRT can be easily installed within Eclipse, as follows:

1. From the main menu of the Eclipse IDE, select Help ➤ Software Updates.

2. Select the Available Software tab, and then expand Ganymede ➤ Charting and Reporting.

3. Click BIRT Report Designer Framework, and then click Install.

Depending on the speed of your network, the installation may take a while, as BIRT has a lot of dependencies, such as the Data Tools Platform (DTP), Eclipse Modeling Framework (EMF), Web Standard Tools (WST), iText, Apache Derby, Mozilla Rhino (for scripting), and others.

Report Anatomy

A report usually consists of four main parts:

Data source: A data source provides access to many kinds of tabular data. A single report can include any number of data sources, or disparate data sources can be combined into virtual data sources. BIRT supports the following:

- Flat files (comma-separated value style)
- Any database compliant with Java Database Connectivity (JDBC)
- Web services (a WSDL descriptor and a SOAP endpoint URL for the web service are required)
- XML data (an XML file or URL and corresponding schema are required)

Data transforms: Data can be sorted, summarized, filtered, and grouped to fit the users' needs.

Business logic: The business logic provides the means to convert raw data into information useful for the users.

Presentation: BIRT provides a wide range of options for displaying data, such as tables, charts, and text.

Three basic things are needed by all reports: a data source, a query against the source, and a report layout. To help you get started, BIRT includes a sample database called Classic Models, which we will use for the examples in this chapter.

Getting Your Feet Wet with the Report Designer

You can access the Report Designer through the Report Design perspective of the workbench. Figure 9-2 shows an example of the Report Design perspective for creating a report. It consists of four views:

Data Explorer: Use this view to add data and parameters to your report. From this view, you can set up the following for your report:

- A data source, such as a database or flat file
- A dataset, which represents a data query against the data source (invoice data, for example)
- A data cube, which is a structure for fast analysis of data, such a summary of the entire product inventory by city over time
- Report parameters, which are runtime input values, such as an order number to display invoice data

Palette: The Palette view contains report UI elements, such as labels, images, data lists, tables, charts, and cross-tabs. Elements can be dragged into the Layout view, and are usually bound to a data element from a dataset.

Property Editor: This view displays properties of the various report elements.

Layout: This is a powerful WYSIWYG editor. It has tabs to display the report layout, source, and preview.

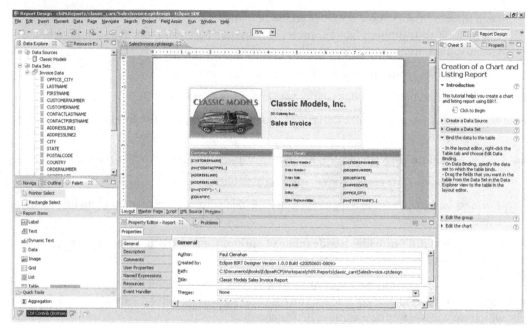

Figure 9-2. *Report Designer showing the Data Explorer, Palette, Property Editor, and Layout views*

Creating a Simple Report

To get started, we'll walk through an example of creating a simple report of the inventory of BIRT's Classic Models sample database.

1. From the Eclipse IDE main menu, select File ➤ New ➤ Other ➤ Report Project.

2. Switch to the Report Design perspective when prompted.

3. In the Data Explorer view, right-click Data Sources and select New Data Source. Select the Classic Models sample database. Click Finish.

4. Right-click Data Sets and select New Data Set. Enter a name (for example, `ProductInventory`). Make sure the dataset type is SQL query and the data source you chose in step 3 is selected. Click Next.

5. In the Edit Data Set window, enter the following SQL fragment to select inventory data (from the CLASSICMODELS.PRODUCTS table) sorted by name and price:

```
select *
from CLASSICMODELS.PRODUCTS
order by CLASSICMODELS.PRODUCTS.PRODUCTNAME
  ,CLASSICMODELS.PRODUCTS.MSRP
```

6. Your query should appear as shown in Figure 9-3. Click OK to continue.

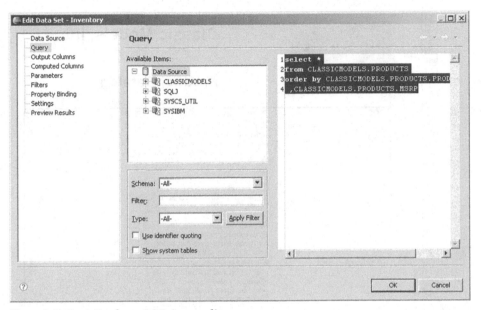

Figure 9-3. *Data Explorer SQL query editor*

7. Now you need to create a new blank report layout. To do so, select File ➤ New ➤ Report. Enter a name, and then click Finish. The layout should be displayed in the WYSIWYG editor. (Alternatively, you could also select one of the built-in report templates.)

8. Bind data elements to the report layout. Use the Palette view to add a data table that will display data from the query. Then simply drag and drop elements from the dataset you created in step 4 to the data table in the Layout view. Drag PRODUCTNAME to the first column, PRODUCTDESCRIPTION to the second column, and so on, until you are satisfied with the presentation.

9. Customize the presentation to your liking (add headings or images using the Palette view, for example). Images can be embedded from files, URIs, and other sources.

10. Preview the report from the Layout view's Preview tab or by selecting Run ➤ View Report from the main menu. BIRT provides many preview format types, including Word (DOC), HTML, PDF, PostScript, PowerPoint (PPT), Excel (XLS), and others. Figure 9-4 shows the sample report previewed in PDF format.

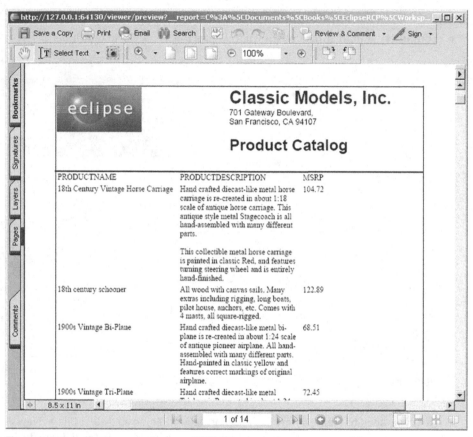

Figure 9-4. *Previewing a report as a PDF document*

Now that you've tried a simple report, let's create one that is a bit more complex.

Creating a Complex Report

In this section, we will create a report to show a pie chart of total sales by product line from the Classic Models sample database. The backbone of any report is the data, which usually represents a SQL query from a database. Consider the following SQL to extract total sales by product line:

```
select PRODUCTS.PRODUCTLINE,
    SUM(ORDERDETAILS.QUANTITYORDERED * ORDERDETAILS.PRICEEACH)
      AS "TOTAL SALES"
from PRODUCTS, ORDERDETAILS
where PRODUCTS.PRODUCTCODE = ORDERDETAILS.PRODUCTCODE
group by PRODUCTS.PRODUCTLINE
```

This query selects the PRODUCTLINE and the sum of the QUANTITY * PRICEEACH (labeled as TOTAL SALES) of the PRODUCTS and ORDERDETAILS tables, grouped by PRODUCTLINE. With this query, we can easily build a total sales by product line report, shown as a pie chart.

1. To create a new report, select File ➤ New ➤ Report, enter a file name, and click Finish.

2. Within the Data Explorer view, create a data source to the Classic Models sample database, as explained in the previous section.

3. To create a new dataset for the total sales by product line, from the Data Explorer view, right-click Data Sets and select New. Enter the SQL shown at the beginning of this section into the editor. You can preview the results of this query, as shown in Figure 9-5.

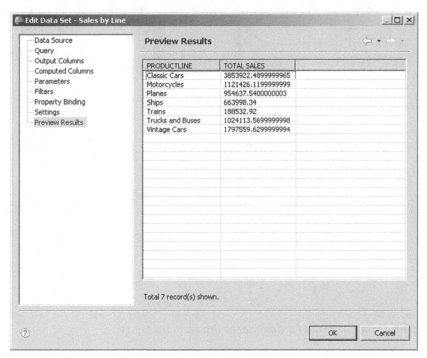

Figure 9-5. *Query results for the total sales by product line query*

4. Drag and drop the chart icon from the Palette view into the Layout view.

5. Customize the chart. Double-click the chart within the editor, set the type to Pie and the Dimension to 2D with Depth.

6. Click the Select Data tab. Choose the "Use Data from" option and select the dataset created in step 3 (Sales by Product Line). The query will be displayed in the preview area.

7. Bind the query data by dragging the TOTAL SALES column header into the pie chart's Series Definition. Drag the PRODUCTLINE into the Category Definition, as shown in Figure 9-6.

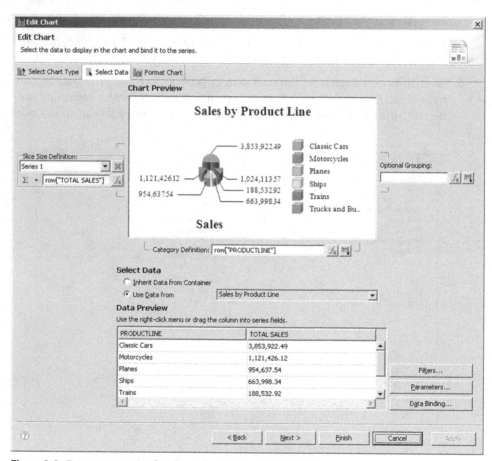

Figure 9-6. *Data properties for the Sales by Product Line chart*

8. Click the Format Chart tab. Change the data series label, chart title, and other format items, as desired. Then click Finish.

9. Select the Preview tab in the Layout view to inspect the results, as shown in Figure 9-7.

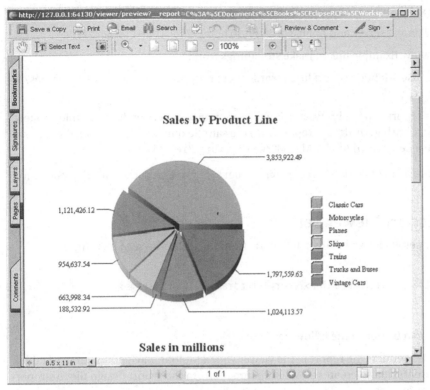

Figure 9-7. *Sales by Product Line chart from the sample database*

Using BIRT Within a Servlet Container

BIRT can also be used as a report server within a servlet container such as Apache Tomcat, or a Java EE server such as JBoss. To do this, you must deploy the BIRT Runtime into the servlet container, and then copy your reports to a server folder. With the server in place, you can use the report viewer servlet to display your reports, or you can create custom reports using BIRT's JSP tag library within your web application. The next sections explain how to deploy a report server, display your reports using the report viewer servlet, and build a custom report viewer using the JSP tag library.

Deploying the BIRT Runtime

This section shows how to build a report server by deploying the BIRT Runtime within the Tomcat servlet container.[1] Here are the steps:

1. Download the latest BIRT Runtime from the Eclipse web site, `http://download.eclipse.org/birt/downloads/` (the file name should be `birt-runtime-2_3_0.zip`).

2. Unzip the folder to a working directory.

---

1. See "Installing the BIRT Viewer in Tomcat" at `http://www.eclipse.org/birt/phoenix/deploy/viewerSetup.php`.

3. Copy the WAR archive (`birt.war`) to the `TOMCAT_HOME/webapps` folder.

4. Start the Tomcat server and open a browser to `http://localhost:8080/birt/`.

5. Click the View Example link to make sure things work.

6. Copy your user-defined report files (`.rptdesign` or `.rptdoc`) to `TOMCAT_HOME/webapps/birt/report`.

7. View your reports from a browser using the report viewer servlet. For example, to view the `ProductCatalog.rptdesign` report from the sample database (assuming the report design has been copied to `TOMCAT_HOME/webapps/birt/report`), use this URL:

   `http://localhost:8080/birt/frameset?__report=report/ProductCatalog.rptdesign`

Using the Report Viewer Servlet

The report viewer servlet is used to display reports from the web browser.[2] Its format is as follows:

`http://localhost:8080/birt/<mapping>?<servlet_params>&<user_params>`

where:

- `<mapping>` can be one of the following:

  - `frameset` renders the report in the viewer with a toolbar, navigation bar, and table of contents. It also creates a report document from the report design file to support the Ajax features.

  - `run` renders the report without toolbar, navigation bar, or table of contents. Moreover, it does not create a report document. It does use Ajax, however.

  - `preview` previews a report design or document in an output format (such as PDF, DOC, or HTML).

- `<servlet_params>` are the servlet parameters sent in the URL. They start with two underscores (`__`). Table 9-1 describes the most important parameters.[3]

- `<user_params>` are defined within the report design (for example, the order number for an order details report). User parameters defined as required in the report design but not passed in the URL will cause the viewer to display a user parameter entry page (which makes sense, because you cannot view order details without an order number, for example).

You configure the report viewer servlet within the `${birt home}/WEB-INF/web.xml` file. Some of the most important parameters are described in Table 9-2.[4]

---

2. See "Using the BIRT Report Viewer" at `http://www.eclipse.org/birt/phoenix/deploy/viewerUsage2.2.php`.
3. For a complete list of parameters, see the Parameters section of "Using the BIRT Report Viewer" at `http://www.eclipse.org/birt/phoenix/deploy/viewerUsage2.2.php#parameters`.
4. For a compete list of parameters, see the Web Viewer Web.xml Settings section of "Using the BIRT Report Viewer" at `http://www.eclipse.org/birt/phoenix/deploy/viewerUsage2.2.php#webxml`.

Table 9-1. *Some Report Viewer Servlet Parameters*

Parameter	Description
__bookmark	A bookmark within the report to load. The page with the bookmark will be loaded automatically.
__document	The name for the report document. It can be an absolute path or a path relative to the working folder.
__fittopage	Whether a generated PDF should fit the report contents to a page (true or false).
__format	Output format (such as pdf, html, doc, ppt, or xls).
__id	Unique viewer ID.
__isnull	Specifies that a report parameter is null.
__locale	The locale (en-US by default).
__masterpage	Whether the report master page should be used (true or false).
__navigationbar	Whether the navigation bar appears in the frameset viewer (true by default).
__overwrite	Whether to force an overwrite of the existing report document (true or false). Overrides the setting in web.xml. (By default, overwriting takes places whenever the report design is changed.)
__page	A specific page to render.
__pagerange	A specific page range to render.
__report	The name of the report design to process. It can be an absolute path or a path relative to the working folder.
__resourceFolder	The resource folder (used to contain libraries, images, and resource files) to use. Overrides the default setting in web.xml.
__rtl	Whether to show the report in right-to-left format (false by default).
__title	The report title.
__toolbar	Whether the report toolbar appears in the frameset viewer (true by default).

Table 9-2. *Some Report Viewer web.xml Configuration Parameters*

Parameter	Description	Default
BIRT_RESOURCE_PATH	Resource location directory	${birt home}
BIRT_VIEWER_DOCUMENT_FOLDER	Directory in which to generate report documents	${birt home}/webapp/documents
BIRT_VIEWER_IMAGE_DIR	Directory for image and chart output	${birt home}/report/images
BIRT_VIEWER_LOCALE	Locale	en-US
BIRT_VIEWER_LOG_DIR	Directory for the engine log directory	${birt home}/logs.
BIRT_VIEWER_MAX_ROWS	Maximum number of rows to retrieve from a dataset	All
BIRT_VIEWER_SCRIPTLIB_DIR	Directory for report script JAR libraries	${birt home}/scriptlib

Continued

Table 9-2. *Continued*

Parameter	Description	Default
BIRT_VIEWER_WORKING_FOLDER	Default directory for report designs (can be an absolute or relative path; if relative, the path will be prepended to the report name)	reports
WORKING_FOLDER_ACCESS_ONLY	Whether reports will be searched relative to the working folder; a setting of true prevents users from entering full paths to reports	false

Using the JSP Tag Library

BIRT provides even more flexibility through a JSP tag library. This tag library is most useful when writing custom report JSPs within your web application. The library is composed of five major JSP tags:[5]

- `<birt:viewer>`: Displays a complete viewer (with a toolbar and navigation bar) within an IFRAME using the /run or /frameset mapping (described in the previous section). Table 9-3 shows some of the important attributes of this tag.

- `<birt:report>`: Displays a preview report (with a toolbar) inside an IFRAME or DIV. It uses the /preview mapping without creating a report document. This tag takes most of the attributes listed in Table 9-3, as well as those listed in Table 9-4.

- `<birt:param>`: Defines parameters within the report tag. Table 9-5 lists some attributes of this tag.

- `<birt:parameterPage>`: Used to create a custom parameter page for user-defined report parameters.

- `<birt:paramDef>`: Used within a parameterPage tag to retrieve HTML for complex parameter types, such as radio button, check box, or cascaded parameters.

Table 9-3. *Some <birt:viewer> JSP Tag Attributes*

Attribute	Description
id	Unique viewer ID.
pattern	The mapping: run or frameset (frameset by default).
baseURL	Used to determine the location of the viewer application. Not required if the tags are used in the same context as the BIRT viewer. When the tags are used in a separate context but in the same application server, baseURL may contain a value such as "/ WebViewerExample".
format	The output format, such as PDF, HTML, or XLS.
isHostPage	When true, the viewer tag will occupy the entire page; when false (the default), multiple reports can be contained in one JSP page.

---

5. Tables 9-3, 9-4, and 9-5 show the most important attributes for the JSP tags. For a complete list, see the Viewer Tag Library section of "Using the BIRT Report Viewer" at http://www.eclipse.org/birt/phoenix/deploy/viewerUsage2.2.php#tags.

Attribute	Description
scrolling	The IFRAME scrolling style: auto, yes, or no.[a]
position	The IFRAME position style when the report viewer has a navigation bar and toolbar:static, absolute, relative, or fixed.[a]
height	The height of the IFRAME in pixels.[a]
width	The width of the IFRAME in pixels.[a]
top	The top margin of the IFRAME in pixels.[a]
left	The left margin of the IFRAME in pixels. [a]
reportDesign	The name of the report design file. This can be relative, set to a full path, or set to a URL.
reportDocument	The name of the report document file. This can be relative, set to a full path, or set to a file URL.
pageNum	The page number you wish to display (for multipage reports).
showParameterPage	Whether the parameter page is displayed.
title	The title for the report container page.

[a] If isHostPage *is* true, *these values are ignored.*

■Note Most of the attributes in Table 9-3 also apply to the <birt:report> tag. The exceptions are showToolBar, showNavigationBar, and showTitle.

Table 9-4. *Some <birt:report> JSP Tag Attributes*

Attribute	Description
resourceFolder	The resource folder (which stores libraries and images). It overrides the value specified in web.xml.
reportContainer	Defines the report HTML container: an IFRAME or a DIV element.
showParameterPage	Specifies whether the report parameter page is displayed. (Report parameters can be the order ID for an order details report, for example.)

Table 9-5. *Some <birt:param> JSP Tag Attributes*

Attribute	Description
id	Unique viewer ID.
name	Report parameter name. This must match the report design file.
isLocale	Whether the report parameter value is a locale/format-related string (true or false).
value	The value for the report parameter. If not supplied, the default value for the parameter is used.
displayText	The display text for the parameter.

Using the JSP tag library within your web application is easy. Here is how:

1. Copy the `WEB-INF/tlds/birt.tld` file to your `WEB-INF/tlds` directory.

2. Copy `coreapi.jar`, `modelapi,jar`, `viewerservlets.jar`, `engineapi.jar`, and `com.ibm. icu_3.6.1v*.jar` from `WEB-INF/lib` to the new `WEB-INF/lib` directory.

3. Add the following reference to your `web.xml` file:

```
<jsp-config>
 <taglib>
  <taglib-uri>/birt.tld</taglib-uri>
  <taglib-location>/WEB-INF/tlds/birt.tld</taglib-location>
  </taglib>
</jsp-config>
```

Listing 9-1 shows a simple JSP page that uses BIRT's JSP tag library. The page uses the `<birt:viewer>` tag to process the `SalesInvoince.rptdesign` report using the `/frameset` URL mapping. The report will prompt for an order number as an argument and set the output to HTML. The result is shown in Figure 9-8.

Listing 9-1. *A Report Viewer JSP Using the BIRT Tag Library (SalesInvoice.jsp)*

```
<%@ page language="java" contentType="text/html; charset=ISO-8859-1"
    pageEncoding="ISO-8859-1"%>
<%@ taglib uri="/birt.tld" prefix="birt" %>
<!DOCTYPE html PUBLIC "-//W3C//DTD HTML 4.01 Transitional//EN"
  "http://www.w3.org/TR/html4/loose.dtd">
<html>
<head>
<meta http-equiv="Content-Type" content="text/html; charset=ISO-8859-1">
<title>Sales Invoice Report Viewer</title>
</head>
<body>

<birt:viewer id="birtViewer" reportDesign="report/SalesInvoice.rptdesign"
  pattern="frameset"
  height="600"
  width="800"
  format="html">
</birt:viewer>

</body>
</html>
```

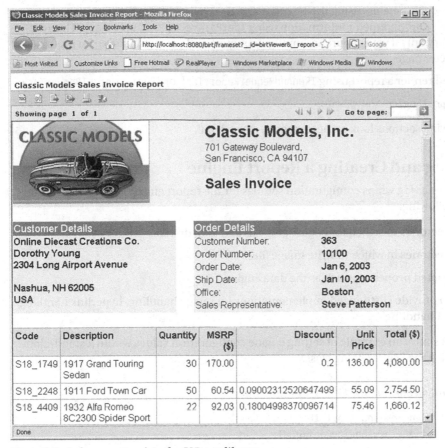

Figure 9-8. *Sales report using the JSP tag library*

Using the Report Engine API

There is another way of using BIRT if you do not wish to use the GUIs it provides. The Report Engine API is a tool for developers to use BIRT within a stand-alone Java application, a servlet, or an RCP application.

Using the API usually involves the following steps:

1. Set report engine configuration values, such as the engine home directory and log configuration (not required within RCP), with `EngineConfig`.

2. For a stand-alone application or servlet, set the report engine home and start the Eclipse Platform.

3. Create an instance of the report engine to perform multiple tasks.

4. Open a report design document using one of the `openReport` methods of the report engine.

5. Set report parameters using the `IRunTask` and the `IRunAndRenderTask` interfaces, or extract report parameter information using `IGetParameterDefinitionTask`. This is necessary only if your report has input parameters and you are building an input parameter page.

6. Run and render a report using `IRunAndRenderReportTask` or `IRunTask` and `IRenderTask`.

7. Call `ReportEngine.shutdown()`.

The following sections look at these steps in more detail.

Configuring and Creating a Report Engine

The class `EngineConfig` wraps configuration settings for the report engine. The configuration includes the following:

- The directories to search for engine plug-ins and data drivers
- The directories in which to write image files
- Data-related properties, such as the data engine
- Ways to provide customized implementations for image handling, hyperlink handling, and font handling

Listing 9-2 shows an example of setting engine configuration values within a stand-alone application using the `EngineConfig` class.

Listing 9-2. *Setting Report Engine Configuration Values*

```
// Configure the engine and start the Platform
EngineConfig config = new EngineConfig( );

// Set the engine home. Not required for RCP
config.setEngineHome( "C:/birt-runtime-VERSION/ReportEngine" );

// Set the log configuration. Use ( null, Level ) if you do not want a log file
config.setLogConfig("c:/birt/logs", Level.FINE);

// Start Eclipse. Not required for RCP
Platform.startup( config );

// Create an engine ...
```

Next, you create a report engine instance using the public interface `IReportEngine`.[6] Here is where you customize the report generation and rendering process. Through the report engine, reports can be generated and rendered to different output formats. Queries can also be executed for preview purposes, without requiring the generation of a full report.

Listing 9-3 shows how to create a report engine using the factory class `IReportEngineFactory`.

---

6. See the Report Engine API at http://www.birt-exchange.com/documentation/BIRT_220/EngineJavadoc/engine/api/org/eclipse/birt/report/engine/api/IReportEngine.html.

Listing 9-3. *Creating a Report Engine*

```
// Get a report engine factory
IReportEngineFactory factory = (IReportEngineFactory) Platform
    .createFactoryObject( IReportEngineFactory.EXTENSION_REPORT_ENGINE_FACTORY );

// Get a report engine
IReportEngine engine = factory.createReportEngine( config );
engine.changeLogLevel( Level.WARNING );
```

What Kinds of Operations Can Be Done with the Report Engine?

The report engine provides the developer a high degree of control over reports. BIRT reports are classified using two public interfaces: IReportDocument for a report document (.rptdocument) or IReportRunnable for a report design (.rptdesign). The method for opening a report document is IReportEngine.openReportDocument(), and the method for opening a report design is IReportEngine.openReportDesign().

IReportEngine is capable of creating five different types of operations, also known as *tasks*:

- The data extraction task allows data extraction from a report document.

- The get parameter definitions task obtains report parameter definitions.

- The render task renders the report to a specific output format.

- The run task runs a report to generate a report document.

- The run and render task runs and renders a report directly to an output format.

These tasks are discussed in more detail in the following sections.

Creating a Data Extraction Task

The IDataExtractionTask, created with createDataExtractionTask(IReportDocument), allows the extraction of data from a report document. If you don't specify a report component ID or report component instance ID, the extraction will be based on all the data stored in the report. You can also use the getMetaData() method to get metadata for each result set and use that to further manipulate the data returned.

Listing 9-4 shows a data extraction task to display the first two columns of the first result set of a document.

Listing 9-4. *Data Extraction Task*

```
// Open report document
IReportDocument iReportDocument = engine.
    openReportDocument("c:/report.rptdocument");

// Create data extraction task
IDataExtractionTask iDataExtract = engine.createDataExtractionTask(iReportDocument);
```

```
// Get list of result sets
ArrayList resultSetList = (ArrayList)iDataExtract.getResultSetList( );

// Choose first result set
IResultSetItem resultItem = (IResultSetItem)resultSetList.get( 0 );

String dispName = resultItem.getResultSetName( );
iDataExtract.selectResultSet( dispName );

IExtractionResults iExtractResults = iDataExtract.extract();

IDataIterator iData = null;

try
{
 if ( iExtractResults != null )
 {
    iData = iExtractResults.nextResultIterator( );

    //Iterate through the results
    if ( iData != null  ) {
        while ( iData.next( ) )
          {
              Object objColumn1 = iData.getValue(0);
              Object objColumn2 = iData.getValue(1);
              System.out.println( objColumn1 + " , " + objColumn2 );
          }
          iData.close();
    }
 }
}
catch( Exception e)
{
  e.printStackTrace();
}

iDataExtract.close();
```

Creating a Parameter Definition Task

The IGetParameterDefinitionTask task, created with createGetParameterDefinitionTask
(IReportRunnable), retrieves parameter definitions, default values, and dynamic selection lists
from a report. Parameter definitions provide access to the parameter definition information
entered at design time.

Listing 9-5 shows an example of a task that opens a report design and iterates through the
parameters and parameter groups.

Listing 9-5. *Report Parameter Definition Task*

```
// Open a report design
IReportRunnable design = engine.openReportDesign("C:/path/report.rptdesign");

IGetParameterDefinitionTask task = engine.
        createGetParameterDefinitionTask( design );
Collection params = task.getParameterDefns( true );

Iterator iter = params.iterator( );

// Iterate over parameters
while ( iter.hasNext( ) )
{
    IParameterDefnBase param = (IParameterDefnBase) iter.next( );

    // Group section found
    if ( param instanceof IParameterGroupDefn )
    {
            // Get group name
            IParameterGroupDefn group = (IParameterGroupDefn) param;
            System.out.println( "Parameter Group: " + group.getName( ) );

            // Get the parameters within a group
            Iterator i2 = group.getContents( ).iterator();

            while ( i2.hasNext( ) ) {
               IScalarParameterDefn scalar = (IScalarParameterDefn) i2.next( );
               System.out.println(" " + scalar.getName());
            }
    }
    Else {
            // Parameters are not in a group
            IScalarParameterDefn scalar = (IScalarParameterDefn) param;
            System.out.println(param);
    }
}

task.close();
```

Creating a Render Task

The IRenderTask task, created with createRenderTask(IReportDocument), renders a report document to one of the output formats supported by the report engine. It can render just a page or range of pages, or the entire report (if no page is specified).

The report engine uses an *emitter* to generate the output. You use the HTMLRenderOption or PDFRenderOption class, for HTML or PDF output, respectively.

When rendering HTML with HTMLRenderOption, you need to be sure that images are handled properly. There are two ways to handle images: with HTMLCompleteImageHandler or with HTMLServerImageHandler. HTMLCompleteImageHandler (the default) writes images to disk when rendering a report:

```
HTMLRenderOption options = new HTMLRenderOption();

options.setOutputFileName("output/report.html");
options.setImageDirectory("output/image");
options.setOutputFormat("html");
```

HTMLServerImageHandler handles images for a report running in an application server. Use this handler within web applications:

```
HTMLRenderOption options = new HTMLRenderOption();
options.setOutputFileName("output/resample/TopNPercent.html");
options.setOutputFormat("html");

// Write images to app server
options.setImageDirectory("C:\apache-tomcat\webapps\birt\reports\images");

// Append http://localhost:8080/birt/reports/images/ to image hyperlinks
options.setBaseImageURL("http://localhost:8080/birt/reports/images/");
options.setImageHandler(new HTMLServerImageHandler());
```

PDFRenderOption defines output settings for PDF format, as follows:

```
IRenderOption options = new RenderOption();

// Render as PDF
options.setOutputFormat("pdf");
options.setOutputFileName("output/report.pdf");

// PDF options
PDFRenderOption pdfOptions = new PDFRenderOption( options );
pdfOptions.setOption( IPDFRenderOption.FIT_TO_PAGE, new Boolean(true) );
pdfOptions.setOption( IPDFRenderOption.PAGEBREAK_PAGINATION_ONLY
  , new Boolean(true) );

task.setRenderOption(options);
```

RenderOptionBase defines options for rendering a report to an output format, such as whether to render HTML with a style sheet. Future options may include image formats in PDF (vector or bitmap), font embedding, and others.

■Note Custom emitters for other output formats can be created by implementing the interface org. eclipse.birt.report.engine.api.IRenderOption. In fact, this is how the PDF and HTML renderers are implemented. However, this could be a fairly complex task.

Listing 9-6 shows an example of creating a render task to output the report in HTML and PDF format.

Listing 9-6. *Report Render Task (HTML and PDF)*

```
// Open a report document
IReportDocument iReportDocument = engine.openReportDocument("report.rptdocument");

// Create render task
IRenderTask task = engine.createRenderTask(iReportDocument);

// Set parent classloader report engine
task.getAppContext().put(EngineConstants.APPCONTEXT_CLASSLOADER_KEY
  , RenderTaskExample.class.getClassLoader());

// Render as HTML
IRenderOption options = new RenderOption();
options.setOutputFormat("html");
options.setOutputFileName("output/report.html");

// HTML options
HTMLRenderOption htmlOptions = new HTMLRenderOption( options);
htmlOptions.setImageDirectory("output/image");
htmlOptions.setHtmlPagination(false);

// Create task
IRenderTask task = engine.createRenderTask(document);

task.setRenderOption(options);
task.setPageRange("1-2");
task.render();

// Render as PDF too
options.setOutputFormat("pdf");
options.setOutputFileName("output/report.pdf");

// PDF options
PDFRenderOption pdfOptions = new PDFRenderOption( options );
pdfOptions.setOption( IPDFRenderOption.FIT_TO_PAGE, new Boolean(true) );
pdfOptions.setOption( IPDFRenderOption.PAGEBREAK_PAGINATION_ONLY
  , new Boolean(true) );

task.setRenderOption(options);
task.render();

iReportDocument.close();
```

Creating a Run Task

Use the IRunTask task, created with createRunTask(IReportRunnable), to run a report and generate a report document, which is saved to disk. The report document can then be used with the IRenderTask to support features such as paging. Listing 9-7 shows an example of creating a run task.

Listing 9-7. *Run Task, Used to Create a Report Document*

```
// Open document
IReportRunnable design = engine.openReportDesign("report.rptdesign");

// Create task to run the report
// Use the task to execute the report and save to disk.
IRunTask task = engine.createRunTask(design);

// Set parent classloader for engine
task.getAppContext().put(
     EngineConstants.APPCONTEXT_CLASSLOADER_KEY,
     RunTaskExample.class.getClassLoader());

// Run the report and destroy the engine
task.run("c:/work/test/report.rptdocument");

// Close task
task.close();
```

Creating a Run and Render Task

The IRunAndRenderTask task, created with createRunAndRenderTask(IReportRunnable), combines the previous two tasks to run and render a report. This task does not create a report document. Listing 9-8 shows an example of creating a run and render task.

Listing 9-8. *Run and Render Report As PDF Task*

```
// Open the report design
IReportRunnable design = engine.openReportDesign("Reports/SalesInvoice.rptdesign");

// Create task
IRunAndRenderTask task = engine.createRunAndRenderTask(design);

// Set parent classloader for engine
task.getAppContext().put(
     EngineConstants.APPCONTEXT_CLASSLOADER_KEY,
     RunAndRenderTaskExample.class.getClassLoader());
```

```
// Set report parameters and validate
task.setParameterValue("Oredr Number", (new Integer(10100)));;
task.validateParameters();

// Render to PDF
PDFRenderOption options = new PDFRenderOption();

options.setOption( IPDFRenderOption.FIT_TO_PAGE, new Boolean(true) );
options.setOption( IPDFRenderOption.PAGEBREAK_PAGINATION_ONLY,
    new Boolean(true) );

options.setOutputFileName("output/resample/SalesInvoice.pdf");
options.setOutputFormat("html");
task.setRenderOption(options);

// Run and render report
task.run();
task.close();
```

The previous sections have explained the basics of creating programmatic reports using the BIRT engine. The next section demonstrates these concepts with a practical exercise.

Hands-on Exercise: Report Generation from the OSGi Console

As you've learned, BIRT provides a powerful set of UI tools to design and render reports. In this exercise, let's try to do something different by building a report generator within the OSGi console. The idea is to type a simple console command with arguments such as report design, output format, and report parameters, and have an output document on disk.

In this exercise, you will learn how to extend the OSGi console with custom user commands, as well as how to create a report generator class using the BIRT Runtime API.

Extending the OSGi Console

To begin, create a new plug-in project using the Plug-in Project wizard. Name the new project something like ch06.Reports. Uncheck the "This plug-in will make contributions to the UI" option, and set "Would you like to create a rich client application?" to No. (This plug-in will be run within the OSGi framework (Equinox); thus, it won't be an RCP.)

The new plug-in must be modified to extend the OSGi console. This will allow the user to type custom commands when running in console mode. When an object wants to provide a number of commands to the console, it must implement the interface org.eclipse.osgi.framework.console.CommandProvider, and define the commands as methods starting with a _ character and taking a CommandInterpreter as argument. At runtime, the console will find all the public commands. For example, the next fragment defines the command `hello`:

```
public Object _hello( CommandInterpreter intp ) {
  return "hello " + intp.nextArgument();
}
```

Note When implementing the `CommandInterpreter` interface, the plug-in class must override public `String getHelp()` to return help text that explains the command.

The goal is to add a report command to generate a report document using the BIRT Runtime. Open the plug-in `Activator` class (`Activator.java`) and insert a report command, as shown in Listing 9-9.

Listing 9-9. *Plug-in Activator with a Report Command*

```
public class Activator extends Plugin implements CommandProvider {

    // The plug-in ID
    public static final String PLUGIN_ID = "ch09.Reports";

    // The shared instance
    private static Activator plugin;

    /**
     * The constructor
     */
    public Activator() {
    }

    @SuppressWarnings("unchecked")
    public void start(BundleContext context) throws Exception {
        super.start(context);
        plugin = this;

        Hashtable properties = new Hashtable();
        context.registerService(CommandProvider.class.getName(), this,
                properties);
    }

    public void stop(BundleContext context) throws Exception {
        plugin = null;
        super.stop(context);
    }
```

```java
    public static Activator getDefault() {
        return plugin;
    }

    @Override
    public String getHelp() {
        return "---BIRT Console Commands---"
            + "\n\treport <input_file> <output_file> <format> <user_params>"
            + "\n\t\tuser params: name1=value1&name2=value2&...";
    }

    /**
     * Report command
     *
     * @param ci
     * @throws Exception
     */
    public void _report(CommandInterpreter ci) throws Exception {
        // Generate report here...
    }
}
```

Listing 9-9 shows a plug-in activator that defines the _report command, which will render a report from the command line. This class also registers the CommandProvider service (within the start() method), with the specified properties, with the framework:

```java
context.registerService(CommandProvider.class.getName(), this, properties)
```

Generating the Report

The plug-in needs a report generator to use the BIRT Runtime to create a document based on command arguments. This requires two additions to the plug-in:

- BIRT dependencies in the plug-in manifest
- A ReportGenerator Java class to generate the actual document(s)

Add the following BIRT dependencies within the plug-in manifest:

- org.eclipse.birt.core
- org.eclipse.birt.report.engine

To use the Classic Models sample database, add the following:

- org.eclipse.birt.report.data.oda.sampledb

To render charts within a document, add four packages:

- org.eclipse.birt.chart.runtime
- org.eclipse.birt.chart.device.pdf

- org.eclipse.birt.chart.device.svg
- org.eclipse.birt.chart.engine

To support multiple output formats, add five more packages:

- org.eclipse.birt.report.engine.emitter.html
- org.eclipse.birt.report.engine.emitter.pdf
- org.eclipse.birt.report.engine.emitter.postscript
- org.eclipse.birt.report.engine.emitter.ppt
- org.eclipse.birt.report.engine.emitter.prototype.excel

Listing 9-10 shows ReportGenerator.java, a class that uses a report engine (IReportEngine) to provide reporting functionalities. This class uses IRunAndRenderTask to run and render a report to one of the output formats supported by the engine. This task supports report parameters sent through the command line, and output options such as format or file name defined through the IRenderOption interface.

Listing 9-10. *ReportGenerator.java: A Class to Generate a Report Document Using the BIRT Runtime*

```
public class ReportGenerator {
    IReportEngine engine;

    public ReportGenerator() {
        final EngineConfig config = new EngineConfig();

        IReportEngineFactory factory = (IReportEngineFactory) Platform
            .createFactoryObject(
                    IReportEngineFactory.EXTENSION_REPORT_ENGINE_FACTORY);

        engine = factory.createReportEngine(config);
    }

    /**
     * Run and render report task
     * @param designDocPath
     *             Design document
     * @param params
     *             Report params as a query string name1=val1&name2=val2,...
     * @param outFormat
     *             pdf, html, etc.
     * @param out
     *             Output file
     * @throws EngineException
     */
```

```java
@SuppressWarnings("unchecked")
public void runAndRender(String designDocPath, String outFileName
        , String outFormat, String params)
        throws EngineException
{
    // Open the report design
    IReportRunnable design = engine.openReportDesign(designDocPath);

    // Create task to run and render the report,
    IRunAndRenderTask task = engine.createRunAndRenderTask(design);

    // Set parent classloader for engine
    task.getAppContext().put(
            EngineConstants.APPCONTEXT_CLASSLOADER_KEY,
            ReportGenerator.class.getClassLoader());

    if (params != null) {
        task.setParameterValues(splitParams(params));
        task.validateParameters();
    }

    // Render options
    IRenderOption options = new RenderOption();
    options.setOutputFormat(outFormat);
    options.setOutputFileName(outFileName);

    task.setRenderOption(options);

    // Run and render report
    task.run();
    task.close();
}

public void destroy() {
    engine.destroy();
}

/**
 * Extract report params from a query string. Values must be integer
 * @param queryString
 *              name1=val1&name2=val2&....
 * @return
 */
private static HashMap<String, Object> splitParams(String queryString) {
    String[] pairs = queryString.split("&");
    HashMap<String, Object> params = new HashMap<String, Object>();
```

```
    if (pairs == null)
        return null;

    for (int i = 0; i < pairs.length; i++) {
        String[] keyVal = pairs[i].split("=");

        if (keyVal == null)
            throw new IllegalArgumentException(
                    "Invalid params quer string:" + queryString);
        // Values must be integers
        params.put(keyVal[0], new Integer(keyVal[1]));
    }
    return params;
}

}
```

The ReportGenerator.java class in Listing 9-10 has four major methods:

- ReportGenerator(): This is the ReportGenerator constructor. Its role is to create a report engine factory (IReportEngineFactory), which is used to create a report engine (IReportEngine).

- runAndRender(String designDocPath, String outFileName, String outFormat, String params): This method opens a report document specified by designDocPath. It then creates an IRunAndRenderTask task and sets report parameters, if any. It sets the render options output file name (outFileName) and format (outFormat; for example, PDF). Finally, it starts the task to generate the output report.

Note Report parameters are sent in a string, such as name1=val1&name2=val2,..., which must be split into a Java HashMap object for the engine to process.

- destroy(): This method cleans up by destroying the engine and releasing resources.
- splitParams(String queryString): This is a utility method to split the user parameter string into a Java HashMap that can be understood by the engine.

All the pieces are now in place. The final step is to add logic to the Activator class to call the report generator when the user types a report command, as shown in Listing 9-11.

Listing 9-11. *Plug-in Activator _report Command Subroutine*

```
public void _report(CommandInterpreter ci) throws Exception {
    String in = ci.nextArgument();
    String out = ci.nextArgument();
    String fmt = ci.nextArgument();
    String params = ci.nextArgument();
```

```
  if (in == null) {
    ci.println("Invalid arguments.\n" + getHelp());
    return;
  }

  try {
    ReportGenerator generator = new ReportGenerator();
    generator.runAndRender(in, out, fmt, params);
    generator.destory();

    ci.println(out);

  } catch (Exception e) {
    e.printStackTrace();
  }
}
```

In Listing 9-11, arguments are read from the command interpreter and passed to the report generator, which will create a report output file. In this case, the input arguments are a report design document (.rptdesign), an output report document, the output format (PDF), and report arguments. For example, to render the top 10% selling items (TopNPercent) report from the Classic Models sample database, use this command:

```
osgi> report <path to report>/TopNPercent.rptdesign
c:/Documents/TopNPercent.pdf pdf "Top Percentage=10&Top Count=3"
```

Note that TopNPercent.rptdesign is a report created using the built-in templates from the Report Designer.

Running the Report Generator Plug-in

To run the report generator plug-in, create an OSGi framework launch configuration, as follows:

1. Select Run ➤ Run Configurations.

2. Right-click OSGi Framework and select New.

3. Enter a descriptive name, such as Report Generator.

4. Under Bundles. check the ch09.Reports plug-in. Click Add Required Bundles, and then click Validate Bundles to make sure all dependencies are selected.

5. Click Apply and Run.

6. At the console prompt, type help to see the command arguments. To render a report design, use the following format:

   ```
   report <input_file> <output_file> <format> <user_params:name1=
      value1&name2=value2&...>
   ```

Summary

This chapter covered using BIRT. The following are the important points:

- BIRT is a powerful reporting system for RCP, stand-alone, or web applications.

- Reports can be lists of data, charts, spreadsheets, documents, and compound reports.

- BIRT consists of the Report Designer UI, a Runtime API, and a Chart engine.

- The Report Designer is the tool of choice to create reports. It consists of Data Explorer, Palette, Property Editor, and Layout views.

- BIRT can also be used as a report server within a Java EE server such as Tomcat or JBoss.

  - To use BIRT within Tomcat, copy the file `birt.war` from the report runtime to the `TOMCAT_HOME/webapps` folder, and then simply browse to `http://localhost:8080/birt/`.

  - To view user reports within the Java EE report servlet, copy any design documents to your web application reports folder, and then simply browse to `http://localhost:8080/birt/frameset?__report=folder/report.rptdesign&param1=value1`.

- The servlet URL mapping can be `frameset` (to create a report within an IFRAME with a toolbar and report document), `run` (to create a report without a navigation bar), and `preview` (to create a report without toolbars).

- BIRT provides even more flexibility through a JSP tag library. The library is composed of five major tags:

  - `viewer` to display a complete viewer with a navigation bar and toolbars

  - `report` to display a preview report inside an IFRAME or a DIV without a document

  - `param` to define parameters

  - `parameterPage` to create a custom parameter page

  - `paramDef`, used within a `parameterPage` to retrieve HTML for complex parameter types such as radio buttons, check boxes, and cascaded parameters

- The Report Engine API is a tool for developers to use BIRT within a stand-alone Java application, a servlet, or an RCP application. Use the Report Engine API as follows:

  - Set report options with `EngineConfig`.

  - Set the engine home and start the Eclipse Platform, if running stand-alone or within Java EE.

  - Create an instance of the `ReportEngine` to perform multiple tasks.

  - Open a report design using one of the `openReport` methods of `ReportEngine`.

  - Set report parameters using the `IRunTask` and the `IRunAndRenderTask` interfaces, or extract report parameter information using `IGetParameterDefinitionTask`.

  - Run and render a report using `IRunAndRenderReportTask` or `IRunTask` and `IRenderTask`.

  - Clean up with `ReportEngine.shutdown()`.

■ ■ ■

## CHAPTER 10

Automated Updates

The Eclipse update manager is a powerful framework to publish bundles of plug-ins (known as *features*) to an update site so that clients can download and install them directly into an RCP application. Couple this with the possibility of building plug-ins automatically outside the workbench (also known as a *headless build*), and you have a complete solution to automate distribution of your RCP application.

In this chapter, you will learn how to build a feature and update site project to provide web updates to an RCP application, as well as how to build RCP plug-ins outside the workbench using the headless build system.

Updating and Installing Software the Eclipse Way

Eclipse provides facilities for adding new software to the platform or updating software in the system, thus providing a convenient way to deliver updates to your users. The install update process usually involves the following steps:

Define and configure a product: This is the first step when packaging and delivering an RCP application. Eclipse provides a standard for packaging, configuring, and installing using the product extension point (org.eclipse.core.runtime.products). This extension point describes information such as application name and startup class, as well as custom properties such as window images, splash screen, and About dialog information. The product configuration also defines the plug-ins that compose the product, as well as dependencies, information about the binary launcher, and runtime configuration data.

Build a feature project: A feature is a way of grouping and describing different functionality that makes up a product. Grouping plug-ins into features allows the product to be installed and updated using the Eclipse update system. Features may also include fragments that are useful for packaging locale translations.

Build an update site project: An update site allows users to discover and install updated versions of products and features. In addition, the platform update UI allows users to maintain a list of update servers that can be searched for new features.

The following sections describe these steps in more detail.

Defining and Configuring a Product

A product is usually packaged and delivered as one or more features that include all the code and plug-ins needed to run them. After the product is installed, the user launches it and is presented with a workbench configured specifically for the purpose supported by the product.

Note Product providers are free to use the JRE and installation tool of their choice when building an RCP product.

The typical disk layout of a product is shown in Table 10-1.

Table 10-1. *Typical Disk Layout of an RCP Application*

Name	Type	Description
.eclipseproduct	File	Marker file used to mark a directory into which an Eclipse-based product has been installed.
artifacts.xml	File	Bundle pool contents. It is used to avoid duplication of software and other artifacts when multiple Eclipse-based applications are installed on the same computer.
eclipse.exe	File	Application launcher (its name can be customized).
eclipse.ini	File	Launch arguments. The file name must be the same as the launcher, with the extension ini.
configuration	Folder	Runtime configuration data.
features	Folder	Installed features.
plugins	Folder	Installed plug-ins.
p2	Folder	Files for Eclipse 3.4's new provisioning system, dubbed p2 (described in more detail in the "Software Update UI Tools" section later in this chapter).

Describing a Product

The preferred mechanism to describe a product is the org.eclipse.core.runtime .products extension point. You commonly define this extension point in the master plug-in that configures the workbench. For example, the web browser product created with plug-ins in Chapters 2 and 3 is shown in Listing 10-1 and Figure 10-1.

Listing 10-1. *Product Extension Point for the Web Browser RCP*

```
<extension
     id="product"
     point="org.eclipse.core.runtime.products">
  <product
       application="ch03.WebBrowser.application"
       name="Web Browser RCP">
```

```
        <property
              name="windowImages"
              value="16-earth.png,32-earth.png">
        </property>
        <property
              name="appName"
              value="Web Browser RCP">
        </property>
        <property
              name="startupForegroundColor"
              value="000000">
        </property>
        <property
              name="startupMessageRect"
              value="7,252,445,20">
        </property>
        <property
              name="startupProgressRect"
              value="5,275,445,15">
        </property>
        <property
              name="preferenceCustomization"
              value="plugin_customization.ini">
        </property>
        <property
              name="aboutImage"
              value="icons/128-earth.png">
        </property>
        <property
              name="aboutText"
              value="Web Browser Application&#x0A;Copyright 2008">
        </property>
      </product>
   </extension>
```

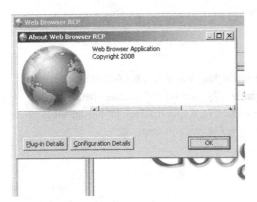

Figure 10-1. *Web Browser RCP showing window images and About dialog settings*

The `org.eclipse.core.runtime.products` extension point defines the properties shown in Table 10-2.

Table 10-2. *Properties of the org.eclipse.core.runtime.products Extension Point*

Name	Description
application	The fully qualified name of a class that implements `org.eclipse.equinox.app.IApplication`, which represents the executable entry point to the application.
windowImages	The path to two comma-separated images (16×16 and 32×32 pixels) used as window icons. Paths can be relative to the plug-in or absolute to another plug-in using the format `plugin:/plug-in-name/path/file-name`.
appName	The name of the product.
startupForegroundColor	The font color of messages displayed on the splash screen.
startupMessageRect	The bounding box for messages within the splash screen.
startupProgressRect	The bounding box for the splash screen progress bar. This box is defined by comma-separated numbers that specify the top-left point, width, and height of the progress bar. The same applies to the `startupMessageRect`.
preferenceCustomization	The name of a properties file containing default preference values for the product. This file should be placed in the master plug-in (the plug-in that defines the GUI of your RCP).
aboutImage	The About dialog image.
aboutText	The About dialog text.

Using Your Own Splash Screen

You can customize your application's splash screen by creating a file named `splash.bmp` and locating it in the plug-in declaring the product. If you wish to add a progress bar showing the plug-in load sequence, create the file `plugin_customization.ini` in the same location, and add the following property:

```
org.eclipse.ui/SHOW_PROGRESS_ON_STARTUP = true
```

■**Tip** The step of adding a custom splash screen can be automated by selecting the Add branding option from the Plug-in Project wizard when creating your RCP plug-in. Also, if you need a locale-specific image, put it in the `nl` directory beneath the plug-in's directory. For example, a splash screen for the Japanese locale (`jp_JA`) should be placed in the plug-in's directory `nl/jp/JA/splash.bmp`.

Grouping Plug-ins in Features

In the real world, an RCP application can be composed of many plug-ins working together to perform a useful function. For example, BIRT (described in the previous chapter) consists of more than 50 plug-ins. To isolate this kind of common functionality, Eclipse groups plug-ins into features. Thus, instead of installing 50 plug-ins to do reports, users need to install or update only the BIRT feature.

Features do not contain code. They contain only a list of plug-ins for the product, packaged in a archive and described using a manifest file (feature.xml). This fragment shows the basic syntax of a feature:

```
<?xml version="1.0" encoding="UTF-8"?>
<feature
      id="org.eclipse.myfeature"
      label="My Feature"
      version="1.1.0"
      provider-name="ACME Inc."
      >

<description>Feature Description</description>
<license url="http://license.com">License Text</license>
<url>
    <update label="ACME Update Site" url="http://update.acme.org/updates/3.3"/>
    <discovery label="ACME Update Site" url="http://update.acme.org/updates/3.3/">
</url>

<!-- Plug-ins that make the feature -->
<!-- One tag per plug-in -->
<plugin
      id="com.plugin1"
      download-size="0"
      install-size="0"
      version="0.1.31"
      unpack="false"/>
<!-- more plugins here -->
</feature>
```

All features are described by a required unique ID and label. Version and provider are optional information. Other tags include the following:[1]

- <license>: Specifies your license text with an optional URL.

- <url>: An optional tag that defines zero or more URLs specifying site(s) containing feature updates or new features.

- <update>: Defines the URL and label to go to for updates to this feature.

---

1. For a complete list of tags and attributes, as well as the feature document DTD, see the feature reference guide at http://help.eclipse.org/ganymede/index.jsp?topic=/org.eclipse.platform.doc.isv/reference/misc/feature_manifest.html.

- `<discovery>`: Defines the URL and label to go to for new features. You can use this element to reference your own site or a site with complementary features.

- `<plugin>`: Identifies the plug-ins that compose the feature (multiple plug-ins will require multiple tags). Plug-ins are identified by a required ID and version. Optional attributes include download and install size. The optional `unpack` attribute specifies that the plug-in is run from a JAR.

Grouping Plug-ins Within Fragments

Fragments are ideal for shipping extra functionality without repackaging or reinstalling the original plug-in, and for packing language translations.

Fragments are described using a fragment manifest file, `fragment.xml`. Fragments attach themselves to a host plug-in, and their contents are included to the host classpath at runtime.

If you are packing translations, you should use the following:

Platform core mechanism: This mechanism defines a directory structure that uses locale-specific subdirectories for files that differ by locale. Translated files are placed in a folder called `nl` beneath the plug-in. For example, French translations will be placed under `nl/fr` or `n/fr/FR` for France and `n/fr/CA` for Canadian French.

Java resource bundles: This is the standard Java approach to handling property resource bundles. Translated files are contained in a JAR file and given a locale-specific name (for example, `messages_fr_FR.properties`). The files are in package-specific subdirectories and may appear in the plug-in itself or in one of its fragments.

`plugin.properties` *mechanism*: `plugin.properties` provides translations for strings in the plug-in manifest files (which are `plugin.xml` and `MANIFEST.MF`). `plugin.properties` must be located in the root of the plug-in or in the root of a fragment of this plug-in.

Building an Update Site Project

An update site can be used to make your project available on a web server so that users can download and install it directly into Eclipse using the update manager. Creating an update site involves defining an update site project, which packs all features and plug-ins into JARs along with a site map (`site.xml`). Eclipse provides powerful tools for this task. You'll learn how to create an update site project in this chapter's hands-on exercise.

■**Caution** Updating software from a remote, nontrusted server may be a security risk. Be careful when connecting to an unknown update site and examining its content.

Software Update UI Tools

Since Eclipse 3.4, the update manager has been rewritten to a completely new provisioning platform dubbed p2. p2 was created for two main reasons:

- To simplify the work flow of the update manager, and make it simpler and more streamlined to use (hence the term provisioning updates)

- To provide bundle pooling, which allows you to share plug-ins across multiple Eclipse installations, thus eliminating duplicates (very helpful if you have multiple Eclipse installations)

The internals of p2 are transparent to the user. However, new applications and update sites can be optimized for use with p2 for managing code repositories.

■**Note** Eclipse recommends using the new update manager, rather than the legacy update manager (before version 3.4). The problem with the new update manager is that p2 needs a new disk layout, which will require changes for legacy applications.

You can also use a command-line tool provided by p2 to completely automate software installations or updates (commonly used from a scheduled script).

Using the Software Updates and Add-ons Dialog

The Software Updates and Add-ons dialog provides a UI for performing provisioning operations using p2, as shown in Figure 10-2. To access this dialog, select Help ➤ Software Updates.

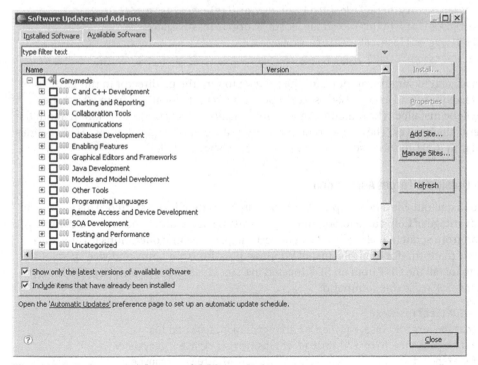

Figure 10-2. *Software Updates and Add-ons dialog*

The Software Updates and Add-ons dialog has two main tabs:

Installed Software: From this tab, you can update and uninstall features or revert to a previously installed configuration of the platform. You can also configure automatic updates by setting an update schedule, download, and notification options.

Available Software: This tab lets you browse the Ganymede code repository for features or filter names by keyword. It also allows you to add a new local or remote update site, or manage the sites used to find available software.

Installing Software from the Command Line

p2 provides a director application to perform provisioning operations from the command line. This application is capable of provisioning a complete installation from scratch or simply extending your application. Depending on your needs, this application can be executed either inside or outside the target product being provisioned.

Installing Inside the Target Application

Installing inside the target application allows you to add new components to an existing product. For example, the next fragment shows the command used to install the C/C++ Development Tools (CDT) into the SDK.

```
eclipse.exe
  -application org.eclipse.equinox.p2.director.app.application
  -metadataRepository http://download.eclipse.org/releases/ganymede/
  -artifactRepository http://download.eclipse.org/releases/ganymede/
  -installIU org.eclipse.cdt.feature.group
  -version <version>
```

The application argument indicates the product to run (the p2 director in this case). metadataRepository and artifactRepository specify the remote locations from which the product will be installed. The metadata repository usually contains only information about the components themselves. The artifact repository stores the component code. installIU defines the install unit (CDT in this case) and the version you wish to install.

Installing Outside a Target Application

When you install outside a target application, the target product is not started. This approach has the advantage of being able to both modify an existing installation and create a complete installation from scratch. It also allows you to perform provisioning operations on any platform for any platform (for example, install Windows plug-ins from Linux and vice versa). For example, to install the CDT from an SDK located in C:\eclipseSDK1 into another SDK located in D:\eclipseSDK2, use this command:

```
c:\eclipseSDK1\eclipse.exe
  -application org.eclipse.equinox.p2.director.app.application
  -metadataRepository http://download.eclipse.org/releases/ganymede/
  -artifactRepository http://download.eclipse.org/releases/ganymede/l
```

```
-installIU org.eclipse.cdt.feature.group
-version <version>
-destination d:/eclipseSDK2/
-profile SDKProfile
-Declipse.p2.data.area=d:/eclipseSDK2/p2
```

Now suppose that you wish to provide multiple-platform Eclipse installations from a single disk. For example, to install a Linux Eclipse SDK into C:/eclipse-linux-sdk from a Windows SDK located in C:/eclipse-SDK, use the following command:

```
c:\eclipse-SDK\eclipse.exe
    -application org.eclipse.equinox.p2.director.app.application
    -metadataRepository http://download.eclipse.org/eclipse/updates/3.4
    -artifactRepository http://download.eclipse.org/eclipse/updates/3.4
    -installIU org.eclipse.sdk.ide
    -destination c:/eclipse-linux-sdk/
    -profile SDKProfile
    -profileProperties org.eclipse.update.install.features=true
    -bundlepool c:/eclipse-linux-sdk/
    -p2.os linux
    -p2.ws gtk
    -p2.arch x86
    -vmargs
    -Declipse.p2.data.area=d:/eclipse-linux-sdk/p2
```

See Table 10-3 for parameter descriptions.

Table 10-3. *p2 Director Command-Line Arguments*

Parameter	Description
-application org. eclipse.equinox.p2. director.app.application	The p2 director application ID.
-metadataRepository	A comma-separated list of metadata repositories where the installable units to be installed can be found. For example, the metadata repository for Eclipse Ganymede (3.4) is http:// download.eclipse.org/eclipse/updates/3.4.
-artifactRepository	A comma-separated list of artifact repositories where the artifacts can be found.
-installIU	The ID (or unique name) of the installable unit (IU) to install. An installable unit is a component you wish to process. For example, the installable unit ID for the entire SDK is org.eclipse. sdk.ide. The installable unit ID for the CDT is org.eclipse.cdt. feature.group. If you want to install a feature, the identifier of the feature must be suffixed with .feature.group.
-version	The version of the installable unit to be installed.
-destination	The folder in which the targeted product is located. It may be a new folder for a new installation or an existing folder for an update.

Continued

Table 10-3. *Continued*

Parameter	Description
-profile	The profile ID containing the description of the targeted product. This ID is usually found in the eclipse.p2.profile property contained in the config.ini file of the targeted product. For the Eclipse SDK, the ID is SDKProfile.
-Declipse.p2.data.area	Points to the location of the profile registry containing the description of the profile set in -profile. Eclipse recommends setting this to <destination>/p2. This property must be set as a VM argument.
-bundlepool	The location where the plug-ins and features will be stored. This value is taken into account only when a new profile is created. For an application where all the bundles are located in the plugins/ folder of the destination, set this argument to <destination>.
-p2.os	The operating system to use when the profile is created. This will be used to filter which operating system-specific installable units need to be installed.
-p2.ws	The windowing system to use when the profile is created; for example, win32 for Windows or gtk for Linux. This will be used to filter which windowing system-specific installable units need to be installed.
-p2.arch	The architecture to use when the profile is created. This will be used to filter which architecture-specific installable units need to be installed.
-roaming	Indicates that the product resulting from the installation can be moved. This property makes sense only when the destination and bundle pool are in the same location, and eclipse.p2.data.area is set to <destination>/p2. This value is taken into account only when the profile is created.

Product Build Automation with the Headless Build System

When an RCP product is made of many plug-ins, it makes no sense to build it within the IDE. Clearly, an automated build system is needed. The PDE provides a headless build system to accomplish this task. In fact, Eclipse uses the org.eclipse.releng.eclipsebuilder plug-in and a set of control files for the automated build of all parts of its platform.

To use a headless build to build a product, you will need the following:

- An Eclipse installation

- CVS client version 1.10 or higher

- Zip and unzip executables

A builder (org.eclipse.releng.eclipsebuilder) is provided by Eclipse. You can download it remotely with this command:

```
cvs -d :pserver:anonymous@dev.eclipse.org:/cvsroot/eclipse
export -r HEAD org.eclipse.releng.eclipsebuilder
```

You can start a headless build from the command line or an Ant script with a command such as the following:

```
set ECLIPSE_HOME=<PATH TO ECLIPSE>

java -cp %ECLIPSE_HOME%\org.eclipse.equinox.launcher_<version>.jar
  org.eclipse.core.launcher.Main
 -application org.eclipse.ant.core.antRunner
 -buildfile build.xml
 -Dcomponent=<LOCATION OF BUILD FILES>
 -Dbaseos=win32
 -Dbasews=win32
 -Dbasearch=x86
 -Djavacfailonerror=true
 -Dpde.build.scripts=%ECLIPSE_HOME%/plugins/org.eclipse.pde.build_<version>/scripts
 -DbaseLocation=%ECLIPSE_HOME%
```

The previous fragment defines the basic arguments of a headless build:

- ECLIPSE_HOME: The path to your Eclipse installation. An environment variable is commonly used to store this path.

- org.eclipse.equinox.launcher_<version>.jar: The JAR that contains the build launcher (org.eclipse.core.launcher.Main). It must be included in your classpath. Note that the version changes depending on your installation.

- -application: Defines the application to run—in this case, an Ant build script.

- -buildfile: The master Ant build script (build.xml) to drive the process.

- -DbuildDirectory: The location where the build files will be created (for example, C:\build\).

- -Dbaseos, -Dbasews, and -Dbasearch: The base operating, windowing system, and architecture (for example, win32, win32, and x86). This is useful to create packs for multiple operating systems.

- -Djavacfailonerror: Tells the build to abort on compilation errors.

- -Dpde.build.scripts: The location of the build scripts. These are provided by Eclipse and are located in ECLIPSE_HOME%/plugins/org.eclipse.pde.build_<version>/scripts.

- -DbaseLocation: The location of your Eclipse installation.

See Table 10-4 for a list of arguments.

It is best to put the build command in a shell script, especially when you have a lot of arguments.

Tip To run only a particular phase of the build process (after modifications to the build files for example), simply append the phase name to the -buildfile argument in the command line: java org. eclipse.core.launcher.Main -application org.eclipse.ant.core.antRunner -buildfile *<BUILD_FILE>* *<PHASE_NAME>*. The phase names are preBuild, fetch, generate, process, assemble, package, and postBuild.

The following sections describe the underpinnings of the build system. We'll start with configuration files and runtime arguments, and then cover the build phases. Understanding this process is required if you wish to perform custom steps on any of the phases (to create a binary installer, for example). Otherwise, the build simply packs the required files in a zip archive.

Build Configuration

The build configuration is driven by series of files for which Eclipse provides templates located in the folder ECLIPSE_HOME\plugins\org.eclipse.pde.build_<version>\templates\ headless-build. This folder contains the following files:

- allElements.xml: An optional file that is primarily useful when you must build multiple top-level components such as multiple features.

- build.properties: A critical file that defines the parameters describing how and where to execute the build. These parameters can be specified in the command line; however, there are so many that is best to put them in this file.

- customAssembly.xml: An optional file to define targets called before and after the binary files are gathered. It is useful to insert license files or digitally sign the JARs.

- customTargets.xml: An optional file that can be used to control all the phases of the build. It can also be used to download base build components (such as a build target platform), check out map files from a build repository, clean a build, gather build logs, test the build, and publish the build to a specific location.

For a basic build, you need only build.properties. Complex builds may use any or all of these files. They must be edited by the user and stored in the build configuration directory (specified by the -Dbuilder argument in the command line).

The headless build provides two extra files, located in the $ECLIPSE_HOME/plugins/org. eclipse.pde.build_*<version>*/scripts folder:

- build.xml: The main Ant build script.

- genericTargets.xml: Used to control the phases of the build process.

■ **Tip** Basic templates for `customTargets.xml` and `build.properties` can be found under `ECLIPSE_ HOME/org.eclipse.pde.build_<version>/templates/headless-build`.

Table 10-4 describes the most useful build configuration parameters.[2] See the hands-on exercise later in this chapter for a real-world example of using them.

Table 10-4. *Some Headless Build Command Options*

Name	Description
buildDirectory	The relative path to a directory where the source for the build will be exported, where scripts will be generated, and where the end products of the build will be located. On Windows systems, this directory should be close to the drive root to avoid path-length limitations, particularly at compile time.
baseLocation	A directory separate from ${buildDirectory} that contains prebuilt plug-ins against which to compile. ${baseLocation} must not contain any features, plug-ins, or fragments that are already or will be located in ${buildDirectory}.
baseos, basews, basearch, basenl	The os, ws, arch, and nl values of the prebuilt Eclipse found in ${baseLocation}.
configs	An ampersand-separated list of configurations to build for an element, where a configuration is specified as <os>, <ws>, or <arch>; for example, configs="win32,win32,x86 & linux, motif, x86 & linux, gtk, x86". It is typically used to build a feature that is os, ws, and arch-specific. A nonplatform-specific configuration is specified with "*,*,*".
collectingFolder	The directory in which build features and plug-ins are gathered. This is typically set to "eclipse".
archivePrefix	The top-level directory in the assembled distribution. This is typically set to "eclipse".
buildType	A letter used to identify builds: I (integration), N (nightly), S (stable), R (release), or M (maintenance).
buildId	The build name. The default is set to "build" in the template build. properties.
buildLabel	Refers to the name of the directory that will contain the end result of the build. It is set to ${buildType}.${buildId} in the template build.properties. This directory will be created in ${buildDirectory}.
timestamp	A timestamp used to fill in the value for buildid in about.mappings files. Also used to name build output directory; for example, I-build-<timestamp>.
mapVersionTag	Sets the tag attribute in a call to the Ant cvs task to check out the map file project.

Continued

---

2. For a complete list of build configuration parameters, see the Builder Configuration Properties section at http://help.eclipse.org/stable/index.jsp?topic=/org.eclipse.pde.doc.user/reference/ pde_builder_config.htm.

Table 10-4. *Continued*

Name	Description
fetchTag	Sets the tag or branch when exporting modules used in the build. For example, setting fetchTag=HEAD will fetch the HEAD stream of the source for all features, plug-ins, and fragments listed in the map files, instead of fetching the tag specified in the map entry for that element. For example, this is used in the Eclipse build process to produce the nightly build.
bootclasspath	Sets the value for the attribute bootclasspath in calls to the Ant javac task in a plug-in's build.xml file.
javacDebugInfo	Sets the value for the attribute debug in calls to the Ant javac task in a plug-in's build.xml file. Determines if debug information is included in the output JARs. Set to on in the template build.properties.
javacFailOnError	Sets the value for the attribute failonerror in calls to the Ant javac task in a plug-in's build.xml file. When this is set to false, the build will continue, even if there are compilation errors.
javacSource	Sets the value for the attribute source in calls to the Ant javac task in a plug-in's build.xml file. Sets the value of the -source command-line switch for javac version 1.4. Used when compiling the JARs for the plug-ins. The default is set to 1.3 in the build.xml file generated for plug-ins and fragments.
javacTarget	Sets the value for the attribute target in calls to the Ant javac task in a plug-in's build.xml file. Sets the value of the -target command-line switch for javac. Used when compiling the JARs for the plug-ins. The default is set to 1.1 in the build.xml file generated for plug-ins and fragments.
javacVerbose	Sets the value for the attribute verbose in calls to the Ant javac task in a plug-in's build.xml file. Asks the compiler for verbose output. The default is set to true.
zipargs	Arguments to send to the zip executable. Setting it to -y on Linux systems preserves symbolic links.

Build Phases

Behind the scenes, the build system is divided in a series of steps or phases. These phases are useful to customize the build (for example, to fetch files from a server or create a binary installer) and can be run from the command line. The build phases are as follows:

preBuild and fetch: The most important task of these phases is to fetch the plug-ins that constitute the product as well as all dependencies. This is accomplished by fetching a map file. The map file is a Java property file that contains mappings of plug-ins, features, or fragments to their CVS locations and access methods. Adding a new plug-in or fragment to the product requires updating the map files with the new element. Map files are described in more detail in the "Creating a Release Engineering Project" section later in this chapter.

generate: After features and plug-ins have been fetched to the build directory, the build scripts are generated in the same way as they would be with the PDE GUI.

process and assemble: These two phases mark the start of the compilation process with a call to processElement in genericTargets.xml. This, in turn, calls the build.jars target (which is hidden from the user) in build.xml within the feature directory to start compilation. After compilation, the assembly is started from the assembleElement target in genericTargets.xml. Most the work is just delegated to the headless build. The assemble phase creates a series of scripts to drive the process. These scripts are hidden from the user.

Note   The assemble script copies all the build results to a temporary subdirectory in the build target directory and then zips them. The files being collected are feature manifest files (feature.xml), plug-in manifest files (plugin.xml), and the built JAR files. The inclusion of arbitrary files can be specified with the bin. includes property of the plug-in's build.properties file.

---

package: When the packer is run (by setting runPackager=true in build.properties), this phase defines targets to run before and after the packer starts. It is helpful if your build results need to contain binary features and plug-ins that come from the baseLocation.

postBuild: This phase allows you to perform actions with the build output, such as build an operating system-dependent installer.

These concepts can be better understood with a practical exercise. The next section will get you started with a hands-on example.

Hands-on Exercise: Automated Updates and Builds for RCP

Let's put the concepts from the previous sections to the test. The goal of this exercise is to build an automated update site for the OpenGL product created in Chapter 8. The projects to be created include a feature project that contains product plug-ins and an update site project to perform the actual updates locally or remotely.

The exercise will demonstrate how to deploy the product to multiple operating systems using the IDE, as well as a how to create a headless build.

Creating a Feature

As mentioned earlier, a feature is a collection of plug-ins that perform a common task. This is critical for installing or updating products that have many plug-ins, as they can manipulated as a single entity. A feature project does not contain any code. It merely describes the set of plug-ins that provide a function.

Follow these steps to create a feature project:

1. Select File ➤ New ➤ Project ➤ Plug-in Development ➤ Feature Project. Click Next.

2. Enter a project name (ch10.OpenGL.Feature) and add feature information, as shown in Figure 10-3. Click Next.

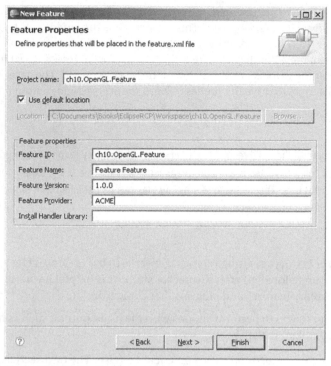

Figure 10-3. *Defining feature properties*

3. Select the plug-ins that make the feature—ch08.OpenGL and ch08.OpenGL.Natives in this case—as shown in Figure 10-4. Click Finish.

Note Make sure ch08.OpenGL.Natives includes the native libraries for deployment. Otherwise, the native OpenGL code will not be deployed, and the plug-in will fail to start. To ensure that these libraries are included, open the manifest editor for the project, click the Build tab, and under Binary Build, make sure all the DLL and SO files are checked.

Creating an Update Site

An update site project allows you to define one or more features to install or update. To create this project, follow these steps:

1. Select File ➤ New ➤ Project ➤ Plug-in Development ➤ Update Site Project. Click Next.

2. Enter a project name (ch10.OpenGL.UpdateSite) and check "Generate a web page listing all available features within this site," as shown in Figure 10-5. This will create an index HTML page for deployment to a web server. Click Finish.

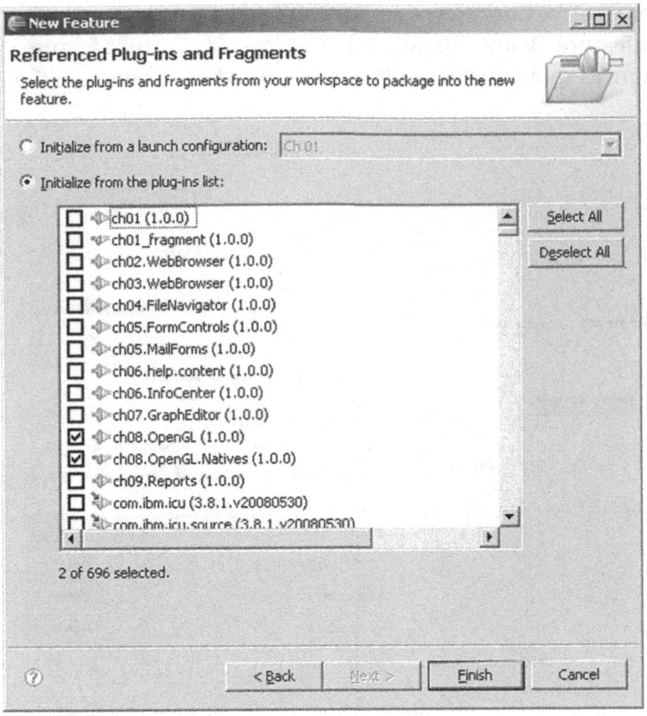

Figure 10-4. *Selecting feature project plug-ins*

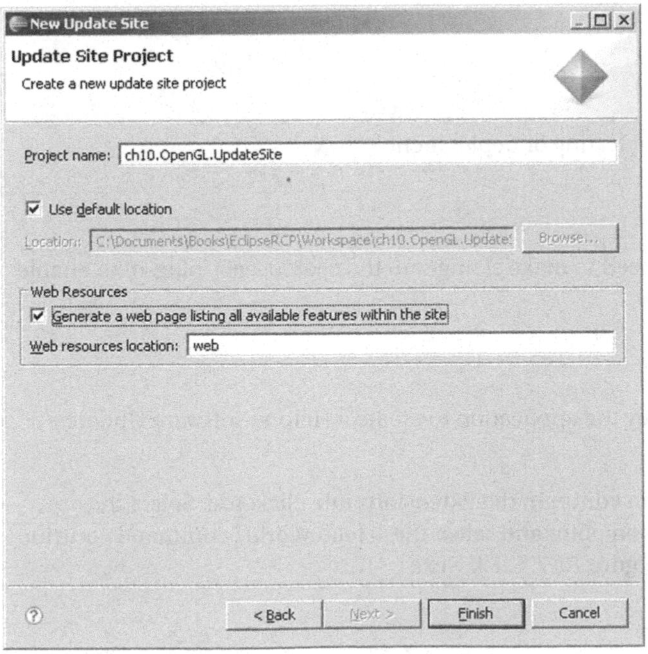

Figure 10-5. *Using the Update Site Project wizard*

3. The site map editor will be presented. Click New Category and add a new category called OpenGL to describe the feature. Below this, add the ch10.OpenGL.Feature feature created in the previous section, as shown in Figure 10-6. Click Build All to generate the site files.

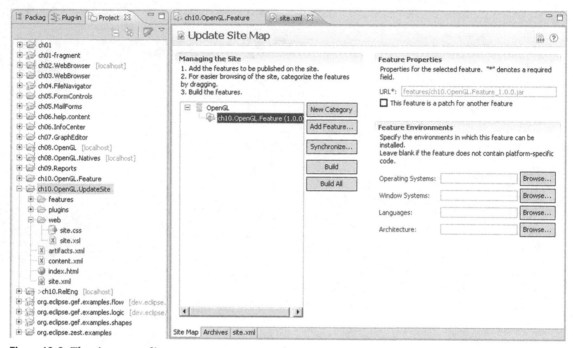

Figure 10-6. *The site map editor*

At this point, the site is ready for testing or deployment.

Testing and Publishing

Before testing the update site, you need to make changes to the ch08.OpenGL plug-in to enable software updates.

Adding a Software Updates Menu

New extension points are required by the application to create a Help ➤ Software Updates menu. Add them as follows:

1. Open the ch08.OpenGL plug-in editor. In the Extensions tab, click Add. Select the org. eclipse.ui.commands extension point and select the "Hello World" command contribution template, as shown in Figure 10-7. Click Next.

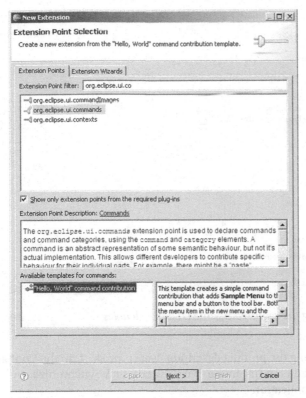

Figure 10-7. *Extension wizard showing the command template*

2. Rename the Handler class name to UpdatesHandler, and then click Finish.

3. A new sample menu will be added to the menu bar. Using the plug-in editor, rename Sample Menu to Help, and Sample Command to Software Updates. Optionally, rename the Sample Category that contains the command to Updates Category (see Listing 10-2 at the end of this section for the extension points XML).

4. Modify the command handler class UpdatesHandler to remove the sample message from UpdatesHandler.execute and start the Updates wizard, as shown in the next fragment:

```
public Object execute(ExecutionEvent event) throws ExecutionException {
  IWorkbenchWindow window = HandlerUtil.getActiveWorkbenchWindowChecked(event);
  UpdateManagerUI.openInstaller(window.getShell());

  return null;
}
```

5. Add the org.eclipse.update.ui dependency to the Dependencies tab of the plug-in manifest, as shown in Figure 10-8. This is required for compilation.

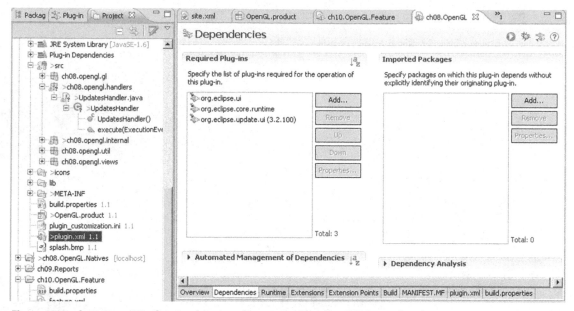

Figure 10-8. *ch08.OpenGL plug-in showing the required update UI dependencies*

6. Test the changes by opening the product descriptor OpenGL.product. In the Configuration tab, click Add Required Plug-ins. In the Overview tab, click Synchronize, and then click Launch an Eclipse application.

Caution   You must click Add Required Plug-ins in the Configuration tab of the product editor. Otherwise, dependencies will not be added, and the product will fail to start.

---

7. When the application starts, open Help ➤ Software Updates to access the Updates wizard, as shown in Figure 10-9.

   Listing 10-2 shows the extension points required to add the Help ➤ Software Updates menu to the ch08.OpenGL plug-in.w

---

Note   Make sure the ID of the command is the same for the menu, command, and handler extension points.

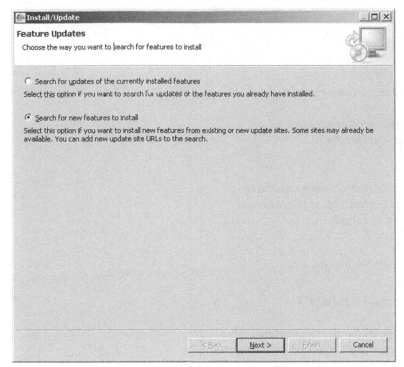

Figure 10-9. *The Updates wizard*

Listing 10-2. *Extension Points to Add the Software Updates Option to the ch08.OpenGL Plug-in's Help Menu*

```
<extension
        point="org.eclipse.ui.menus">
     <menuContribution
         locationURI="menu:org.eclipse.ui.main.menu?after=additions">
       <menu
           label="Help"
           mnemonic="H">

    .  <command
             commandId="ch08.OpenGL.commands.updatesCommand"
             id="ch08.OpenGL.menus.sampleCommand"
             mnemonic="S">
         </command>

         <command
             commandId="org.eclipse.ui.help.aboutAction"
             style="push">
         </command>
```

```
            </menu>
        </menuContribution>
    </extension>

    <extension
        point="org.eclipse.ui.commands">
        <category
            id="ch08.OpenGL.commands.category"
            name="Updates Category">
        </category>
        <command
            categoryId="ch08.OpenGL.commands.category"
            id="ch08.OpenGL.commands.updatesCommand"
            name="Software Updates">
        </command>
    </extension>

    <extension
        point="org.eclipse.ui.handlers">
        <handler
            class="ch08.opengl.handlers.UpdatesHandler"
            commandId="ch08.OpenGL.commands.updatesCommand">
        </handler>
    </extension>
```

Now that the RCP product has enabled software updates, the update site can actually be tested. But first, we need to export the product, along with all required dependencies and binary files.

Deploying the Product Using the Delta Pack

As mentioned in previous chapters, the delta pack is an Eclipse tool used to export products for multiple platforms within the IDE. The tricky part is that this tool is not part of the default installation, which means you must install it manually.

■**Tip** To check for the delta pack within your IDE, open a product configuration file and select the Product Export wizard. If the export options include "Export for multiple platforms," this means that the pack is installed.

If you don't have a delta pack, download it from the Eclipse site (click Downloads ➤ Eclipse IDE ➤ By Project ➤ Eclipse Platform ➤ Latest Release ➤ Delta Pack). Then unzip the pack in the root folder of your Eclipse installation. Finally, restart the workbench.

■**Caution** When unzipping the pack, do not overwrite existing files. Otherwise, your workbench may fail to start.

To export the ch08.OpenGL product, open the OpenGL.product file and start the Eclipse Product Export wizard. Enter a destination directory and check "Export for multiple platforms," as shown in Figure 10-10. Click Next. Select your target platforms, and then click Finish.

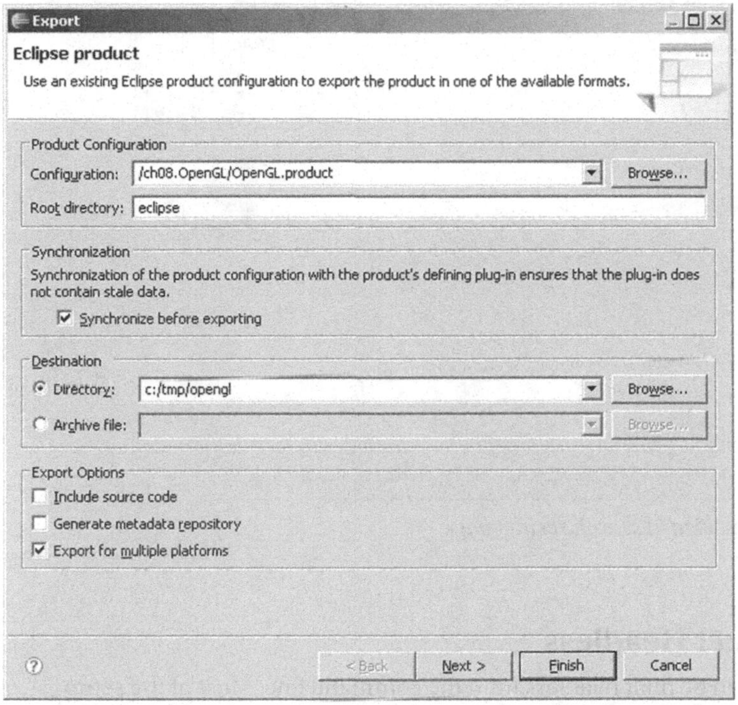

Figure 10-10. *Delta pack export wizard for the OpenGL sample plug-in*

The build process will deploy all the required files to run the RCP application. Browse to the target directory and run the RCP application by double-clicking the eclipse binary.

Running and Connecting to the Update Site

It's now time to try the update site, as follows:

1. Run the OpenGL RCP application and select Help ➤ Software Updates to start the Updates wizard.

2. In the wizard, select "Search for new features to install" (see Figure 10-9), and then click Next.

3. On the Updates Sites page, click New Local Site, and then browse to the update site project created in the previous section. Click Finish.

4. The Search Results page will display the features available for install, as shown in Figure 10-11. Follow the wizard's instructions, and then restart the workbench. The features are now up-to-date.

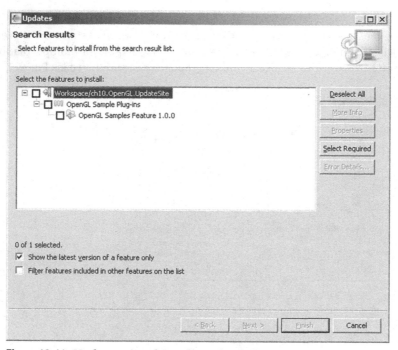

Figure 10-11. *Updates wizard search results page*

Building the Product Headless

The ch08.OpenGL product can be built headless from the command line. Most of the setup necessary for such a build can be done through a few modifications to the template build. properties provided in the PDE build.

Note To build a product headless, an Eclipse installation with the delta pack is required.

To build the ch08.OpenGL product headless, follow these steps:

1. Create a master build directory, such as C:\tmp\build.

2. Create two folders within the root: buildDirectory and buildConfig. The first folder will contain the plug-ins to build. The latter will contain the configuration file build. properties.

3. Beneath buildDir, create two folders: plugins and features. Copy the product plug-ins ch08.OpenGL and ch08.OpenGL.Natives to buildDir/plugins.

4. Create a build configuration file build.properties in buildConfig, as shown in Listing 10-3. This file defines the build parameters.

5. Create a batch file named build.bat to start the process, as shown in Listing 10-4.

6. Run build.bat. Follow all steps carefully; otherwise, the build will fail. Keep in mind that an Eclipse installation with the delta pack is required.

7. After the run completes, a zip archive (OpenGL.RCP-win32.win32.x86.zip) will be created under buildDir\I.OpenGL.RCP. Unzip this archive and run launcher.exe to test the product.

Listing 10-3 shows the build.properties file for this example. Make sure the following properties are set up correctly (if they are not, the build will fail):

- product must point to the product configuration.

- baseLocation must be set to your Eclipse installation.

- buildDirectory must point to the directory where the build will take place.

- archivePrefix has a name for your product build file name.

Listing 10-3. *Headless Build Configuration File (build.properties)*

```
## Build configuration
topLevelElementType = feature

# The id of the top level element we are building
topLevelElementId = ch08.OpenGL

product=/ch08.OpenGL/OpenGL.product
runPackager=true

# Set the name of the archive that will result from the product build.
#archiveNamePrefix=

# The prefix that will be used in the generated archive.
archivePrefix=OpenGLRCP

# The location under which all of the build output will be collected.
collectingFolder=${archivePrefix}

# The list of {os, ws, arch} configurations to build. This
# value is a '&' separated list of ',' separate triples.  For example,
#     configs=win32,win32,x86 & linux,motif,x86
configs=win32,win32,x86
```

```
# Arguments to send to the zip executable
zipargs=

# Arguments to send to the tar executable
tarargs=

# The directory into which the build elements are fetched
buildDirectory=${user.home}/eclipse.build

# Type of build. Used in naming the build output. Typically this value is
# one of I, N, M, S, ...
buildType=I

# ID of the build. Used in naming the build output.
buildId=OpenGL.RCP

# Label for the build. Used in naming the build output
buildLabel=${buildType}.${buildId}

# Timestamp for the build. Used in naming the build output
timestamp=007

# Base location for anything the build needs to compile against.  For example,
# in most RCP apps or a plug-in, the baseLocation should be the location of a
# previously installed Eclipse against which the application or plug-in code will be
# compiled and the RCP delta pack.
base=<path/to/parent/of/eclipse>
baseLocation=${base}/eclipse

# Os/Ws/Arch/nl of the Eclipse specified by baseLocation
baseos=win32
basews=win32
basearch=x86

# This property indicates whether you want the set of plug-ins and features to be
# considered during the build to be limited to the ones reachable from the features
# and plug-ins being built
filteredDependencyCheck=false

# This property indicates whether the resolution should be done in development mode
# (i.e. ignore multiple bundles with singletons)
resolution.devMode=false


skipBase=true
eclipseURL=<url for eclipse download site>
```

```
eclipseBuildId=<Id of Eclipse build to get>
eclipseBaseURL=${eclipseURL}/eclipse-platform-${eclipseBuildId}-win32.zip


# This section defines CVS tags to use when fetching the map files from the
# repository. If you want to fetch the map file from repository / location, change
# the getMapFiles target in the customTargets.xml
skipMaps=true
mapsRepo=:pserver:anonymous@example.com/path/to/repo
mapsRoot=path/to/maps
mapsCheckoutTag=HEAD

#tagMaps=true
mapsTagTag=v${buildId}


############# REPOSITORY CONTROL ###############
# This section defines properties parameterizing the repositories where plug-ins,
# fragments bundles and features are being obtained from.

# The tags to use when fetching elements to build.
skipFetch=true


############# JAVA COMPILER OPTIONS #############

# Specify the output format of the compiler log when eclipse jdt is used
logExtension=.log

# Whether or not to include debug info in the output jars
javacDebugInfo=false

# Whether or not to fail the build if there are compiler errors
javacFailOnError=true

# Enable or disable verbose mode of the compiler
javacVerbose=true

# Extra arguments for the compiler. These are specific to the Java compiler
# being used.
#compilerArg=

# Java compiler version
javacSource=1.6
javacTarget=1.6
```

Listing 10-4. *Batch File to Build ch08.OpenGL Headless*

```
@echo off

:: Change this to fit your system
:: Eclipse Installation with delta pack
set ECLIPSE_HOME=C:\eclipse-SDK\eclipse-GANYMEDE

:: Build master folder
set ROOT_BUILD=C:\Documents\Books\EclipseRCP\Workspace\ch10.Local.Build

:: Depending on your Eclipse version you may have to change this...
:: Name of the Equinox launcher plug-in under ECLIPSE_HOME/plugins
set LAUNCHER=org.eclipse.equinox.launcher_1.0.100.v20080509-1800.jar

:: Eclipse plug-in that contains the PDE build scripts (depends on Eclipse version)
set PDE_BUILD=org.eclipse.pde.build_3.4.0.v20080604

:: Launch class path (no need to change this)
set CP=%ECLIPSE_HOME%/plugins/%LAUNCHER%

:: Main Program
set MAIN=org.eclipse.core.launcher.Main
set APP=org.eclipse.ant.core.antRunner

:: Product Build file
set BUILDFILE=%ECLIPSE_HOME%/plugins/
    %PDE_BUILD%/scripts/productBuild/productBuild.xml

:: Build directory. It must contain the user developed plug-ins and features
set BUILD_DIR=%ROOT_BUILD%\buildDir

:: Directory that has build.properties
set BUILD_CONF=%ROOT_BUILD%\buildConfig

:: Run time args: Base location, build directory, etc.
set ARGS=-DbaseLocation=%ECLIPSE_HOME%
    -DbuildDirectory=%BUILD_DIR% -Dbuilder=%BUILD_CONF%

java -cp %CP% %MAIN% %ARGS% -application %APP%  -buildfile %BUILDFILE%
```

Building the Product Headless from a CVS Repository

The previous section showed how to build an RCP application headless assuming that all plug-ins and features (both to build and prebuilt) referenced by the product file are already locally available on disk. However, in the real world, organizations mostly use a source code repository such as CVS. This section focuses on the infrastructure offered by the PDE build to fetch the source code from a Windows CVS repository as part of the build process.

Installing CVS on a Windows System

The first thing needed for this headless build is a CVS server for Windows. CVSNT is a Windows version control system licensed under the GNU General Public License, which can be used to quickly set up a code repository.[3]

To set up a CVS server in Windows, follow these steps:

1. Download CVSNT (from `http://www.march-hare.com/cvspro/`) and install it. Then restart your computer.

2. Create a new code repository to store the code for the OpenGL product. Run the CVSNT control panel by choosing Start ➤ Programs ➤ CVSNT ➤ Control Panel. Create a repository (`/cvs`, for example) to point to the disk location of your choice, as shown in Figure 10-12.

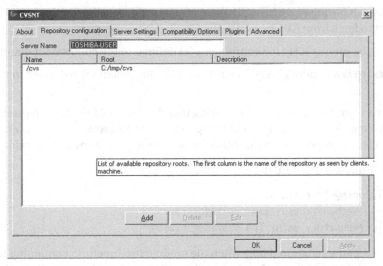

Figure 10-12. *CVSNT control panel showing a configured repositories*

3. Assuming that CVSNT has been installed in the default location (`C:\Program Files\ CVSNT`), add a CVS user to commit code to the repository by opening a command prompt and typing the following:

```
C:\"Program Files"\CVSNT\cvs passwd -a -r <LOCAL_ACCOUNT> cvsuser
Adding user cvsuser@localhost
New Password:
Verify Password:
```

Note that `LOCAL_ACCOUNT` must be an existing user account on the Windows machine where CVSNT is installed.

---

3. CVSNT for Windows is available from `http://www.march-hare.com/cvspro/`.

4. Configure a read-only user (anonymous) to check out code without a password. This is necessary because the automated build sends an empty password by default when fetching code. anonymous is the standard name for read-only access. Add anonymous to the $CVSROOT/CVSROOT/readers file for read-only access and anonymous::<LOCAL_ACCOUNT> to $CVSROOT/CVSROOT/passwd to set an empty password. Note that LOCAL_ACCOUNT must be the name of a local Windows user.

Creating a Release Engineering Project

A release engineering (commonly referred as *releng*) project is the Eclipse naming convention for the project that hosts configuration files for automated headless builds. In order to know where to get things, PDE uses map files. A map file is a Java property file that maps feature and plug-in IDs to a location and a tag in a repository. The format of the map file is as follows:

```
<elementType>@<elementID>[,<elementVersion>] = <repository-specific content>
```

The various placeholders are as follows:

- elementType can be one of feature, plugin, or fragment, depending on the type of component to fetch from CVS.

- elementID is the unique ID of the component (as defined in the component manifest).

- elementVersion is an optional version string for the component (also defined in the manifest).

- The repository-specific information is a string that defines CVS information used to fetch the component. For example, the string :pserver:anonymous@localhost:/cvs will fetch from the /cvs repository in the local computer using the anonymous account.

The map file entries use this format:

```
feature|fragment|plugin@elementId =
  <cvs tag>,<access method>:<cvsuser>@<cvs repository>,
  <cvs password>[,<repository path> (no starting slash) ]
```

The <repository path> is required only when the module (or directory) containing the source for the element does not match the elementId or if the directory is not at the root of the repository.

For example, the next fragment shows the map file required to build the ch08.OpenGL product.

```
feature@ch10.OpenGL.Feature=CVS,tag=HEAD,cvsRoot=:pserver:anonymous@localhost:/cvs,
plugin@ch08.OpenGL=CVS,tag=HEAD,cvsRoot=:pserver:anonymous@localhost:/cvs,
fragment@ch08.OpenGL.Natives=CVS,tag=HEAD,cvsRoot=:pserver:anonymous@localhost:/cvs,
```

This fragment describes the ch08.OpenGL product, which is made up of a feature, the actual OpenGL plug-in, and a fragment containing native libraries for Windows and Unix.

Now, let's create the release engineering project to host the build configuration:

1. Select File ➤ New ➤ Project ➤ General ➤ Project. Click Next.

2. Enter a name (ch10.RelEng), and then click Finish.

3. Create a folder called maps and a file within it (rcp.map) with the properties described in the previous fragment.

4. Grab the headless build configuration files (build.properties and customTargets. xml) from your Eclipse distribution ECLIPSE_HOME/plugins/org.eclipse.pde. build_<version>/templates/headless-build and save them in ch10.RelEng.

5. Customize the build files. No changes are required to customTargets.xml. Listing 10-5 shows the changes to build.properties required for fetching code from repositories. Be extremely careful with build.properties, as any mistake will cause the build to fail.

Listing 10-5. *Changes to build.properties for Fetching Code from Repositories*

```
topLevelElementType=feature
topLevelElementId=ch10.OpenGL.Feature

product=OpenGL.product
runPackager=true

archivePrefix=OpenGLRCP
configs=win32,win32,x86

buildId=OpenGL.RCP

#skipMaps=true
mapsRepo=:pserver:anonymous@localhost/cvs
mapsRoot=ch10.RelEng
mapsCheckoutTag=HEAD

#skipFetch=true

# Java 1.6 is required by the OpenGL product
javacSource=1.6
javacTarget=1.6
```

Make sure to comment the skipFetch and skipMaps properties. The mapsRepo property defines the connection arguments to the CVS server. The OpenGL product requires Java 1.6.

Committing the Product

Now we can use the CVS client within the Eclipse workbench to commit the OpenGL RCP to the new repository, as follows:

1. Select Window ➤ Show View ➤ Other ➤ CVS ➤ CVS Repositories.

2. In the CVS Repositories view, right-click the background and select New ➤ Repository Location. This will display the Add CVS Repository dialog, as shown in Figure 10-13.

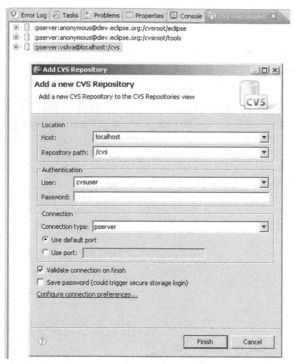

Figure 10-13. *Eclipse IDE CVS Repositories view and Add CVS Repository wizard*

3. Enter the repository information. Set the host to localhost, repository path to /cvs, the user to the previously created user (cvsuser), and the password to the one set earlier. Click Finish.

4. Commit the OpenGL product plug-ins and features. Right-click each project (ch08. OpeGL, ch08.OpenGL.Natives, ch10.OpenGL.Feature, and ch10.RelEng), select Team ➤ Share Project from the context menu, and follow the CVS Commit wizard instructions.

Running the Build

To run the build, we need a batch script (build.bat). But first, the product file (ch08.OpenGL/ OpenGL.product) must be copied to the build directory. Assuming the build directory C:\tmp, the Eclipse installation C:\eclipse-SDK\eclipse-GANYMEDE, and the workspace C:\Documents\ EclipseRCP\Workspace, Listing 10-6 shows the build script.

Listing 10-6. *Headless Build Script for OpenGL.product*

```
@echo off


:: Eclipse home. Update this to match your versions
set ECLIPSE_HOME=C:\eclipse-SDK\eclipse-GANYMEDE
set LAUNCHER=org.eclipse.equinox.launcher_1.0.100.v20080509-1800.jar
set PDE_BUILD=org.eclipse.pde.build_3.4.0.v20080604
```

```
:: Build directory
set BUILD_DIR=C:\tmp\build

:: Configuration directory
set BUILD_CONF=C:\Documents\EclipseRCP\Workspace\ch10.RelEng

set MAIN=org.eclipse.core.launcher.Main
set APP=org.eclipse.ant.core.antRunner
set CP=%ECLIPSE_HOME%/plugins/%LAUNCHER%

set BUILDFILE=%ECLIPSE_HOME%/plugins/
  %PDE_BUILD%/scripts/productBuild/productBuild.xml
set ARGS=-DbaseLocation=%ECLIPSE_HOME%
  -DbuildDirectory=%BUILD_DIR% -Dbuilder=%BUILD_CONF%

java -cp %CP% %MAIN% %ARGS% -application %APP%  -buildfile %BUILDFILE%
```

■**Note** Do not forget to copy the product file (OpenGL.product) to the build directory. Otherwise, the build will fail.

Summary

In this chapter, we have studied the Eclipse build system used to build plug-ins automatically outside the Eclipse IDE. Eclipse itself is built headless and, since it is a collection of plug-ins, this functionality is available to any RCP application. Here are the important points to keep in mind:

- Eclipse provides a convenient way to deliver updates to your users using products, features, fragments, and update sites.

- A *product* packs and delivers one or more features, which include all the code and plug-ins needed to run them. It also lets you customize the presentation and runtime parameters of the application.

- A *feature* describes a grouping of plug-ins that perform a common task. Features are useful for working with (installing and updating) a lot of plug-ins as a single entity.

- *Fragments* are separately packaged files that attach to a host plug-in. They are useful for adding functionality missing from the original release, without needing to repackage or reinstall, and packaging national language translations.

- Since Eclipse 3.4, the update manager has been reworked with a brand-new provisioning system, including a software updates UI and a command-line tool to perform provisioning tasks such as installing, updating, and removing software.

- The headless build system provides automated build capabilities for complex applications with hundreds of plug-ins. Building such applications within an IDE makes no sense. It includes a plug-in (org.eclipse.releng.eclipsebuilder) specifically created for the task and requires a CVS server for code storage and zip/unzip tools.

- The headless build is divided in phases: preBuild, fetch, generate, process, assemble, package, and postBuild. It requires two input files: customTargets.xml and build. properties. customTargets.xml acts as callback where the user can perform customs tasks for each phase. Build.properties describes runtime parameters such as target location, operating system configuration, compilation arguments, and so on.

  - The prebuild and fetch phases extract the plug-ins that constitute the product as well as all dependencies. These phases require a bundle map file, which describes plug-in IDs and the CVS server locations.

  - The generate and assemble phases perform the actual code compilation and assembly of plug-ins and their dependencies.

  - The postBuild phase is used for performing actions with the build output, such as building an operating system–dependent installer.

Index

▉Numerics

2D graphics
  advanced graphics editor exercise
    overview, 195–196
    RCP product, 196–200
    testing, 206
    Zest plug-in, 200–206
  Draw2d, 173–175
  GEF
    displaying figures, 176
    EditPolicies, 185–187
    overview, 175–176
    palettes, 187–190
    shapes example, 176–185
  Zest, 190–195
3D chart scene
  BarValue class, 232
  ChartScene class, 233–236
  display lists, 228–230
  GLU, 231–232
  overview, 228
3D graphics
  Earth navigator project
    finding latitude and longitude, 251–255
    flying to locations, 250–251
    navigator view, 248–250, 256–258
    overview, 242
    setting up, 245–248
    WWJ, 242–245
  OpenGL scenes
    3D chart scene, 228–236
    overview, 209–212
    RCP view, 241–242
    refreshing, 241
    rotating and moving, 236–240
    setting up for, 212–219
    wire cubes, 220–228
  SWT, 209–211

▉A

<A> tag, 122
About dialog, 66
aboutImage property, 294
aboutText property, 294
absolute coordinate system, 175
AbstractLayoutAlgorithm class, 193
AbstractUIPlugin class, 22, 138
action bar advisor, 63
Action providers, 79
ActionBarAdvisor class, 61, 142
activator class, 54, 138, 284, 288
Activator.java file, 8

add( ) method, 111
Add branding option, 294
addBookmark( ) method, 48
addBookmark function, 48
addControlListener method, 221
addDisposeListener method, 221
addEntity( ) method, 195
addHyperlinkListener(IHyperlinkListener)
    method, 117
Add-ons dialog, 297–298
addPages( ) method, 126
addRelationship( )method, 195
addStandaloneView method, 105, 218
adjust method, 240
advisor classes
  modifying, 70–71
  RCP application, 61–63
allElements.xml file, 302
<anchor> element, 148
Apache Derby application, 263
Apache Tomcat servlet container, 269
APIs (application program interfaces), 3
appid parameter, 251
application argument, 298, 301
-application org.eclipse.equinox.p2.director.app.
    application parameter, 299
application program interfaces (APIs), 3
application property, 294
ApplicationActionBarAdvisor class, 70–71, 162
ApplicationWorkbenchAdvisor class, 70
ApplicationWorkbenchWindowAdvisor class,
    70–71
applyStateIterator( ) method, 251
appName property, 294
arch ${target.arch} argument, 13
archivePrefix property, 303, 315
Arguments tab, 13
-artifactRepository parameter, 298, 299
artifacts.xml file, 292
assemble phase, 305
automated updates
  automated updates and builds exercise
    building product headless, 314–322
    features, creating, 305–306
    publishing, 308–314
    testing, 308–314
    update site project, 306–308
  Eclipse process
    defining product, 292–294
    grouping plug-ins, 295–296
    overview, 291
    update site project, 296
  overview, 291

product build automation with headless build
    system
    build configuration, 302–304
    build phases, 304–305
    overview, 300–302
Software Update UI tools
    Add-ons dialog, 297–298
    installing software from command line,
        298–299
    overview, 296–297
Available Software tab, 18, 298
Axis class, 229

■B

<B> tag, 122
BarValue class, 212, 232
base parameter, 232
basearch command, 303
baseLocation property, 303, 315
basenl command, 303
baseos command, 303
baseURL attribute, 272
basews command, 303
Basic RCP Application page, 214
batch script, 322
beginTask( ) method, 88
bindings, 36–37, 209
bin.includes property, 305
BIRT (Business Intelligence and Report Toolkit)
    OSGi console
        extending, 283–285
        generating reports, 285–289
        report generator plug-in, 289
    overview, 261
    Report Designer
        anatomy of, 263
        creating reports, 264–268
        installing, 262–263
        overview, 261–262
    Report Engine API
        configuring, 276
        IDataExtractionTask task, 277–278
        IGetParameterDefinitionTask task, 278–279
        IRenderTask task, 279–281
        IRunAndRenderTask task, 282–283
        IRunTask task, 282
        overview, 275–276
    servlet containers
        deploying runtime, 269–270
        JSP tag library, 272–274
        overview, 269
        report viewer servlet, 270
BIRT_RESOURCE_PATH parameter, 271
BIRT_VIEWER_DOCUMENT_FOLDER parameter,
    271
BIRT_VIEWER_IMAGE_DIR parameter, 271
BIRT_VIEWER_LOCALE parameter, 271
BIRT_VIEWER_LOG_DIR parameter, 271
BIRT_VIEWER_MAX_ROWS parameter, 271
BIRT_VIEWER_SCRIPTLIB_DIR parameter, 271
BIRT_VIEWER_WORKING_FOLDER parameter,
    272

<birt:param> tag, 272
<birt:paramDef> tag, 272
<birt:parameterPage> tag, 272
<birt:report> tag, 272
<birt:viewer> tag, 272–274
__bookmark parameter, 271
boolean doubleBuffer property, 210
boolean stereo property, 210
bootclasspath command, 304

 tag, 122
branding products, 65–66
build.bat file, 315
buildConfig file, 314–315
buildDir folder, 315
buildDirectory command, 303
buildDirectory folder, 314–315
buildfile argument, 301
buildId command, 303
buildLabel command, 303
build.properties file, 302, 305, 315
build.properties property, 314, 321
buildType command, 303
build.xml file, 302
BundleContext object, 9, 22–23
-bundlepool parameter, 300
bundles, defined, 3
Business Intelligence and Report Toolkit. *See* BIRT
business logic, 263

■C

cancel( ) method, 84
Cascading Style Sheets (CSS), 6
category attribute, 147
category element, 29
category extension, 73
CDT (C/C++ Development Tools), 298
change listeners, job, 89
ChartScene class, 211, 233–236
ChartView class, 216
child EditParts, 176
city parameter, 251
class attribute, 26, 36, 94
Classic Models sample database, 263, 266
classpath dependencies, 218–219
ClearColor function, 222
CNF (Common Navigator Framework)
    classes, 78
    Common Navigator view
        contributing to, 80–82
        extending, 82–83
    configuration, 79
    file system navigator project
        classes, 96–105
        extension points, 94–96
        project template, 93–94
    overview, 77–78
collectingFolder command, 303
Color object, 5
ColumnLayout class, 107, 115
command line
    building product headless from, 314–318
    installing software from, 298–299

commanded attribute, 37
commandID attribute, 36
CommandInterpreter interface, 283
command-line tool, 297
commands
    plug-in, 35–38
    RCP application, 73–75
Common Navigator Framework. *See* CNF
CommonNavigator class, 78
Commons Logging service, 18
CommonViewer class, 78
CompiledShape class, 212, 232
compute( ) method, 195
concurrency infrastructure
    jobs
        locks, 86
        operations, 84
        overview, 84
        scheduling rules, 85–86
        states, 84
    overview, 83
    virtual race example
        job change listeners, 89
        Job class, 87–88
        job families, 89
        overview, 86
        progress reporting, 88
        Race class, 89–92
config.ini file, 66
configs command, 303
configuration folder, 66, 292
configuration parameters, 303
Configuration tab, 142, 310
connection EditParts, 176–177, 183–184
ConnectionCreateCommand.java command, 185
ConnectionRequest class, 187
Console argument, 13
console command, 283
contains(ISchedulingRule rule) method, 85
content binding, 95–96
content EditParts, 176
Content extensions, 79
Content provider classes, 96
content providers, 101–104
Content trigger, 96
contentProvider attribute, 95
Contents plug-in, 157, 160–162
context help information, 150–154
contextId attribute, 37
contexts.xml file, 152
contributorClass attribute, 32
<control> tag, 123
controllers, defined, 176
core platform, 3–4
<country> element, 150
CreateConnectionRequest class, 187
createDataExtractionTask(IReportDocument)
    method, 277
createExternalGLContext( ) method, 221
createFormContent( ) method, 126
createGetParameterDefinitionTask(IReport-
    Runnable) method, 278

createPageComposite(shell) method, 132
createPalette( ) method, 190
createPartControl( ) method, 29, 50, 100, 109, 132,
    137, 241, 250
createRenderTask(IReportDocument) method,
    279
createRunAndRenderTask(IReportRunnable)
    method, 282
createRunTask(IReportRunnable) method, 282
createToolBar( ) method, 137
createWindowContents( ) method, 128–129
CSS (Cascading Style Sheets), 6
CubeScene class, 237
CubesView class, 216
customAssembly.xml file, 302
customTargets.xml file, 302, 321
CVS repository, 318–322
CVSNT, 319
$CVSROOT/CVSROOT/passwd file, 320
$CVSROOT/CVSROOT/readers file, 320
/cvsroot/tools path, 197

■D

Data Explorer view, 263–264, 267
data sources, defined, 263
Data Tools Platform (DTP), 263
Data transforms, 263
Dbasearch argument, 301
DbaseLocation argument, 301
Dbaseos argument, 301
Dbasews argument, 301
DbuildDirectory argument, 301
Dbuilder argument, 302
-Declipse.p2.data.area parameter, 300
default perspective
    CNF classes, 104–105
    GEF, 199
    RCP application, 58–59, 70
delta pack, 68, 312–313
Dependencies tab, 10, 198, 309
Derby application, 263
DESCRIPTION style, 119
-destination parameter, 299
destroy( )method, 288
<discovery> tag, 296
Display object, 104, 109
displayText attribute, 273
Djavacfailonerror argument, 301
DnD (drag-and-drop) functionality, 77
__document parameter, 271
doc.zip file, 146
doGet method, 12
Dpde.build.scripts argument, 301
drag-and-drop (DnD) functionality, 77
DragTracker class, 187
draw( ) method, 229
Draw2d, 173–175
drop-down menus, 112–113
DTP (Data Tools Platform), 263
Dynamic loading, 4
DYNAMIC_HELP action, 144

E

Earth navigator project
    finding latitude and longitude, 251–255
    flying to locations, 250–251
    navigator view, 248–250, 256–258
    overview, 242
    setting up, 245–248
    WWJ, 242–245
eclipse binary, 313
Eclipse Forms API. *See* Forms API
Eclipse IDE main menu, 144, 196, 264
Eclipse Modeling Framework (EMF), 263
Eclipse Rich Client Platform. *See* RCP
Eclipse Web Tools Platform (WTP), 49
Eclipse workbench, 2–6
ECLIPSE_HOME argument, 301
$ECLIPSE_HOME/plugins/org.eclipse.pde.
        build_<version>/scripts folder, 302
ECLIPSE_HOME\plugins\org.eclipse.pde.
        build_<version>\templates\headless-
        build folder, 302, 321
eclipse.exe file, 292
eclipse.ini file, 292
eclipse-linux-sdk command, 299
eclipse.navigator.view view, 81
.eclipseproduct file, 292
eclipse-SDK command, 299
eclipseSDK1 command, 298
eclipseSDK2 command, 298
eclipse-SDK\eclipse-GANYMEDE command, 322
Edit Data Set window, 265
editors, 6, 31–32
EditPart component, 176–184
EditPartViewer component, 176
EditPolicy component, 176–177, 185–187
elementID placeholder, 320
elementType placeholder, 320
elementVersion placeholder, 320
Ellipse figure, 178
EllipticalShape class, 177
EMF (Eclipse Modeling Framework), 263
emitters, 279
Enable API Analysis check box, 54
EngineConfig class, 276
Equinox OSGi. *See* OSGi
Execution Environment drop-down menu, 54
expandable composites, 117–118
ExpandableComposite.addExpansionListener
        class, 118
expansionStateChanged method, 118
extension points
    adding to plug-ins
        commands, 35–38
        editors, 31–32
        overview, 24–25
        perspectives, 25–28
        pop-up menus, 33–34
        view actions, 29–30
        views, 28–29
    CNF, 94–96
    defined, 4, 21
    for RCP applications, 55–59
    web browser plug-in exercise, 68–70

Extension Wizards tab, 24
extensions attribute, 179
Extensions tab, 10, 55
extradir attribute, 147

F

families, job, 89
features
    creating, 305–306
    defined, 24, 67, 291
features folder, 292, 315
feature.xml file, 24
fetch phase, 304
fetchTag command, 304
figures, 173
file attribute, 147, 153
FileBean class, 98–99, 102
filters, 79
findFigureAtExcluding(int x, int y, Collection
        exclude) method, 175
findFigureAt(int x, int y, TreeSearch) method, 175
findFigureAt(Point p) method, 175
findFigureAt(x, y) method, 175
__fittopage parameter, 271
fitWithinBounds( )method, 195
flyTo( ) method, 250–251
Font object, 5
Form class, 109
form text control, 121–124
<form> element, 122
format attribute, 272
Format Chart tab, 268
__format parameter, 271
FormAttachments class, 132
FormColors class, 114
FormEditor class, 126
form.getMenuManager( ).add(IAction) method,
        112
form.getToolBarManager.add(IAction) method,
        112
Forms API
    appearance, 111–115
    complex forms, 124–126
    controls
        common, 109–110
        expandable composites, 117–118
        form text control, 121–124
        hyperlinks, 116–117
        overview, 115
        sections, 118–121
    Mail Template exercise
        mail view, 134–138
        navigation view, 132–134
        overview, 127
        window contents, 129–132
        workbench window, 128–129
    overview, 107–109
Forms object, 107
FormText class, 119
FormToolkit class, 109
fragments, plug-in, 24
fragment.xml file, 296
/frameset URL mapping, 274

■G

GEF (Graphical Editing Framework)
    EditPolicies, 185–187
    figures, displaying, 175–176
    overview, 175–176
    palettes, 187–190
    shapes example
        Connection EditParts, 183–184
        overview, 176–179
        Shape EditParts, 180–183
        Shapes EditPart factory, 179–180
generate phase, 304
genericTargets.xml file, 302
Geocoding API
    creating layer navigator view with, 256–258
    finding latitude and longitude with, 251–255
Geographic Names Information System (GNIS),
    243
GET request, 251
getChildren( ) method, 99, 102
getConnectionCompleteCommand( ) method, 187
getConnectionCreateCommand( ) method, 187
getDefault( ) method, 64
getDefaultPageInput method, 81
getElements( ) method, 102
getFormColors( ) method, 115
getImageData method, 104
getImageDescriptor( ) method, 138
getInitialInput( ) method, 100
getMetaData( ) method, 277
getModelSourceConnections( )method, 183
getModelTargetConnections( )method, 183
getParent( ) method, 102
getParentBeans( ) method, 97
getParentBeans method, 102
getPartForElement( )method, 180
getToolBarManager( ) method, 111
getView function, 48
GL Cubes View class, 216
GL drawables, 210
GL_AMBIENT value, 236
GL_DIFFUSE value, 236
GL_POSITION value, 236
glBlendFunc parameter, 235
GLCanvas class, 209
glColorMaterial parameter, 236
GLContext class, 226
GLData class, 209
glEndList class, 228
gljava binding, 211
glLightfv parameter, 236
Global actions, 63
Globe object, 243, 250
GLScene class, 211, 220–224
GLScene constructor, 220
gluNewQuadric parameter, 235
gluQuadricNormals parameter, 235
GLUT (OpenGL Utility Toolkit), 222, 227
GLUT class, 212, 227
GNIS (Geographic Names Information System),
    243
GNU General Public License, 319
gradient colors, 114–115

Graph Editor product file, 206
Graph object, 191, 204
Graph1View class, 202
GraphConnection component, 191
Graphical Editing Framework. *See* GEF
graphical user interface (GUI) toolkit, 4
GraphicalNodeEditPolicy class, 185, 187
graphics. *See* 2D graphics; 3D graphics
GraphNode component, 191
GridLayout class, 134
GridLayoutAlgorithm class, 193
GUI (graphical user interface) toolkit, 4

■H

handleEvent(Event) method, 237
Handler class, 309
handlers, 35–36, 73–75
hasChildren( ) method, 99, 102
headless build system
    defined, 291
    example
        from command line, 314–318
        from CVS repository, 318–322
    product build automation with, 300–305
        build configuration, 302–304
        build phases, 304–305
        overview, 300–302
height attribute, 273
height parameter, 232
Hello RCP template, 214
Help command, 15, 309
Help menu, 162–163
help system
    configuring product to use, 141–144
    content, adding, 144–150
    context help support, adding, 150–154
    customizing, 154–156
    infocenters, creating, 156–169
    overview, 141
HELP_CONTENTS action, 144
HELP_DATA property, 155
HELP_SEARCH action, 144
helpData.xml file, 155
hit testing, 175
HorizontalTreeLayoutAlgorithm class, 193
href attribute, 123, 147, 149
HTML (Hypertext Markup Language), 6
html content directories, 162
html folder, 146
HTMLCompleteImageHandler class, 280
HTMLRenderOption class, 279
HTMLServerImageHandler class, 280
HTTP response content, 49
hyperlinks, 116–117
Hypertext Markup Language (HTML), 6

■I

IAdaptable interface, 83, 97
icon attribute, 26
id attribute, 26, 28, 35, 38, 94–95, 179, 272–273
__id parameter, 271
IDataExtractionTask task, 277–278
IDE (integrated development environment), 1

IDs drop-down menu, 66
IFigure interface, 175
IFile class, 33
IFormColors.H_BOTTOM_KEYLINE1 constant, 114
IFormColors.H_BOTTOM_KEYLINE2 constant, 114
IFormColors.H_GRADIENT_END constant, 114
IFormColors.H_GRADIENT_START constant, 114
IFormColors.TITLE constant, 114
IGetParameterDefinitionTask task, 276, 278–279
IHyperlinkListener interface, 117
IJobChangeListener interface, 89
Image object, 5
<img> tag, 122
INavigatorContentService class, 78
includes statement, 81, 96
index file, help system, 148–149
infocenter exercise
    Contents plug-in, 157–162
    customizing, 168–169
    help system dependencies, 163–164
    Infocenter plug-in
        adding Help menu to, 162–163
        adding product configuration file to, 159–160
        creating, 158–159
        deploying, 166
        testing, 164–166
    overview, 156
    splitting documentation into topic HTML/
        XHTML files, 156–157
    starting from command line, 166–168
Infocenter folder, 159
initGL( ) method, 221, 225
initGLContext method, 221
initialize method, 81
inputChanged( ) method, 102
install {URL} command, 15
Installed Software tab, 298
-installIU parameter, 299
int alphaSize property, 210
int blueSize property, 210
int greenSize property, 210
int redSize property, 210
int stencilSize property, 210
integrated development environment (IDE), 1
interface org.eclipse.draw2d.IFigure plug-in, 174
internationalization, help system, 150
IRenderOption interface, 286
IRenderTask interface, 276, 279–281
IReportEngineFactory class, 276
IRunAndRenderReportTask interface, 276
IRunAndRenderTask interface, 276, 282–283, 286
IRunTask interface, 276, 282
isCanceled( ) method, 88
isConflicting( ) method, 85–86
isDirectory( ) method, 98
isHostPage attribute, 272
__isnull parameter, 271
iText application, 263
IViewActionDelegate interface, 30
IWorkbenchPage.VIEW_ACTIVATE argument, 75
IWorkbenchWindowConfigurer class, 128

J
Java development tools (JDT), 4
Java EE server, 269
Java Native Interface (JNI), 209
Java OpenGL (JOGL), 211
Java resource bundles, 296
Java Runtime Environment (JRE), 54
Java Virtual Machine (JVM) environment, 3
javacDebugInfo command, 304
javacFailOnError command, 304
javacSource command, 304
javacTarget command, 304
javacVerbose command, 304
java.io.File object, 98
javax.servlet.http.HttpServlet class, 12
JDT (Java development tools), 4
JFace toolkit, 5
JNI (Java Native Interface), 209
Job class, 84, 87–88
JobChangeAdapter argument, 89
jobs, 84–86
JOGL, 211–212, 218–220, 228, 236, 240–242
JOGL (Java OpenGL), 211
join( ) method, 84
JRE (Java Runtime Environment), 54
JSP tag library, 269, 272–274
JVM (Java Virtual Machine) environment, 3

K
key bindings, 73–75
KeyListener listener, 237
keyPressed method, 240

L
label attribute, 147
labelProvider attribute, 95
<language> element, 150
Launch an Eclipse application link, 67, 200
Layer interface, 244
Layout view, 264–265, 267–268
left attribute, 273
legacy update manager, 297
<li> tags, 122
<license> tag, 295
Lightweight Java Game Library (LWJGL), 211
<link> element, 148
list argument, 228
local actions, 63
__locale parameter, 271
localhost property, 322
location parameter, 251–252
LocationListener class, 49
locationURI attribute, 38, 72
locks, 86
log4j.properties file, 16
logging services, 16–18
LWJGL (Lightweight Java Game Library), 211

M
Mail Template exercise
    mail view, modifying, 134–138
    navigation view, modifying, 132–134

overview, 127
  window contents, customizing, 129–132
  workbench window, customizing, 128–129
makeActions method, 142
managed forms, 124
MANIFEST.MF file, 4, 8, 23, 59, 166
manifests, 23–24
<mapping> element, 270
mapsRepo property, 321
mapVersionTag command, 303
master/details form, 125
__masterpage parameter, 271
menu bar, updating, 142–144
menu contributions, 37–38
menu extension points, 72–73
messages, 113–114
-metadataRepository parameter, 299
metadataRepository property, 298
minimized attribute, 28
mipmaps, 231
mode argument, 228
model, 83, 176
Model interface, 244
model-view-controller (MVC) architecture, 5, 175
mouseDown method, 237, 240
MouseEvents class, 236
mouseMove( ) method, 237, 240
MouseMoveListener listener, 237
mouseUp method, 237, 240
moving scenes, 236–240
Mozilla Rhino application, 263
multipage editors, 125–126
MVC (model-view-controller) architecture, 5, 175

N

name attribute, 26, 29, 35, 94–95, 273
National Geospatial-Intelligence Agency, 243
__navigationbar parameter, 271
navigator class, 96, 99–101
navigator root, 97
navigator view, 132–134, 246–247, 256–258
NavigatorActionService class, 78
NavigatorRoot class, 100, 102
New Extension wizard, 24
New Production Configuration wizard, 65
new Separator(IWorkbenchActionConstants.MB_
    ADDITIONS) action separator, 47
NewAction class, 33
newBrowser command, 73
NewBrowserHandler class, 74
nl ${target.nl} argument, 13
nl directory, 294
NO_LAYOUT_NODE_RESIZING constant, 205
NONE state, 84

O

objectContribution menu, 33
Open Perspective dialog, 26
OpenGL scenes
  3D chart, 228–236
  overview, 209–212
  RCP view, 241–242
  refreshing, 241

rotating and moving, 236–240
  setting up for, 212–219
  wire cubes, 220–228
OpenGL Utility Toolkit (GLUT), 222, 227
OpenGL.product file, 310, 313
openIntro method, 62
openReport methods, 275
openReportDesign( ) method, 277
openReportDocument( ) method, 277
operations, job, 84
ORDERDETAILS tables, 267
org.eclipse,jface.viewers.IContentProvider inter-
    face, 121
org.eclipse.birt.chart.device.pdf package, 285
org.eclipse.birt.chart.device.svg package, 286
org.eclipse.birt.chart.engine package, 286
org.eclipse.birt.chart.runtime package, 285
org.eclipse.birt.core package, 285
org.eclipse.birt.report.data.oda.sampledb package,
    285
org.eclipse.birt.report.engine package, 285
org.eclipse.birt.report.engine.emitter.html pack-
    age, 286
org.eclipse.birt.report.engine.emitter.pdf package,
    286
org.eclipse.birt.report.engine.emitter.postscript
    package, 286
org.eclipse.birt.report.engine.emitter.ppt package,
    286
org.eclipse.birt.report.engine.emitter.prototype.
    excel package, 286
org.eclipse.core runtime plug-in, 2
org.eclipse.core.command.AbstractHandler exten-
    sion point, 36
org.eclipse.core.runtime plug-in, 3
org.eclipse.core.runtime.applications extension
    point, 57, 195
org.eclipse.core.runtime.jobs.ISchedulingRule
    interface, 85
org.eclipse.core.runtime.products extension point,
    195, 292, 294
org.eclipse.core.runtime.products file, 168
org.eclipse.equinox.app.IApplication class, 57
org.eclipse.equinox.http.registry.servlets extension
    point, 6
org.eclipse.equinox.launcher_<version>.jar argu-
    ment, 301
org.eclipse.gef.examples.flow extension point, 196
org.eclipse.gef.examples.logic extension point, 196
org.eclipse.gef.examples.shapes plug-in, 174, 176,
    196
org.eclipse.gef.examples.shapes.ShapesEditor
    class, 179
org.eclipse.help.base/banner property, 156
org.eclipse.help.base/banner_height property, 156
org.eclipse.help.base/help_home property, 156
org.eclipse.help.contexts extension point, 151,
    152–153
org.eclipse.help.index extension point, 146
org.eclipse.help.standalone.Infocenter class, 166
org.eclipse.help.toc extension point, 146, 162
org.eclipse.jdt.ui.PackageExplorer view, 28
org.eclipse.opengl.GLCanvas class, 210

org.eclipse.opengl.GLData class, 210
org.eclipse.osgi plug-in, 3
org.eclipse.osgi.framework.console.Command-
    Provider interface, 283
org.eclipse.releng.eclipsebuilder plug-in, 300
org.eclipse.swt.awt package, 245
org.eclipse.swt.events.MouseAdapter class, 236
org.eclipse.swt.opengl package, 209
org.eclipse.swt.program.Program class, 104
org.eclipse.ui plug-in, 2
org.eclipse.ui.actions.ActionFactory class, 144
org.eclipse.ui.bindings extension point, 35–36
org.eclipse.ui.commands extension point, 35, 308
org.eclipse.ui.editors extension point, 31
org.eclipse.ui.file.exit command, 73
org.eclipse.ui.forms.events.HyperlinkAdapter
    class, 117
org.eclipse.ui.handlers extension point, 35
org.eclipse.ui.help.aboutAction command, 73
org.eclipse.ui.menus extension point, 35, 37
org.eclipse.ui.navigator plug-in, 199
org.eclipse.ui.navigator.CommonNavigator class,
    78–80, 83, 93
org.eclipse.ui.navigator.navigatorContent exten-
    sion point, 83
org.eclipse.ui.navigator.resourceContent view, 81
org.eclipse.ui.navigator.resources plug-in, 77, 80,
    199
org.eclipse.ui.navigator.resources.linkHelper
    extension, 81
org.eclipse.ui.navigator.viewer extension point,
    83, 196
org.eclipse.ui.newWizards extension point, 196
org.eclipse.ui.perspectives extension point, 26, 39,
    58, 70, 196
org.eclipse.ui.PlatformUI class, 58
org.eclipse.ui.popupMenus extension point, 33
org.eclipse.ui.views extension point, 28–29, 39, 94,
    196, 216
org.eclipse.update.ui dependency, 309
org.eclipse.zest.examples extension point, 196
org.eclipse.zest.examples plug-in, 200
os ${target.os} argument, 13
OSGi
    commands, 15–16
    creating plug-in, 9–12
    logging services, 16–18
    overview, 3, 6
    report generation from, 283–289
    starting plug-in project, 6–8
    testing plug-in, 12–14
OSGi manifest, 4, 59–60
osgi.noShutdown argument, 13
output format, 283
output parameter, 251
Overview tab, 310
__overwrite parameter, 271

■P

<p> tag, 122
p2 folder, 292
-p2.arch parameter, 300
-p2.os parameter, 300

-p2.ws parameter, 300
package phase, 305
packaging products, 67–68
__page parameter, 271
pageNum attribute, 273
__pagerange parameter, 271
paint( ) method, 175
paintBorder( ) method, 175
paintChildren( ) method, 175
paintClientArea( ) method, 175
paintFigure( ) method, 175
Palette factory, 177
Palette view, 264–265, 267
palettes, GEF, 187–190
pattern attribute, 272
PDE (Plug-in Developer Environment), 4
PDFRenderOption class, 279–280
Perspective class, 58, 97
perspective extension point, 39–40
perspective factory, 40, 96
Perspective.java class, 218
perspectives, 6, 25–28
placement attribute, 38
Platform core mechanism, 296
PlatformObject class, 83, 97
PlatformUI.createAndRunWorkbench(Display,
    ApplicationWorkbenchAdvisor) class, 61
plugin attribute, 153
plug-in class, 22–23, 63–65
Plug-in Content page, 53, 144, 196
Plug-in Developer Environment (PDE), 4
plug-in fragments, 24
plug-in manifest, 4, 60–61
Plug-in Name field, 53
Plug-in Options section, 8
Plug-in Project wizard, 6, 144, 157, 294
Plug-in Provider field, 54
Plug-in Version field, 53
plugin_customization.ini file, 154, 156, 168–169, 294
<plugin> tag, 296
plugin.properties mechanism, 296
plug-ins
    defined, 4
    Eclipse model, 21–24
    extension points
        commands, 35–38
        editors, 31–32
        overview, 24–25
        perspectives, 25–28
        pop-up menus, 33–34
        view actions, 29–30
        views, 28–29
    OSGi console, 9–14
    overview, 21
    web browser plug-in exercise
        content, 41–48
        enhancing, 49–50
        overview, 38–39
        perspective extension point, 39–40
        perspective factory, 40
        testing, 48
        views, 41–48
Plug-ins and Fragments section, 142

plugins folder, 292, 315
plugin.xml file, 23, 59, 63, 151–152, 218, 247
pop-up menus, 33–34
position attribute, 273
postBuild phase, 305
postWindowCreate method, 62
postWindowOpen method, 62
postWindowRestore method, 62
preBuild phase, 304
preferenceCustomization property, 168, 294
preWindowOpen( ) method, 62, 128
preWindowShellClose method, 62
primary attribute, 147
process phase, 305
product build automation, 300–305
product configuration file, 75, 159–160
product property, 315
ProductCatalog.rptdesign report, 270
production configuration, 214–216, 246
PRODUCTLINE table, 267
PRODUCTS table, 267
-profile parameter, 300
progress reporting, 88
projects, defined, 6
Property Editor view, 264
PropertyChangeListener interface, 183
provisioning updates, 297

■ Q
quad parameter, 232
quadrics, 231
qualifiers, 53

■ R
race( ) method, 92
Race class, 89–92
RaceRunner class, 88
ratio attribute, 28
RCP (Rich Client Platform)
    applications
        advanced graphics editor exercise, 195–200
        advisor classes, 61–63
        branding, 65–66
        defining, 65–66
        Earth navigator project, 246
        extension points for, 55–59
        features, 67
        OpenGL scenes, 212–214
        OSGi manifest, 59–60
        overview, 53
        packaging, 67–68
        plug-in class, 63–65
        plug-in manifest, 60–61
        testing, 67–68
        web browser plug-in exercise, 68–75
    architecture
        core platform, 3–4
        Eclipse workbench, 6
        Equinox OSGi, 3
        JFace, 5
        overview, 2
        SWT, 4–5
    benefits of, 1–2

        versus Eclipse workbench, 2
    OSGi console
        commands, 15–16
        creating plug-in, 9–12
        logging services, 16–18
        overview, 6
        starting plug-in project, 6–8
        testing plug-in, 12–14
    overview, 1
RCP view, 241–242
rcp.example.mail.MailApplication class, 56–57
Rectangle figure, 178
RectangularShape class, 177
Refresher class, 211
refreshing scenes, 241
refreshVisuals( ) method, 180, 183
register method, 89
relationship attribute, 28
relative attribute, 28
relative coordinate system, 175
release engineering project, 320–321
render( ) method, 241
RenderOptionBase class, 280
_report command, 285
report design, 283
Report Designer
    anatomy of, 263
    creating reports, 264–268
    installing BIRT, 262–263
    overview, 261–262
Report Engine API
    configuring, 276
    IDataExtractionTask task, 277–278
    IGetParameterDefinitionTask task, 278–279
    IRenderTask task, 279–281
    IRunAndRenderTask task, 282–283
    IRunTask task, 282
    overview, 275–276
__report parameter, 271
report viewer servlet, 270
reportContainer attribute, 273
reportDesign attribute, 273
reportDocument attribute, 273
ReportGenerator( ) method, 288
ReportGenerator.java class, 285–286, 288
<repository path> tag, 320
Resource encapsulator, 96
resource management, 4
resourceFolder attribute, 273
__resourceFolder parameter, 271
Rhino application, 263
Rich Client Platform. See RCP
-roaming parameter, 300
root EditParts, 176
rotating scenes, 236–240
__rtl parameter, 271
run( ) method, 84, 86, 241
runAndRender(String designDocPath, String
        outFileName, String outFormat, String
        params) method, 288
RUNNING state, 84
runtime kernel, 2
runtime plug-in model, 4

■S

SalesInvoince.rptdesign report, 274
sample.actions.ViewActionDelegate1 class, 30
sample.views.SampleView view, 28
SceneController interface, 244
SceneGrip class, 211, 226, 236–237
schedule( ) method, 84, 92
scheduling rules, 85–86
scheme attribute, 38
schemeId attribute, 37
ScrolledForm control, 109
scrolledForm.reflow(true) method, 118
scrolling attribute, 273
SDK (Software Development Kit), 4
sections, 118–121
Section.TWISTIE state, 121
Select Data tab, 268
<selection> element, 179
sequence attribute, 37
servlet containers, 269–274
<servlet_params> element, 270
setLayoutData( ) method, 133
setShow* methods, 128
setTarget( )method, 187
shape EditParts, 177, 180–183
Shape instances, 183
ShapeEditPart class, 178, 183
Shapes EditPart factory, 177, 179–180
ShapesCreationWizard class, 179
ShapesEditPartFactory class, 178
ShapeTreeEditPart class, 178
ShapeTreeEditPartFactory class, 178
showParameterPage attribute, 273
showView( ) method, 75
shutdown( ) method, 276
skipFetch property, 321
skipMaps property, 321
sleep( ) method, 84
SLEEPING state, 84
slices parameter, 232
Software Development Kit (SDK), 4
Software Update Manager, 18
Software Update UI tools
    Add-ons dialog and, 297–298
    installing software from command line, 298–299
    overview, 296–297
Software Updates command, 309
Software Updates menu, 308–312
<span> tag, 122
splash screen, 66, 294
splash.bmp file, 66, 294
splitParams(String queryString) method, 288
SpringLayout object, 195
SpringLayoutAlgorithm class, 194–195
ss command, 15
stacks parameter, 232
Standard Widget Toolkit (SWT), 4–5, 211–212, 218–220, 228, 236, 240–242
start [<id>|<name>] command, 15
start method, 23, 58
startupForegroundColor property, 294
startupMessageRect property, 294
startupProgressRect property, 294

state parameter, 251
states, job, 84
stop [<id>|<name>] command, 15
stop method, 23
street parameter, 251
StyledText widget, 124
SWT (Standard Widget Toolkit), 4–5, 211–212, 218–220, 228, 236, 240–242
SWT graphics context (GC), 174
SWT.WRAP style, 124
system jobs, 92

■T

table of contents (TOC), 144–146
TableWrapLayout class, 107, 115, 132, 134, 137
target application, 298–299
Target Platform, 12
targetID view, 27, 29
Templates page, 144, 196
testing
    advanced graphics editor exercise, 206
    automated updates and builds exercise, 308–314
    Infocenter plug-in, 164–166
    RCP applications, 67–68
    via OSGi console, 12–14
    web browser plug-in exercise, 48
timestamp command, 303
title attribute, 149, 273
__title parameter, 271
TOC (table of contents), 144–146
TOC file, 147–148, 160–162
<toc> element, 147, 162
toc.xml file, 166
Tomcat servlet container, 269
TOMCAT_HOME/webapps folder, 270
toolbar extension points, 72–73
__toolbar parameter, 271
toolbars, 111–112
toolkit = new FormToolkit(getFormColors(Display)) method, 115
toolkit.createTree( ) method, 133
toolkit.paintBordersFor(text.getParent( )) method, 109
top attribute, 273
top parameter, 232
topic attribute, 147
<topic> element, 147
TopNPercent.rptdesign class, 289
toString( )method, 98
TOTAL SALES column header, 268
trapping HTTP response content, 49
TreeGraphView class, 202
TreeLayoutAlgorithm class, 193, 205

■U

UI (user interface) concepts
    CNF
        classes, 78
        configuration, 79
        overview, 77–78
        using, 79–83

concurrency infrastructure
    jobs, 84–86
    overview, 83
    using, 86–92
file system navigator project
    classes, 96–105
    extension points, 94–96
    overview, 93
    project template, 93–94
    overview, 77
uninstall [<id>|<name>] command, 15
unpack attribute, 296
update site, 291, 306–308, 313–314
<update> tag, 295
Updates Category command, 309
UpdatesHandler class, 309
URL bookmarks, 50
<url> tag, 295
user interface concepts. *See* UI concepts
User jobs, 92
<user_params> element, 270

V

validate( ) method, 174
value attribute, 273
-version parameter, 299
view actions, 29–30
View class, 241, 250
View Example link, 270
View interface, 244
View toolbar, 47
viewerActionBinding element, 83
viewerContentBinding element, 81, 83
viewerContribution menu, 33
views
    adding, 28–29, 41–48
    creating, 216–218
    defined, 6

W

W3C (World Wide Web Consortium), 115
WAITING state, 84
wakeUp( ) method, 84
WAR archive, 270
web browser plug-in exercise
    content, 41–48
    enhancing, 49–50
    overview, 38–39
    perspective extension point, 39–40
    perspective factory, 40

RCP application for, 68–75
testing plug-in, 48
views, 41–48
Web Browser widget, 46–47
Web Standard Tools (WST), 263
Web Tools Platform (WTP), 49
WebBrowserPerspective class, 70
WebBrowserView.java file, 49
WEB-INF/tlds directory, 274
WEB-INF/tlds/birt.tld file, 274
web.xml file, 274
width attribute, 273
windowImages property, 294
wire cubes scene, 220–228
wireCube( ) method, 227
wizard extension, 179
workbench window advisor, 61–62, 128–129
WorkbenchAdvisor class, 61, 81
WorkbenchWindowAdvisor class, 61–62, 92
WORKING_FOLDER_ACCESS_ONLY parameter,
    272
workspaces, defined, 6
World Wide Web Consortium (W3C), 115
World Wind Java (WWJ), 242–248
World Wind SDK, 242
WorldWindow interface, 243
WorldWindowGLCanvas class, 243, 245
ws ${target.ws} argument, 13
WST (Web Standard Tools), 263
WTP (Web Tools Platform), 49
WWJ (World Wind Java), 242–248

X

XYLayoutManager class, 183

Y

Yahoo Geocoding API
    creating layer navigator view with, 256–258
    finding latitude and longitude with, 251–255
YGeoSearch class, 252

Z

Zest
    components of, 191–192
    layouts, 193–195
    overview, 190–191
    plug-in, 200–206
zip parameter, 251
zipargs command, 304

You Need the Companion eBook

Your purchase of this book entitles you to buy the companion PDF-version eBook for only $10. Take the weightless companion with you anywhere.

We believe this Apress title will prove so indispensable that you'll want to carry it with you everywhere, which is why we are offering the companion eBook (in PDF format) for $10 to customers who purchase this book now. Convenient and fully searchable, the PDF version of any content-rich, page-heavy Apress book makes a valuable addition to your programming library. You can easily find and copy code—or perform examples by quickly toggling between instructions and the application. Even simultaneously tackling a donut, diet soda, and complex code becomes simplified with hands-free eBooks!

Once you purchase your book, getting the $10 companion eBook is simple:

❶ Visit **www.apress.com/promo/tendollars/**.

❷ Complete a basic registration form to receive a randomly generated question about this title.

❸ Answer the question correctly in 60 seconds, and you will receive a promotional code to redeem for the $10.00 eBook.

THE EXPERT'S VOICE™

2855 TELEGRAPH AVENUE │ SUITE 600 │ BERKELEY, CA 94705

Offer valid through 9/16/09.